ALL OF MANKIND WILL BE STUNNED!

PASTOR RICK A. BLOMGREN

STUNNED!

Editors: Shirl Thomas, Lee Pound
Text Editor: Kaitlin Barr Nadal
Pagination: Lee Pound
Photography by Figge Photography Studio
Cover Art by Exodus Design Studios
7.7

ISBN: 978-0-9906486-3-5

Contents

Hebrews 4:12–13

12 *For the word of God is living and active and sharper than any two-edged sword, and piercing as far as the division of soul and spirit, of both joints and marrow, and able to judge the thoughts and intentions of the heart.* 13 *And there is no creature hidden from His sight, but all things are open and laid bare to the eyes of Him with whom we have to do.*

Dedications

I dedicate this book to

Jesus the Christ my Lord and Savior

I love you, Jesus, and I thank you for loving me.
You are the King of kings and Lord of lords.
All praise and glory be given to you!

My Bible Teacher, Dr. Fred Beshore (1926–2016)

My dear friend, I also dedicate this book to you.
Thank you for sharing your wisdom, support, encouragement,
love, and understanding of both Jesus and His Bible. I love you,
and I thank God for placing me within your life's path. The
knowledge of the Bible I have learned from you has created the
desire to share this exciting story with others.
You are greatly missed. We will meet again.

1 Timothy 4:16

[16] Pay close attention to yourself and your teaching; persevere in these things; for as you do this you will ensure salvation both to yourselves and for those that hear you.

Introduction

For 45 years I have been intrigued by the subject of the last days; specifically, Bible prophecies explaining the end times. The Bible indicates the last days represents the period from the resurrection of Christ until His return in the future. Through prophecy we are told by God to look for signs so we can know when we are coming close to the end of the last days period.

I am dismayed at the number or prophesy books out today indicating that what is coming must be catastrophic or horrible for living believers. This is not the case per 1 Thessalonians 5:9. Much more is going on. The interpretation of prophecies already offered in the Bible, as presented in this book, shows we have nothing to fear. Will there be challenges? Yes, but our loving God has incredible things planned for believers today to see. Additionally, His plans are specifically designed to bring His "chosen people," the Jews, back to Him. Some Christians might tell you this is not accurate, but how might we know this to be correct? Is the whole story, even to this day, really about the Jews?

At some point we all know God will put an end to sin, we will live with Him perfected for all eternity. Consider the book of Revelation, chapter 21, which talks about the eternal order when all God's work is done and we are with Him. In verse 10 we see the new final perfect Jerusalem coming down to earth out of heaven. In verses 12-14 we are told it has 12 gates and 12 foundation stones. Note in verse 12, the 12 gates each have one name of each of the 12 tribes of Israel (all Jews). In verse 14 the foundations are individually named for the 12 apostles (all Jews). Every time somebody comes into this glorious new City they walk over the name of a Jewish apostle and see the name of a Jewish tribe overhead. Is it possible the eternal order will be Jewish and the Law perfected; ruled by God the Father? I provide my conclusions in this book. **You might be *STUNNED*.** The whole story is more incredible than I could have ever imagined! *All praise and glory be given to Jesus the Christ, my Lord, my Messiah! Amen.*

Rick A. Blomgren, Pastor
President, Revere Today Ministries Inc.
Newport Beach CA

Matthew 13:16–17

[16] But blessed are your eyes, because they see; and your ears, because they hear. [17] For truly I say to you that many prophets and righteous men desired to see what you see, and did not see it, and to hear what you hear, and did not hear it.

CHAPTER 1

OVERVIEW

God is amazing! He has told us the full story of mankind in His Bible. He has shared with us, *in advance*, everything we need to know to navigate through a wondrous time in world history — today. Our Lord is announcing His second coming.

STUNNED

STUNNED is a word that represents two diametrically opposed meanings. The first is overwhelming **shock** or **terror**. The second is **awe** and **astonishment**. A Godly event of monumental proportions, related to Israel, is on the near horizon; it will leave all of mankind **STUNNED**! How an individual will react to this incredible event depends upon their faith and understanding of the Bible as a whole and on their personal trust in the written intentions of **the God of Abraham, Isaac, and Jacob**. For me, **awe** and **astonishment** carry the greatest significance.

I am a born-again Christian and accept the Bible as the singularly true inerrant Word of the living God. I provide compelling evidence to support its accuracy in Appendix A.

My serious in-depth review of Biblical end-time prophecies started 45 years ago. Recently, I realized that I had inadvertently discounted some highly pertinent verses. It is amazing how the smallest, apparently insignificant verses seem to carry incredible truth and weight. For most of my life, I was dogmatic in my belief that mankind was not capable of understanding certain aspects of God's plans for our future. One example is thinking that nobody can know the day or hour of the Lord's return. Then the following verse hit me right between the eyes and created some serious conundrums:

Mark 13:23
[23] *But take heed; behold, I have told you <u>everything in advance</u>.*

I took this one small verse to heart and discovered some amazing insights. It is now clear that there are literally no mysteries listed in the Bible that have not already been fully revealed and defined for believers by our Lord within His precious written Word (*Matthew 13:11*). Upon deeper research into the Bible as a whole, God's magnificent story for mankind went from black and white to Technicolor. **I was STUNNED!** The vibrant detail and specificity related to the Lord's total plan for our specific moment in history, especially for those of us living today, is amazing! Jesus has provided incredibly detailed, clear directions for us so we can navigate accurately in what I believe are mankind's final days. After my recent round of research, I felt embarrassed; I thought I knew the Bible well. How could I have possibly missed God's vibrant in-depth version of His wonderful story for His beloved family?

It became evident that understanding the ramifications required more detailed investigation. I blended both the Old and New Testaments together as not two books but one cohesive document as I believe God intended for it to be. **I was again STUNNED!**

What I learned from this more detailed study is that **the God of Abraham, Isaac, and Jacob**, in His Bible, literally proffers **24 specific end-time prophetic signs to witness** (*signs, see Glossary page 348*), a **Road Map** for the last days. His first prophecy in this series began in 1914. I was astonished when I discovered **the first 12 prophecies have already occurred** with historical precision and accuracy **exactly as prophesied in the Bible; we have witnessed them**. Even more astonishing, the **rebirth of the State of Israel in 1948** was not the first end-time prophecy fulfilled in God's 24-event sequence; **it was purposefully the fourth**. I will explain how and why this is possible, and His reasoning is amazing. **We will soon "witness" the second 12 prophecies arrive** right on God's intended schedule.

The rebirth of the State of Israel on May 14, 1948 was the **first of three major end-time super signs** (*only three of the 24 are super signs*) indicating we will soon experience the literal return of Jesus. When we accept that the entire Bible is God's **all-inclusive guidebook**, prophecy becomes vibrant and understandable.

At first, as I continued to research God's end-time prophecies, I remained skeptical. I was stubborn and wanted to firmly hold to my comfortable, rigid, traditional viewpoints that Christians could not possibly understand certain aspects of the Bible. This new, over-the-top concept that God has provided mankind with specific end-time prophecies or **signs to actually witness** seemed to fly in the face of my stalwart belief system. My original belief was that the only way to justify a **pre-time of Jacob's dis-tress, catching up,** view of the Bible was to latch onto the widely accepted concept of the instantaneous return of Jesus, a secretive surprise return that must occur at any moment **without any signs** preceding the event. This had to be the singularly true Biblical doctrine. Unsettled, I kept returning to this nagging apparent contradiction related to what God tells us in Mark 13:23, where God directly tells us, *"He has told us everything in advance."* Clearly, there was much more to this *"everything."* **I was again STUNNED and awestruck!**

When I finally got my arms around this new, magnificent picture of events being presented by our Lord, I became over-joyed and filled with a new sense of wonder. I discovered His actual plan for end-time events was **intentionally designed to be witnessed**. The numerous theological reasons for this are glori-ous and documented in the coming chapters. **God truly loves us!** Better yet, Christians have also been given **the distinct honor** to be **active participants** on the day the Lord returns, all **for His ul-timate glory**. But how, you say? Why? I will show you. The whole plan is **glorious**! God even offers a special reward for every believer who **loves His appearing** and the study of end-time prophecies. **What I have learned is overwhelming!** It has given me a greater sense for the majesty of Christ.

Through all my research, I am convinced **it is critically im-portant** for Christians to understand that God's 24 end-time prophecies, His **"signs,"** designed for our blessing, are not whim-sical or allegorical. **They are purposeful!**

The arrival of God's 13th prophetic end-times event will leave mankind STUNNED. As a result of this spectacular **super sign**, the second of the Lord's three super events, knowledgeable Christians might acquire some solid assurance that the last days have literally arrived. God intends to leave no room for doubt. This monumental **sign** will change our lives in unimaginable ways. It will have profound repercussions for the entire global community. For Christians, it will create a clear, unambiguous dividing line in the sand. Believers will need to quickly decide where they place their allegiance: either with Jesus and His Bible or with a new counterfeit One World Church that will rapidly consolidate and erroneously tell us what we are to believe the truth really is.

What exactly is God's next impending **super sign** along His Road Map? This event will miraculously resolve today's evolving Middle East upheaval virtually overnight, **rescuing Israel** from all the current potential harm its surrounding enemy countries desire to impose. This earth-shattering event will represent **God's Two-Minute Warning** for humanity, announcing the arrival of the end of the game. God will complete this **spectacular prophetic sign** on His own in one singular astonishing event. He will do this without any help from mankind. It will provide indisputable proof of who He is and that He is indeed real. Chapter 4 is dedicated solely to this one spectacular prophecy.

God holds Israel in high esteem. In Isaiah 46:12, He declares, *"Israel is His Glory."* In Isaiah 48:11, God tells us *"and My glory will I not give to another."* Israel is the apple of God's eye to this very day. These statements make it Biblically clear that <u>the Christian church</u> today <u>has not replaced Israel</u>.

There are a few more issues to share with you before we get into the meat of my subject matter, foundational information re-lated to how I personally analyze what God has graciously shared with us in the Bible for our specific time in history.

If you are not a Bible reader and have not read God's Word personally, please do not let this stop you from proceeding. I provide the actual *Bible text* for more than half of the verses referenced in this book, the ones I use to support my analysis. In some instances, I provide only Biblical reference for support without showing the text. The *New American Standard* version provides all the verses unless otherwise noted.

For Protestants and Catholics alike, the Bible shares critical issues we all need to be aware of. If individual believers in Jesus do not read their Bibles, lovingly given to us by our Lord, and inarguably accept only **traditions**, or what they are told by their leaders, many could easily miss the full intent of God's glorious story. Numerous Christians, in all denominations, may not be fully aware of the vast wealth of wisdom presented for us all in His Word.

If thoughts of the end times have troubled you in the past or you have found the topic of prophecy generally uncomfortable, this exciting new interpretation of God's Biblical prognostications might start to put you at ease regarding the whole subject.

Unfortunately, many people today prefer to ignore altogether this whole topic of Biblical end-times prophecy. Ignoring Scripture doesn't eliminate what it conveys. Sometimes the truth is disconcerting, but here is the good news: God gave us the Bible and His prophecies so Christians can be aware of what is happening and feel at peace. We can then wisely prepare for the inevitable. God does not want us to experience fear of the end times; He actually has something wonderful in mind.

When we take a serious look at the current distress and unrest in our world—totally centered on **Israel**—it seems obvious we are living in the Biblical last days prior to both the prophesied **catching up** and **the time of Jacob's distress**. For centuries, mankind has said the Lord might return in their day. Upon deeper study, the Bible shows us, without a doubt, His final plans for mankind must occur within the **generation** that began with the rebirth of the State of Israel. As mentioned earlier, this rebirth was the fourth of **God's 24 end-time prophetic signs**. Due to this one event, we collectively need no more guessing or speculation. The Bible clearly shows us God wants to finish a few more things **for us to witness** before **His second coming,** which will start the 70th week of Daniel for His beloved Israel.

After reading the New Testament, many believe Jesus came merely to teach us how to live a Godly life. This is in part true, but much more fills its pages. Jesus taught for the long term and, during His ministry, foretold what the future would hold. In conversations with His disciples, Jesus made reference to the destruction of the temple, later followed by a rebuilding. He uses the temple to represent Himself. The destruction is His crucifixion, and the rebuilding refers to His resurrection: rising after three days (*John 2:19–22*), going away for a long time, and then returning at some point in the distant future—which is our time.

God purposefully gave us His prophetic **signs** to specifically **witness** in the last days. Recognizing prophecies that have reached fulfillment is intended to wake up some people. When astute believers comprehend end-time prophecies that have **already reached fulfillment** and begin to **see** God's next predicted events start to happen, they can have full confidence that God is at work.

John 14:29

²⁹ Now I have told you before it happens, so that when it happens, you may believe.

Additionally, what must soon happen within three specific world religions—**Christianity**, **Judaism**, and **Islam**—will play a critical role in foretelling and learning about events that will soon take place. We will explore detailed issues related to their histories, backgrounds, and futures, as this will be vital to understanding what we are about to witness.

In the Bible, God tells us how He hates evil of any kind and that He will soon come to rectify this plague. God plans to do this in a 7-year period called **the time of Jacob's distress** (*Israel's 70th week of Daniel*), which is talked about throughout the Bible. It is specifically detailed in the last book of the New Testament, the book of Revelation. The word **revelation** means **revealing**. Revelation is **not to be feared** but rather **revered**.

I will thoughtfully address some dubious long-held, Christian **doctrines** and **traditions**. When **doctrines** or **traditions** are Biblically **problematic**, God requires us per *Luke 12:54–56* to "*analyze*" our current age. We are to correct marginal thinking **accurately**, using only **His Bible** as our guide.

The Bible states God's boldness in making Himself known; He always does things in astonishing ways. Think about the Exodus as one example. God could have easily provided a fleet of ships to get His people across the sea, but that would not have shown a grand visual representation of His enormousness. God parted the sea, creating a dry path for His people to cross. This also allowed for a dramatic and highly **visual** way to defeat the enemy, a tremendous set of events. What about Noah's flood or the destruction of Sodom? These were not timid events. God's actions created **monumental visual statements**.

A large number of churches today seem comfortably situated on automatic pilot and do not appear to be paying thoughtful attention to God's expressed intentions for our time. The Lord expects us to hold to a higher standard those who teach the Bible, because we expect them to instruct with Biblical accuracy. Could some of our church leaders possibly have missed stated Biblical truths? Have old and tired accepted traditions blinded some of our church leaders to the unique and special time in which we currently live? Is it possible many present-day members of the ministry and clergy have become, for the most part, actually milquetoast on this whole end-times subject? The answer to all three questions is **yes**.

In fact, when some church leaders try to talk about the end times, their congregations become uncomfortable, so it appears these leaders choose to back off the subject, resorting to **feel-good preaching**. With the unchecked continued misconception that prophetic events are most likely allegorical or for some time in the distant future, one should anticipate reasoned discomfort regarding Bible prophecy. Due to this antiquated thinking about God's plans, it's no wonder so many people feel troubled regarding this topic.

In reality, **God's Biblical story is actually more beautiful than we ever could have imagined,** for our comfort, assurance, happiness, and joy, **and all for His infinite glory**! The Lord has actually provided us with precise clarity explaining all about when and how He will return. He has given us specific detailed information we need so we can know, with a high level of certainty, exactly when and how He does intend to return. **His grand plan is spectacular!** Christians have absolutely nothing to dread and much to give thanks for.

When Jesus taught His disciples, He told them they would have a difficult mission and needed awareness of their battle with the Deceiver. Jesus directed them to be "*shrewd*" yet "*innocent.*" These instructions are also highly valid for us today, as our mission in the last days will be challenging:

Matthew 10:16
¹⁶ Behold, I send you out as sheep in the midst of wolves; so be shrewd as serpents and innocent as doves.

In John 8:57–59, Jesus preached truthfully to a group of fellow Jews yet wasn't politically correct for His day. When he was asked a question, His answer was not received well by the crowd. They started picking up stones, and note what is said in verse 59: Jesus did the shrewd thing — He "*hid Himself*" for protection:

John 8:57–59
⁵⁷ So the Jews said to Him, "You are not yet fifty years old, and have You seen Abraham?" ⁵⁸ Jesus said to them, "Truly, truly, I say to you, before Abraham was born, I am."
⁵⁹ Therefore they picked up stones to throw at Him, but Jesus hid Himself and went out of the temple.

God provides direction in the Bible regarding many situations to diverse groups and people. Everything said and taught can and should be gleaned by us today as examples of how to deal with all life's situations. This goes for prophecy as well. God expects us to learn by the examples He shared with others in His Bible and to use this knowledge for our current time:

STUNNED

2 Timothy 3:16–17
16 All Scripture is inspired by God and profitable for teaching, for reproof, for correction, for training in righteousness; 17 so that the man of God may be adequate, equipped for every good work.

Comprehension of God's expressed plans for our time has put my soul at peace. I believe, with all my heart, that God protects us much more than we give Him credit for. The Lord is not punishing Christians or the United States in our tumultuous world today. He genuinely loves us. In these final challenging days, we need to remember this: **our joy and peace must be in Jesus alone, nothing else**. I am thankful God has given us sound direction for our time — one of His multiple blessings.

We who live in the United States have been blessed for so long to have lived in a wonderful, free, mostly God-loving and Biblically moral country. Until recently, we have lived with many blessings. Newly accepted precepts today contradict the Bible's teachings but are accepted as societal norms, causing a major recalibration of morality. What is **right is wrong**, and what is **wrong is right** from a Biblical context (*Isaiah 5:20–21*). Unfortunately, our country is changing drastically and rapidly accelerating morally downhill right before our eyes. For God's Biblical end-time plans to come to fruition, this moral decay must occur. As the world gets progressively darker, we need to prepare, in advance, for the inevitable. Knowledge is powerful, and the Bible is our knowledge. Either we can learn about what will come, accept issues now, and feel joy in the process, or we can suffer as this all unfolds due to a lack of understanding.

Many people today are becoming skeptical of Bible prophecy after being inundated with so many fallacious viewpoints. To add to the problem, many current Millennial Evangelicals are generally distrustful of numerous fundamental Biblical interpretations. Certain young Christians believe the literal meanings of certain Scriptures, in many instances, are intolerant within today's societal culture. They consider parts of the Bible to hold antiquated viewpoints that contradict a perceived highly important element of human existence, **love in any and all relational forms and configurations**. Within this thinking, through some unfortunate **selective omissions** regarding Biblical **truth**, the Bible has in essence been marginalized. Many believe today's **secular bent** of **anything goes** must take precedence so as not to offend **anyone**. By placating mankind in this fashion, **Jesus is actually the one ultimately being offended**.

Some of my friends say we should fight to bring morality back to our country. I understand their sentiments. Unfortunately, we cannot possibly change societal behavior in these last days; the Bible tells us this. Realistically, we cannot put out a forest fire with a garden hose. The wonderful truth in all of this: **Jesus is on the way**; He will fix everything soon. Try looking forward to the big event in full peace and comfort, knowing our Lord is telling us He will soon arrive in a spectacular way.

In our busy lives, so few Christians, in general, open their Bibles regularly anymore. Some people even accept the notion that the Bible may be outdated, that it was written for a different time, and that all religions likely worship the same God. Some have even concluded the Bible may actually be composed of fables or myths—a work of fiction. **Honest Christians know nothing could be further from the truth!** Please pay specific attention to the word *myth* as my story unfolds. God tells us explicitly that this myth concept will become highly accepted and used in great abundance, related to the entire Bible, in the last days.

Matthew 7:13–14
13 *"Enter through the <u>narrow gate</u>; for the gate is wide and the way is broad that leads to destruction, and there are many who enter through it. 14 For the gate is small and the way is narrow that leads to life, and there are few who find it.["]*

Jesus tells us, directly in the Bible, to enter His kingdom by the *"narrow gate"* as *"the gate is wide and the way is broad that leads to destruction."* God tells us about the many people who mistakenly believe they are saved Christians (*Appendix B*). God allows mankind to live barely enough years to fully understand His expressed requirements for salvation . . . just enough time to figure it out. Our lifespan is like a job interview for eternity; we need to get it right. We have only one chance at this.

Mankind secularists and quasi-Christians, collectively in the world today, have started opening the door for the implementation of a new One World Government and Church. They believe this will lead to final world peace . . . exactly what God tells us they will erroneously think in the last days.

1 John 2:15–17
15 Do not love the world nor the things in the world. If anyone loves the world, the love of the Father is not in him. 16 For all that is in the world, the lust of the flesh and the lust of the eyes and the boastful pride of life, is not from the Father, but is from the world. 17 The world is passing away, and also its lusts; but the one who does the will of God lives forever.

Jesus, in Matthew 13, makes reference to the **prophet Isaiah**. This incredible Old Testament prophet explains events in the future related to the end times. In Matthew 13:16–17, we are told the **generation** that will actually *"see"* end-time prophecies happening, as explained in the book of Isaiah, **is blessed**. I want to place emphasis on the word *"see,"* as this has significant meaning. God wants us to *"see"* His prophecies fulfilled in these last days.

Matthew 13:16–17
16 But blessed are your eyes, because they see; and your ears, because they hear. 17 For truly I say to you that many prophets and righteous men

*desired to <u>see what you see</u>, and did not see it,
and to hear what you hear, and did not hear it.*

With the prophesied **rebirth of the State of Israel** in Isaiah 66:7–9, everything related to how we must look at and interpret end-time prophecy radically changed. As I will chronicle, the world **has witnessed** the first series of twelve specific literal end-time prophecies as explained in the Bible. They have become reality. This **rebirth** no longer leaves room for reasoned doubt. God is showing Himself to the world at this time, but is the world paying attention? **Are Christians paying attention?**

The Bible, both Old and New Testaments, is all about Jesus, His identity as the Messiah, His love for all humanity, and particularly *"His glory"* Israel. Scripture tells us about God's redemptive hopes and desires for His entire Jewish family, both natural-born and adopted members—Christians (*Romans 11:17*). Jesus, through His Bible, requires us as Christians to love and care for Israel, to help them find their way home to Him (*Romans 11:11–16*). The Book of Revelation discloses how Israel will finally, at the end of **the time of Jacob's distress**, recognize Jesus as their Messiah (*Appendix D*). The detailed and beautifully designed story shows a loving God.

<u>*Psalm 122:6–7*</u>
*⁶ Pray for the peace of Jerusalem: "May they prosper
who love you. ⁷ May peace be within your walls,
and prosperity within your palaces."*

<u>*Isaiah 40:1–2*</u>
*¹ "Comfort, O comfort My people," says your God. ²"Speak
kindly to Jerusalem; and call out to her, that her warfare has
ended, that her iniquity has been removed.["]*

I make it a rule to use the Bible as my sole support for what I present. As we proceed, I would expect nothing less than Christians reading this book to do the same with the information provided. A person must walk with God in his or her own way and not just that of any organization, old traditions, doctrines, or some other person's individual point of view. God teaches us all, individually, through our personal time in His Word with Him alone. God then asks us to share what we learn with others. After we share, God will do all the heavy lifting.

Additionally, Scriptures actually show us how Jesus explains that understanding His direct instructions for believers in the last days **is a blessed event.** Earlier I mentioned the Lord has a reward for certain believers. God actually offers multiple final **blessings, a gift,** and **His "crown" reward** for living informed Christians who understand the nature of His literal end-time **signs** and their intended purpose. God's **crown reward** is offered only to Christians who **have a passion for end-time prophecy** and **who ultimately understand the Lord's one specific and clear final request of us just prior to His return**. He shows us not only what to do but both how and when to do **this one last request. I will show you what this one last request is; it is literal, and it is amazing!** I urge every believer, do not miss out on **God's final "open book" test** for His beloved family.

In short order, after God rescues Israel, the secular world will start to blame Christians as the ones trying to prevent global peace from expanding. Actually, in the last days, faithful Christians will try to warn the people of the world about difficult times rapidly approaching, desiring only to offer a loving solution. We will try to share the world's happenings with our friends, but the vast majority will not listen and will think of us as delusional. The world on the outside will appear to them as getting its act together, which, unfortunately, to their unexpected surprise, will soon turn out to be horrifically incorrect. God will come soon, **as a thief**, to **steal away a coming false secular world peace**. He will dramatically announce this to humanity in an earth-shattering way. On this coming day, the entire world will be **STUNNED for a second time**. What a harsh surprise, **on that day**, for those

witnessing God's catching up unfold. What a glorious day for Christians. The beginning of God's great final awakening for Israel!

As the global community gets progressively worldlier, the secular masses will almost totally silence Christians. We will need to live within a severely debased and decadent society for a **short time**, but God has provided us with His specific end-times prophetic **Road Map** for a loving reason. By witnessing all of God's **signs** in a general sequence, we will be able to sense the finish line and know, with high confidence, **approximately when He will arrive**. As faithful Christians, we have nothing to fear because God has told us *"everything in advance."*

The exciting contemporary biblical interpretation of end-time prophecy provided in this book is a **positive perspective** that shows the tremendous grandeur of our Lord. In totality, it explains how much God loves us, speaks to us, directs us, and protects us, and how He alone desires to guide us, as believers, in the last days through His total, unconditional love. *"God is love,"* and any view of the end times void of providing comfort for His family would be a theory I do not choose to accept.

1 John 4:16–18
[16] We have come to know and have believed the love which God has for us. <u>God is love</u>, and the one who abides in love abides in God, and God abides in him. [17] By this, love is perfected with us, so that we may have confidence in the day of judgment; because as He is, so also are we in this world. [18] There is no fear in love; but perfect love casts out fear, because fear involves punishment, and the one who fears is not perfected in love.

The Bible tells us the full story of how Jesus will win in the end . . . our glorious hope in our loving Lord.

I am excited about what I have learned and how God has supported me in this entire process. We live in a wonderful and special time in history and are the blessed *"final generation."*

Matthew 24:34

³⁴ *Truly I say to you, this generation will not pass away until all these things take place.*

CHAPTER 2

GOD'S ROAD MAP
24
PROPHECIES

God's **Road Map** explains what He expects
Christians to know and to look for leading up to His
visual **catching up** and the start of
the time of Jacob's distress.

God's **Road Map** brings attention to **24** significant, specific end-time prophecies. **12 have been fulfilled** or have started and must remain ongoing. There are an additional **12** prophecies as explained in the Bible that should begin to occur at **any moment**.

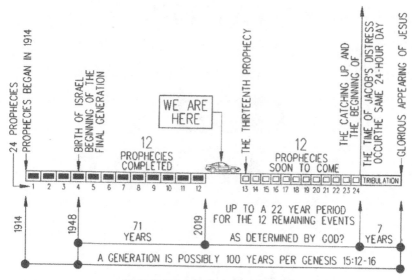

GOD'S ROAD MAP

The first thing that many Christians say today is that they do not believe God is sharing any specific prophetic "signs" related to the end times. A detailed review of the entire Bible reveals this thinking is actually **severely flawed**. God is **shouting out to the world** today for mankind to pay attention to **our season in history**. **Amazing things are happening!**

The next event along **God's Road Map** is the **13th Prophecy**. This one monumental **sign for our season** is about to arrive; **God does not want Christians to be negatively STUNNED**. When God's final 12 prophecies "**signs**" begin to unfold, we can gain a precise understanding of God's intentions.

In the process of explaining God's **24** sequential prophecies, some interpretations of God's Scriptures may, at face value, feel discomforting within **one certain denomination** of our current

Christian Church family. I will explore the history of a group that attends church regularly, predominantly following church-created rituals, doctrines, and traditions. We must all take care not to easily accept only institutional interpretations of the Bible without our own individual verification through personally reading the Scriptures — recorded straight from the original author, God. We should trust but also must verify. I back up my expressed Biblical observations regarding this one current Church's doctrines with Scriptures directly from the Bible. I plan on letting God Himself define His own intentions. The Bible alone holds God's pure truth.

Some Christian Church groups today — including the one alluded to above — seem to discount the idea of Biblical end-time prophecies obtaining fulfillment. They conclude all these events are merely allegorical. Many groups base this belief on manmade doctrines including remnants of the old thinking regarding purgatory, amillennialism, higher criticism, and also replacement theology, where Israel in the New Testament is considered the Christian Church. The Bible completely contradicts all aspects of these false teachings. Anyone who denies the truth of fulfilled and pending prophecies also denies what God's Word literally tells us. God may very likely allow these groups to enter the **time of Jacob's distress** for a false belief that God's literally described Biblical events are not happening. Take great caution regarding false beliefs and place your trust in Jesus and His Bible alone.

God knew false and misguided belief systems would become rampant and increase in the end times. Yet again, for this reason, God provided prophecies, (signs) His **Road Map** for us to "*see*." Once we find awareness of what God has specifically told us in His Word, we must not willfully turn a blind eye to His direct and clear warnings. Everyone must personally gain full knowledge of God's prophecies to recognize and understand their full significance.

Prophecies include concepts that have nothing to do with politics. The only thing that matters is what the Bible tells us all for our current days. The Bible is not a Democratic, Independent, or Republican document *(USA)*. It is the Word of the living God. The Bible contains God's guidance and truths for us all, His beloved creations. He has unnegotiable requirements that mandate thoughtful consideration and specific individual choices during our lifetimes. God also tells us that it does not matter who holds political office as nothing will deter His plans. **The Lord chooses the world's leaders**, so we have no need for concern. Throughout the Bible, God addresses the subject of how to deal with the leaders of our day; this is obviously important to Him. As the world and its coming leaders **progressively** turn boldly against what the Bible tells us is right, we need to remember that God knows what He is doing. We need only to understand how God wants us to deal with this, and Jesus gives us solid direction:

Romans 13:1–3
¹ Every person is to be in subjection to the governing authorities. <u>For there is no authority except from God, and those which exist are established by God.</u> ² Therefore whoever resists authority has opposed the ordinance of God; and they who have opposed will receive condemnation upon themselves. ³ For rulers are not a cause of fear for good behavior, but for evil. Do you want to have no fear of authority? Do what is good and you will have praise from the same.

1 Timothy 2:1–3
¹ First of all, then, I urge that entreaties and prayers, petitions and thanksgivings, be made on behalf of all men, ² for kings and all who are in authority, so that we may lead a tranquil and quiet life in all godliness and dignity. ³ This is good and acceptable in the sight of God our Savior[.]

1 Peter 2:13-17

13 Submit yourselves for the Lord's sake to every human institution, whether to a king as the one in authority, 14 or to governors as sent by him for the punishment of evildoers and the praise of those who do right. 15 For such is the will of God that by doing right you may silence the ignorance of foolish men. 16 Act as free men, and do not use your freedom as a covering for evil, but use it as bond slaves of God. 17 Honor all people, love the brotherhood, fear God, honor the king.

I make no predictions! I offer an interpretation of prophecy using only the Bible as my guide. God explains His intended **Road Map** chronology and timelines for Himself out of His own word. **When prophecy 13 arrives, there will be no need to update this book. Just watch and follow what happens next. The balance of prophecies 14-24 will become self-explanatory.**

Some people today erroneously believe some of us expounding that the end times are upon us are prophets in a literal sense. This is unfortunate. To make matters worse, some contemporary authors are **prophesying**, telling us God has **revealed** to them **new mysteries**, issues never revealed until now for our current last days. This is highly problematic and borders on arrogance. Christians today are so thirsty for knowledge of what God is doing that they are latching onto supposedly newly God-inspired **superfluous revelations** while paying little or no respectful attention to what the **Lord has already boldly revealed** for us in His Word. In actuality, no prophets—in the true sense of the word—live at this time in the world. God needed prophets *(Old Testament prophets and apostles)* only until He completed His entire original inspired text around 95 AD. The Bible, in its original form, tells the whole and complete story, perfectly, as God originally intended. It already includes all pertinent knowledge and instructions, with no need for revisions, new revelations, or modifications by anyone, at any time in history, either past or present. Those of us talking about the end times must always simply use as our guide what God's original designated Old Testament prophets and apostles have already provided for us in the completed Bible. Today, Biblical interpretations or illuminations are **not prophetic events**! God also makes it strikingly clear that to *add* **anything** or conversely to *take* **anything away** from His **completed inerrant Word** carries **grave** and **severe** consequences. God's clear copyright to His Word is vividly expressed in Revelation 22:18-19.

The long period of waiting for the Lord's return described in Isaiah 61:2(a), *"the favorable year of the Lord,"* has lasted almost 2,000 years and will lead us directly to *"the day of vengeance of our God."* The Bible indicates our wait is almost over:

Isaiah 61:1-2
[1] The Spirit of the Lord God is upon me, because the Lord has anointed me to bring good news to the afflicted; He has sent me to bind up the brokenhearted, to proclaim liberty to captives and freedom to prisoners; [2] (a) to proclaim the favorable year of the Lord and (b) the day of vengeance of our God; (c) to comfort all who mourn.

The *"favorable year of the Lord"* 61:2(a) (*also seen in Luke 4:16-21*) refers to the time from the ascension of Jesus up until the time of His visual **catching-up** event. The *"day of vengeance of our God"* **61:2(b)** denotes the coming 7-year **time of Jacob's distress**. This *"favorable year"* is a relational timeframe, meant to indicate a long period of time. How do we know this? We know, per the Bible: *"the day of vengeance of our God"* will last for a defined 7-year period. This 7-year period can then be proportionally likened to a day. Using these two timeframes, in the verses above, both a *"year"* and *"day,"* we can then conclude God established a general time relationship in these verses. A day is likened to 7-years by referring to the *"day of vengeance."* Then a year by comparison becomes a long period of time, a couple thousand years proportionally.

God indicates that we will be able to know this long period of time, *"the favorable year of the Lord,"* is coming to an end when we start to *"see"* God's end-time prophecies happening, His **Road Map**. Therefore, God intended for us to *"see"* His prophecies unfold. He explicitly tells us to literally *"look"* for them in His Bible. We must look for His **signs** showing us this long period of time is coming to an end. **We have arrived!**

The wonders within God's Word will magnify when we see the **final 12** prophetical events arrive, as illuminated in the Bible and chronicled below. Their fulfillment will validate my proposed interpretations.

Here is God's **Road Map**, 24 specific prophecies—some that are simple things to watch for and others that are highly detailed and intricate. **Three of them are "super signs."** All 24 must take place before the visual **catching up** and **the time of Jacob's distress will arrive**. I list them all for you now and will follow up on each with various levels of additional detail. Note again: 12 either have reached completion or are ongoing. **The final 12 will soon begin in God's perfect timing.**

GOD'S ROAD MAP

12 PROPHECIES COMPLETED OR ONGOING

1. TWO MAJOR BIRTH PAINS, WWI AND WWII
2. PREPARING THE LAND OF ISRAEL FOR THE JEWS
3. UNITED NATIONS FORMS
4. REBIRTH OF THE NEW STATE OF ISRAEL—SUPER SIGN #1
   Prophecies 1–4 are covered with more specificity in Chapter 3.
5. RETURN OF THE JEWS TO THE HOLY LAND
6. CAPTURE OF JERUSALEM
7. THE FALLING AWAY (APOSTASY)
8. INCREASE IN TRAVEL AND KNOWLEDGE
9. RISE OF ANTI-SEMITISM
10. MARK OF THE BEAST (TECHNOLOGY)
11. ISRAEL DWELLING SECURELY
12. GAZA ABANDONED

12 PROPHECIES THAT WILL HAPPEN IN SHORT ORDER

13. GOD'S NEXT PROPHECY: EZEKIEL 38 & 39 — SUPER SIGN #2

> This attack against Israel is imminent *(this is not the biblical catching up event)*. This event will resolve today's uprising in the Middle East, by God's hand alone saving His glory Israel.

Prophecies 14 through 23 will happen extremely rapidly after Ezekiel 38 & 39. The **visual catching up** will take place shortly after prophecy 24 begins.

14. **FIRST STAGE OF CONVERSION OF THE JEWS**
15. **REBUILDING OF BABYLON** (Iraq, not Rome)
16. **ONE WORLD GOVERNMENT AND ECONOMY**
17. **ONE WORLD CHURCH AND FALSE PROPHET**
18. **BUILDING OF THE THIRD TEMPLE IN JERUSALEM**
19. **WORLD GOVERNMENT BREAKS INTO 10 KINGDOMS**
20. **RISE OF THE ANTICHRIST** (after the 10 kingdoms)
21. **TIME OF PEACE & SAFETY IN THE UNBELIEVING WORLD**
22. **THE APPEARANCE OF ELIJAH**
23. **FEAR, SCOURGE, THE ANTICHRIST, AND HIS COVENANT**

> Just **prior to the signing** of a covenant between the Antichrist and Israel, the **visual catching up** will dramatically take place. The covenant signing with Israel *(second portion of prophecy #24)* starts the 7-year **time of Jacob's distress**.

24. SIGNS THE DAY OF THE VISUAL CATCHING UP — SUPER SIGN #3

> The **visual catching up** will take place for the whole world to witness. It occurs **mere hours before Israel's covenant is signed** with the Antichrist, starting the Biblical **time of Jacob's distress**. The **visual catching up** and the start of **the time of Jacob's distress by design happen within the same 24-hour day!**

1. TWO MAJOR BIRTH PAINS, WWI AND WWII

Matthew 24:4-8

⁴ And Jesus answered and said to them, "See to it that no one misleads you. ⁵ For many will come in My name, saying, 'I am the Christ,' and will mislead many. ⁶ You will be hearing of <u>wars and rumors of wars</u>. See that you are not frightened, for those things must take place, but that is not yet the end. ⁷ For nations will rise against *nations, and kingdoms against kingdoms, and in various places there will be <u>famines and earthquakes</u>. [8] But <u>all these things</u> are merely the <u>beginning of birth pangs</u>.*

These verses tell us that after a long period of time, *"the favorable year of the Lord"* established in Isaiah 61:2(a), believers will be given major signs of His impending return. When we see *"wars and rumors of wars"* and *"famines and earthquakes,"* *"all these things"* will designate the *"beginning of birth pangs"* (*birth pains*). Birth pangs must then logically lead to a birth.

Two significant major prophetical *"birth pangs"* have happened: World War I (*1914–1918*) and World War II (*1939–1945*). They both had **incredible importance** related **specifically** to the formation and rebirth of the prophesied new **State of Israel** on May 14, 1948. This rebirth officially started God's calendar for the **final generation** of the last days. I will elaborate on this in more detail in Chapter 3. WWI set in motion the availability of the land for the establishment of the rebirth of a new Jewish state. WWII provided a compelling reason for the Jews to return to the land of Israel from all over the world.

2. <u>PREPARING THE LAND OF ISRAEL FOR THE JEWS</u>

Zephaniah 2:1–2
[1] *Gather yourselves together, yes, gather, O nation without shame, [2] before the decree takes effect, the day passes like the chaff, before the burning anger of the Lord comes upon you, before the day of the Lord's anger comes upon you.*

Prior to WWI, Great Britain had control of the land we know today as Israel. After the war, Arthur Balfour of the British government declared this land as a national homeland for the Jewish people. Britain created an official document called the *Balfour Declaration (November 2, 1917)* officially preparing the land for the upcoming rebirth of the State of Israel.

3. UNITED NATIONS FORMS

Luke 21:29–32

[29] *Then He told them a parable: "Behold the fig tree and all the trees; [30] as soon as they put forth leaves, you see it and know for yourselves that summer is now near. [31] So you also, when you see these things happening, recognize that the kingdom of God is near. [32] Truly I say to you, this generation will not pass away until all things take place. [33] Heaven and earth will pass away, but My words will not pass away.["]*

Please notice the word *"see"* in the verses above. God uses this word quite often regarding prophecy.

After WWII, the parable above foretold the formation of the United Nations. The *"fig tree"* symbolically represents **Israel**, and *"all the trees"* refers to the **United Nations**. The United Nations formed in 1945 right after WWII ended. It holds great significance related to both the formation of the current State of Israel, which occurred in 1948, and the ultimate coming formation of the One World Government soon to arrive. The term *"this generation"* will, as mentioned earlier, have great importance.

4. REBIRTH OF THE NEW STATE OF ISRAEL — SUPER SIGN #1

Matthew 24:32–34

[32] *Now learn the parable from the fig tree: when its branch has already become tender and puts forth its leaves, you know that summer is near; [33] so, you too, when you see all these things, recognize that He is near, right at the door. [34] Truly I say to you, this generation will not pass away until all these things take place.*

Israel had been scattered, by God, for over 1,900 years since the destruction of the second temple in Israel in 70 AD. In this Scripture, God says to look for something *"when its branch has already become tender and puts forth its leaves."* This is symbolic of **new life sprouting or rebirth**. Israel is **reborn** on May 14, 1948 . . . chronologically the starting point of the literal **final generation**, God's first super end-times sign. Note that the word "*see*" is used yet again.

5. RETURN OF THE JEWS TO THE HOLY LAND

Ezekiel 37:11–14
[11] *Then He said to me, "Son of man, these bones are the whole house of Israel; behold, they say, 'Our bones are dried up and our hope has perished. We are completely cut off.'* [12] *Therefore prophesy and say to them, 'Thus says the Lord God, "Behold, I will open your graves and cause you to come up out of your graves, My people; and I will bring you into the land of Israel.* [13] *Then you will know that I am the Lord, when I have opened your graves and caused you to come up out of your graves, My people.* [14] *I will put My Spirit within you and you will come to life, and I will place you on your own land. Then you will know that I, the Lord, have spoken and done it," declares the Lord.'"*

Zephaniah 2:1–2
[1] *Gather yourselves together, yes, gather, O nation without shame,* [2] *before the decree takes effect, the day passes like the chaff, before the burning anger of the Lord comes upon you.*

Jeremiah 31:8
[8] *Behold, I am bringing them from the north country, and I will gather them from the remote parts of the earth, among them the blind and the lame, the woman with child and she who is in labor with child, together; A great company, they will return here.*

The return of the Jews to the Holy Land (*the second Exodus*) actually began slowly in the late 1880s and moved at a slow pace until the end of WWII. Hitler killed almost one-half of all the Jews alive during his satanic reign of terror in WWII. After WWII, the Jews no longer felt safe outside of Israel. With anti-Semitism growing rampant, the migration of the Jews back to Israel has happened at an accelerated pace and continues to this day — another key sign indicating the end times have arrived. In Zephaniah 2:2, God says, *"before the burning anger of the Lord comes upon you"* . . . prior to the beginning of **the time of Jacob's distress**.

6. CAPTURE OF JERUSALEM

Luke 21:24
²⁴ and they will fall by the edge of the sword, and will be led captive into all the nations; and Jerusalem will be trampled underfoot by the Gentiles until the times of the Gentiles are fulfilled.

The Gentiles trampled Jerusalem underfoot until June 7, 1967, during the Six-Day War. In that short war, **on that day**, the Jewish people took back control of Jerusalem for the first time in more than 1,900 years, fulfilling the *"time of the Gentiles."*

7. THE FALLING AWAY (APOSTASY)

2 Thessalonians 2:1–3
¹ Now we request you, brethren, with regard to the coming of our Lord Jesus Christ and our gathering together to Him, ² that you not be quickly shaken from your composure or be disturbed either by a spirit or a message or a letter as if from us, to the effect that the day of the Lord has come. ³ Let no one in any way deceive you, for it will not come unless

the apostasy comes first, and the man of lawlessness
is revealed, the son of destruction[.]

1 Timothy 4:1
¹ But the Spirit explicitly says that in later times some
will fall away from the faith, paying attention to
deceitful spirits and doctrines[.]

2 Timothy 4:3-4
³ For the time will come when they will not endure sound
doctrine; but wanting to have their ears tickled, they will
accumulate for themselves teachers in accordance to their own
desires, ⁴ and will turn away their ears from the truth and will
turn aside to myths.

Apostasy, the falling away from faith in Jesus, is happening today on a grand scale. Soon, **one current significant Christian denomination** will as an organization *"fall away from the true faith."* Deceitful *"doctrines"* is a key concept in these verses. This current denomination will follow manmade *"doctrines"* that do not, in fact, line up with what God teaches in His Bible as **truth**. A great deal of evidence supports this thinking. **Road Map** prophecy #17 will address this in additional detail.

I will likely be attacked and ridiculed for the analysis I am about to share in this chapter and specifically in Prophecy #17 regarding the possible future of this <u>one specific, current Christian denomination.</u> However, I offer this information with compassion, not disdain. If anyone starts to feel some irritation or finds what I'm sharing offensive, *<u>I ask only for one kindness</u>.* Please read through it all, trying to maintain objectivity. What the course of future history holds is yet undetermined. What you choose to do with this information individually, in the near future, is between you alone and Jesus. Please be aware and watch what might happen soon.

Hundreds of worldwide organizations have come into existence over the last 200 years, preparing for the coming prophesied

One World Church. Their main goals: to discredit the Bible and its **fundamentals** as **the sole source of truth**. The man of lawlessness, the Antichrist, will come on the scene (**Road Map** prophecy #20) **as apostasy reaches a peak.** The One World Church and the Antichrist both come into existence before the *"day of the Lord"* arrives, **the time of Jacob's distress**.

Hebrews 5:11–14

[11] Concerning him we have much to say, and it is hard to explain, since you have become dull of hearing. [12] For though by this time you ought to be teachers, you have need again for someone to teach you the elementary principles of the oracles of God, and you have come to need milk and not solid food. [13] For everyone who partakes only of milk is not accustomed to the word of righteousness, for he is an infant. [14] But solid food is for the mature, who because of practice have their senses trained to discern good and evil.

The Deceiver continues to water down sin, so some Christians have no problem accepting and justifying any action they choose to pursue—all issues that do not follow Biblical instruction: premarital cohabitation, abortion, cheating, lying, pornography, listening to lustful or hateful music, and basically all unscriptural practices that make people more susceptible to fall away from God's real truth. Through Jesus, Christians, upon asking, receive grace and forgiveness for all these weaknesses—**even after salvation**. What a wonderful and gracious Lord we have. If the Lord can forgive, we need to follow His lead and do the same for our family and friends.

8. INCREASE IN TRAVEL AND KNOWLEDGE

Daniel 12:4

[4] But as for you, Daniel, conceal these words and seal up the book until the <u>end of time</u>; <u>many will go back and forth</u>, and <u>knowledge will increase</u>.

God showed Daniel events that would occur in the distant future during the *"end of time,"* which is our current days. He told him *"many will go back and forth"* (*travel will be easy*). A mere 116 years ago, man traveled by air for the first time. Jets today can take us anywhere on earth within one day. As for knowledge increasing, look at a smartphone: the entire knowledge of the world is available now, if desired, in the palm of your hands.

9.   RISE OF ANTI-SEMITISM

Psalm 83:1–4

¹ O God, do not remain quiet; Do not be silent and, O God, do not be still. ² For behold, Your enemies make an uproar, and those who hate You have exalted themselves. ³ They make shrewd plans against Your people, and conspire together against Your treasured ones. ⁴ They have said, Come, and let us wipe them out as a nation, that the name of Israel be remembered no more.

The majority of the countries currently surrounding Israel have a strong hatred for the Jewish state and its people. This hate is called **anti-Semitism**. Many Islamic people hate Israel and have boldly stated their desire to rid the world of the Jews.

10.   MARK OF THE BEAST (TECHNOLOGY)

Revelation 13:15–18

¹⁶ And he causes all, the small and the great, and the rich and the poor, and the free men and the slaves, to be given a mark on their right hand or on their forehead, ¹⁷ and he provides that no one will be able to buy or to sell, except the one who has the mark, either the name of the beast or the number of his name. ¹⁸ Here is wisdom. Let him who has understanding calculate the number of the beast, for the number is that of a man; and his number is six-hundred and sixty-six.

During the entire 7-year **time of Jacob's distress**, mankind will need to endure difficult times — even in the first half of God's judgment period. I speculate that during the entire time of Jacob's distress, building things and creating new technologies will be the last thing on people's minds. In the early days, they will desire only to survive. The technology actually exists today to keep track of everything we do. National sovereignty restricts world leaders from abusing this power. After **Road Map** prophecy #13, with the completion of the Ezekiel attack, all countries will likely forfeit their sovereignty safety nets.

The Bible tells us that during the **time of Jacob's distress,** at the midpoint, Satan will indwell the Antichrist. He will require all people to take his mark on their bodies or be killed. Anyone who takes the mark can never be with Jesus, according to Revelation 14:9–11. This mark guarantees eternal damnation and is applied to the right hand or forehead. After the midpoint of the time of Jacob's distress, no person should ever take this mark. Nobody can buy or sell without having it during the last half of the time of Jacob's distress. Christians today will not see this.

11.   ISRAEL DWELLING SECURELY

Ezekiel 38:8
8 After many days you will be summoned; <u>in the latter years</u> you will come into the land that is <u>restored from the sword</u>, whose inhabitants have been <u>gathered from many nations to</u> the mountains of <u>Israel</u> which <u>had been a continual waste;</u> but its people were <u>brought out from the nations</u>, and they are <u>living securely</u>, all of them.

Ezekiel 38:11
11 and you will say, 'I will go up against the land of <u>unwalled villages</u>. I will go against those who are at rest, that live securely, all of them living without walls and having no bars or gates[.']

40

Ezekiel 38:14
14 *"Therefore prophesy, son of man, and say to Gog, 'Thus says the Lord God, On that day when My people Israel are <u>living securely</u>, will you not know it?['"]*

Israel has lived securely and safely in **unwalled villages** for almost 71-years as of the revised date of the book. The Hebrew word in the original text for this is *"batach,"* which means a **place of refuge** and **safety**. Currently, no walls **inside** Israel separate internal *"villages."* Israel is also *"living securely"* because of their confidence that they can easily defend themselves from any one of the neighboring countries surrounding them. God did not use *"shalom"* in these verses, which is the word for **peace**. Note that He specifically uses the word for **refuge** and **safety** in the verses above, not **peace**, a significant distinction.

The impending problem: many of the Islamic countries currently surrounding Israel now think (*scheme*) collectively they must rid the world of the Jews . . . exactly what God wants them to believe. This is good news for both Christians and Jews even though the thought of an impending battle may seem frightening. God tells us not to fear, **He will prevail**.

To this point, all of the 12 prophecies discussed either have been fulfilled as singular events or are ongoing and shall remain continuous for God's purposes.

12. GAZA ABANDONED

Zephaniah 2:3-4
3 *Seek the Lord, all you humble of the earth who have carried out His ordinances; seek righteousness, seek humility. Perhaps you will be hidden in <u>the day of the Lord's anger</u>. 4 For <u>Gaza will be abandoned</u> and Ashkelon a desolation; Ashdod will be driven out at noon and Ekron will be uprooted.*

Gaza is a portion of land that existed within the current State of Israel that formed in 1948. This is a simple prophecy, but important. God tells us only to watch, in the last days, for a time when Israel will give land away—specifically Gaza. In 2005, searching for peace, Israelites abandoned control of Gaza (*out of Jewish control*) as prophesied. Note the Jews will abandon Gaza close to the day of the Lord's anger. The *"day of the Lord's anger"* is one of many commonly accepted Biblical terms for **the time of Jacob's distress**. Also, today we are watching the enemies of Israel, who now live in Gaza, shooting thousands of missiles at them. Had Israel not abandoned Gaza—something God did not want—they would not have this problem today.

Road Map Prophecy #13 is coming; it will be an **awesome event**. This **singular event** will change the current course of mankind. **Road Map** prophecies 13–24 are the final 12 events that must soon occur in God's Divine story.

13. GOD'S NEXT PROPHECY: EZEKIEL 38 & 39—SUPER SIGN #2

Ezekiel 39:1–4
[1] *"And you, son of man, prophesy against Gog and say, 'Thus says the Lord GOD, Behold, I am against you, O Gog, prince of Rosh, Meshech and Tubal;* [2] *and I will turn you around, drive you on, take you up from the remotest parts of the north and bring you against the mountains of Israel.* [3] *I will strike your bow from your left hand and dash down your arrows from your right hand.* [4] *You will fall on the mountains of Israel, you and all your troops and the peoples who are with you[.'"]*

(Chapter 4 contains additional Scriptures and detailed analysis).

This interesting, precise, and controversial prophecy explains, in great detail, about a major attack coming at any moment now against Israel by its surrounding enemy neighbors. Ezekiel 38:1–

39:16 tells us how God will both initiate and completely resolve today's imposing, warlike situation including how He will protect and provide a major victory for Israel—a pivotal event in world history. This will be God's second super sign. Road Map prophecies 14–24 will happen after Ezekiel 38:1–39:16, relatively quickly—possibly within a single year. Here are some foundational issues critical to understanding the reasoning for this prophecy to occur at almost any moment.

Today, people belong to many different religions that have a variety of names and definitions professing their particular versions of God, such as Judaism/Christianity, Islam, Buddhism, and Hinduism. Many different internal factions exist within all these major groups. Also, people believe in a multitude of other smaller religions regionally around the world as well.

I will be placing special emphasis on three groups that by God's design, will play major roles in how the end days play out per God's **Road Map**: **Judaism, Christianity**, and **Islam**. Jews and Christians have an intimate connection, because Christianity is actually a splinter group of Judaism. **Christians accept Jesus as the prophesied Jewish Messiah.** These three religions all claim Abraham as their patriarch, but the similarity ends there. To fully comprehend what must soon take place and why, we must understand the distinctions that define and clearly separate these groups. We also need to define how these belief systems will soon play significant roles in world events. I provide substantial evidence that one of these three groups does not believe in the same God, even though they claim, along with the other two, full relationship to the same patriarch Abraham. But how is this possible?

1 Timothy 2:5
5 For there is one God and one mediator between God and mankind, the man Christ Jesus[.]

"One God and one mediator" — God's Son, Jesus. Also, the third part of God — the Holy Spirit — abides within us. **This is the Trinity**: the Father, Son, and Holy Spirit — all one, not three separate Gods. Some people, specifically our Jewish family, have trouble with how one God, as proclaimed in the Bible, can be three entities in one. A popular analogy using water shows this concept quite well: liquid, steam, and ice are three forms of the same thing with different characteristics, yet they are all still water. The three parts of the Trinity have specific importance with different characteristics, also: 1) for our eternity — God the Father, 2) for our salvation — Jesus the Son, 3) for our protection and comfort — the Holy Spirit. God's design is brilliant. But do other Gods exist? No. God has told us **He is the one God**.

As we witness these end times, we need to distrust and disvalue some new upcoming Bible translations during this time of growing apostasy. Some of the most respected Bible translators today have begun to interchange the name of God in some new Christian Bibles with the written word "Allah," to satisfy certain specific populations. Their explanation: use this name to keep current with the language certain people understand. But I find it impossible to even consider the use of the name Allah for the God of Abraham, Isaac, and Jacob, and Isa for Jesus, the Son of God, in any Christian Bible translation.

These translators' websites profess that Jews and Christians used the name Allah in Arabic communities, all through early history. Their sites claim how we wrongly assume that Allah is not an acceptable name for God in Arabic Christian Bibles. I can understand that in the old days many religions found this generic name acceptable, but, for our current time, this thinking causes a serious problem.

The Arabic word for "god" is Allah. Prior to the completion of the Islamic Holy Book, the Quran, in 632 AD, the word "Allah" may have been acceptable as a generic Arabic name for any god. It is believed that Mohamed spoke inspired words to his followers and they scribed all of his thoughts into what is today the Quran.

The Quran has Surahs, chapters and verses similar in format to the Bible. Upon the Quran's completion, the Arabic spoken and written word "Allah" was specifically defined as their sole god. To support my analysis, I will make reference to some Surahs shortly. If desired, you can read the Quran online (*quran.com*).

Mohamed describes Allah, in the Quran, as a god specifically different from the God of the Christians and Jews. Explicitly, "**a god who has no son.**"

It appears that Allah directs the Islamic faithful not to take *"Christians or Jews as allies"* (*Quran, 5:51*). The Quran also defines Allah as a god superior to all other gods. This includes the God of Abraham, Isaac, and Jacob. Allah is Islam's singular god, the god of Abraham and Ishmael, a god who appears, to many of its devoted, to promote Jihad, which is holy war, against people who do not accept only him. This Jihad is happening today on many fronts. I would even venture to say an extremist version of Islam is expanding boldly in an exponential fashion of truly Biblical proportions. This is not by random chance, it is prophetic, and clearly, a piece of God's perfect accurate timeline. The end times are upon us.

Some say it's questionable that Allah requires Jihad in his Quran. If indeed he does not, perhaps his faithful who promote Jihad purposefully break the tenets of both the Quran and Islam. Regardless, biblical level events are formulating.

Some of the Islamic faithful seem to imply that Jihad is a self-defense action. The Quran addresses self-defense actions but may indicate that killing nonbelievers without provocation is an act of bravery. Does this imply that Allah desires these actions to prove a person is worthy of him and of heaven? Interestingly, we currently see many Islamic believers killing each other in the Middle East. This appears as a transgression against Allah in the Quran, unless these deaths occur by accident (*Quran 4:92–93*). It's easy to see that today some people of the Islamic faith are at war with both Jews and Christians and, in some instances, with themselves.

The Bible talks about grace **without requiring works** for salvation. This allows somebody the time to explore and discover their free will selection of a God, within their full natural life span. Nowhere in the Bible does it say Christians must kill somebody as an act required for proving devotion to Jesus or as a work required for entering heaven. Christians in the recent past did kill egregiously for religious purposes. They, however, did so in grave error. God did not condone these horrible past actions in any way. Jesus should hold no blame for the incorrect, misguided actions of sinful, uninformed men.

Using the logic of the translators mentioned earlier, who say Allah is one acceptable name for God in Christian Bibles for certain cultures, what are we to think? Based on the two diametrically opposed approaches to faith listed in the paragraphs above, how can it be justifiable today to accept the name Allah in any format, in any Christian Bible translations, for the God of Abraham, Isaac, and Jacob? It can't.

After the completion of the Quran, the name Allah took on a major change in our lexicon. I understand some Arabic Christians may still refer to God as Allah. I still have difficulty understanding how, with the severe and defined differences, any Christian could use the verbal Arabic word "Allah" so easily for the Father, Son, and Holy Spirit. In 632 AD, the name Allah took on its current specific meaning and definition and has a clear identity.

As Christians, we must not accept the Arabic spoken or written name Allah, in any format, regardless of past history, as a fair current representation of the God of Abraham, Isaac, and Jacob. The Islamic faith certainly would agree with this statement (*Quran 5:72–73*) in my estimation, so maybe we should follow their lead and accept their interpretation of god as quite different from a Christian's.

I'm sure sincere Christian people work for these Bible translation organizations, but they truly need to walk cautiously here. The idea of using the written or spoken name Allah in today's Scriptures for the God of Abraham, Isaac, and Jacob is absurd. Some may argue that apostasy is sneaking in on them. As explained above, after the writing of the Quran and the formation of Islam, we can no longer consider this as simply an update of understandable past language norms; it amounts to dangerous thinking. This current translation controversy, within our faith, indicates a bad sign of the times.

As I see it, we now have an undeniable problem between the Bible and the Quran. I do not see how "extremist" Islam could ever accept the idea of peace with Israel. A one-world religion, as described in the Christian Bible, would contradict the desires of this religion per the Quran if Israel, and Christians for that matter, were still involved.

The God of Abraham, Isaac, and Jacob has stated that a perceived peace with Israel will happen in some form. The tenets of the Quran, on the other hand, dispute this, saying the God of Abraham and Ishmael will destroy Israel. Only one of these two opposing points of view can ultimately be correct. The coming Ezekiel attack will clarify this whole issue. In fact, the Bible tells us, a limited number of Middle East nations will come against Israel at some point in time, attempting to essentially wipe them off the face of the earth (*Psalm 83:4*). Many followers of the Quran truly believe their god requires them to destroy Israel. Looking at the world today, it appears that multiple factions within Islam are preparing, now, to attack Israel in the near future.

Some kind of attack "shall" occur soon, as both the Bible and the Quran predict and our daily news seems to validate. We all need only to wait and watch to see which side wins. It will be interesting to witness how this all plays out.

In the Quran, Allah repeats, many times, he *"does not have a son,"* and he is *"not a part of any three, or triune god entity."* The following list represents Surahs, from the Quran, that back up what I am sharing with you. The following Surahs advocate Islam not accepting the idea of the Trinity (*the Father, Son, and Holy Spirit*). They are 4:171, 5:57, 5:73, 6:101, 9:30, 17:111, 19:35, 19:36, and 19:88–92. Based on these Surahs, it is impossible for the God of Abraham, Isaac, and Jacob to be the same entity as Allah—or for Isa/Jesus to be the same either.

The Quran was scribed around 632 AD, or about 1,400 years ago. The entire Bible used by Christians today, including both Testaments, reached completion around 95 AD, more than 1,900 years ago. It fully explains and defines the God of Abraham, Isaac, and Jacob and established all of His prophetic timelines—a full 500 years before the Islamic Quran came into existence.

Many events (*not doctrines*) in the Quran have similar dates, timeframes, and numerology as the already established written details in the Christian Bible from 500 years earlier. In the Quran, however, Allah appears to have removed the God of Abraham, Isaac, and Jacob and adopted counterfeit versions of already established timeframes for his Quran scribed in 632 AD. Allah, in the younger Quran, appears to have substituted himself and his redefined precepts into the vast majority of already preestablished defined timelines that the Trinity (*Father, Son, and Holy Spirit*) had already claimed long before.

The Quran disputes that Jesus is the Son of God. In the Quran, Jesus is only a prophet. It appears that the Quran—written 500 years after the Bible—when completed, supposedly cleared up errors in the original older Bible. So, did God get His Word in the Bible wrong the first time and need to have somebody revise and correct it? **No.**

Hebrews 6:17–20
[17] In the same way God, desiring even more to show to the heirs of the promise the unchangeableness of His purpose,

interposed with an oath, [18] so that by two unchangeable things in which <u>it is impossible for God to lie</u>, we who have taken refuge would have strong encouragement to take hold of the hope set before us. [19] This hope we have as an anchor of the soul, a hope both sure and steadfast and one which enters within the veil, [20] where <u>Jesus has entered as a forerunner for us</u>, having become a high priest forever according to the order of Melchizedek.

The Lord tells us clearly *"it is impossible for God to lie"* in Hebrews 6:18. This means God has told us that His Word in the older, original Bible is perfect *(1 Cor. 13:9-11)*. *"Jesus has entered as a forerunner for us"* so that we may have hope for our future.

Jesus, the Son of God, was born, died on the cross, and later resurrected per the Bible—long before the Quran was defined. God got it all right the first time. Notice what the Bible tells us about Jesus in Hebrews 13:8.

Hebrews 13:8
[8] *Jesus Christ is the same yesterday and today and forever.*

Jesus and God will never need to modify to catch up with new enlightened times. They are the same, have always been the same, and will always be the same, as they have told us. They are all-powerful and all-knowing and have no need to ever evolve or be redefined.

14. FIRST STAGE OF CONVERSION OF THE JEWS

Ezekiel 39:7
[7] *My holy name I will make known in the midst of My people Israel; and I will not let My holy name be profaned anymore. And the nations will know that I am the Lord, the Holy One in Israel.*

During the Ezekiel attack, God makes himself known. When the attack is quickly completed, God is victorious for Israel. A short period of revival will occur, and many Jews and nonbelievers will profess and accept faith in Jesus. Per the Bible, during this attack it appears God intends to neutralize the Islamic presence, creating a large worldwide spiritual and political void. This will clear a path, opening up the door and paving the way for all of the following outstanding remaining prophecies.

15. __REBUILDING OF BABYLON__ *(in Iraq, not in Rome)*

Zechariah 5:5–11

5 Then the angel who was speaking with me went out and said to me, "Lift up now your eyes and see what this is going forth." 6 I said, "What is it?" And he said, "This is the ephah going forth." Again he said, "This is their appearance in all the land 7 (and behold, a lead cover was lifted up); and this is a woman sitting inside the ephah." 8 Then he said, "This is Wickedness!" And he threw her down into the middle of the ephah and cast the lead weight on its opening.9 Then I lifted up my eyes and looked, and there two women were coming out with the wind in their wings; and they had wings like the wings of a stork, and they lifted up the ephah between the earth and the heavens.
10 I said to the angel who was speaking with me, "Where are they taking the ephah?" 11 Then he said to me, "To build a temple for her in the <u>land of Shinar</u>; and when it is prepared, she will be set there on her own pedestal."

In these verses, God describes the vision of an **ephah** vessel, which is a measuring container able to hold one **ephah** for purchasing and selling. An **ephah** is a Hebrew unit of dry measure equal to about a bushel, 35 liters. In Zechariah, God uses an **ephah** to give us a representation of what will come in relation to the church and government of the last days. Note that by using the un-capitalized word "**ephah**": God is not referring to the son of Midian or any other individual. This use of an **ephah** here is symbolic for **commerce**, and it is also associated with **gloom,** **darkness,** and **wickedness.** God even uses the exact word *"wickedness"* in verse 8; He has chosen a specific term to make His point.

God shows Zechariah this **ephah** container with a heavy lead lid upon it. Zechariah lifts the lid and sees a wicked woman sitting inside the container. The woman sitting within the **ephah** vessel *(apostate Catholicism after Ezekiel 38)* signifies the wickedness contained in commerce and religion, including covetousness and deceit during the future **time of Jacob's distress.**

Zechariah describes two additional women with the appearance of storks *(apostate Judaism and Protestantism)* who lift up and carry away the **ephah** container with its heavy lid, including its inhabitant, and take them to the *"land of Shinar,"* which is the literal **city of Babylon in Iraq**. Upon arrival, the evil woman will remain entrapped inside the **ephah** container until her temple is built. Then, upon her release, she is *"set on her pedestal."* The world will soon prepare Babylon as the place for the One World Church *(her pedestal)* and Government. We will witness this in short order after the Ezekiel 38 attack.

Quickly after the Ezekiel attack, both the One World Government and the One World Church commence consolidation. Some incorrectly believe this will happen in the city of Rome. The Antichrist and his church must be in the *"land of Shinar"* — the actual city of Babylon in current-day Iraq — categorically not Rome, per Zechariah 5:11.

16. ONE WORLD GOVERNMENT AND ECONOMY

Daniel 7:23–24

23 *"Thus he said: 'The fourth beast will be a fourth kingdom on the earth, which will be different from all the other kingdoms and will devour the whole earth and tread it down and crush it.* 24 *As for the ten horns, out of this kingdom ten kings will arise; and another*

*will arise after them, and he will be different
from the previous ones[.'"]*

Almost immediately after Ezekiel 38, the One World Government and Economy will quickly form. Right after the One World Government arrives, it will break into 10 divisions (**Road Map** *prophecy #19*). After the 10 divisions form, then and only then will the Antichrist come on the scene (**Road Map** *prophecy #20*). When we review the verses for the following prophecies, we learn **the Antichrist will arrive before the visual catching up happens.** We can clearly deduce from prophecy that the One World Government and Economy must be in place **before the time of Jacob's distress arrives**, and before the Antichrist will become known to us.

17.   ONE WORLD CHURCH AND FALSE PROPHET

Revelation 17:1–5
*¹ Then one of the seven angels who had the seven bowls came and spoke with me, saying, "Come here, I will show you the judgment of the great harlot who sits on many waters, ² with whom the kings of the earth committed acts of immorality, and those who dwell on the earth were made drunk with the wine of her immorality." ³ And he carried me away in the Spirit into a wilderness; and I saw a woman sitting on a scarlet beast, full of blasphemous names, having seven heads and ten horns. ⁴ The woman was clothed in purple and scarlet, and adorned with gold and precious stones and pearls, having in her hand a gold cup full of abominations and of the unclean things of her immorality, ⁵ and on her forehead a name was written, a mystery, "BABYLON THE GREAT,
THE MOTHER OF HARLOTS
AND OF THE ABOMINATIONS OF THE EARTH."*

This one intricate and involved prophecy follows closely with **Road Map** prophecy #8, apostasy. The Deceiver will successfully weaken and marginalize true faith in Jesus. He will achieve this with cunning, <u>**without the majority of the current-day Church knowing it is happening.**</u> As we will learn now, after the Ezekiel attack, both the One World Church and the False Prophet will smoothly and effortlessly blend onto the scene — not abruptly — but subtly and before the start of **the time of Jacob's distress**.

The Ezekiel attack will create a huge spiritual void, which will quickly be filled by a **co-opted version** of one major Christian church . . . the current denomination that bears the closest resemblance to the original Babylonian Mystery Religion explained in the book of Genesis. This relationship, which I will describe shortly, is a key to what Scripture tells us about the church of the end times in the book of Revelation — a crucial piece of end-time prophecy.

It will become clear to those who study Bible prophecy which denomination must transform into the Church of the end times **<u>after two major things happen:</u>** 1) the Ezekiel attack and 2) this specific church physically moving its headquarters to the city of Babylon in current-day Iraq.

God tells us in 1 Timothy 4:1 that some Christian churches will fall during the apostasy in the last days:

<u>*1 Timothy 4:1*</u>
¹ But the Spirit explicitly says that in later times some will fall away from the faith, paying attention to <u>deceitful spirits</u> and <u>doctrines</u>[.]

We all need awareness about the *"falling away"* and must be diligent in watching the actions of our churches to make sure they do not wander away from Jesus.

All Christians, in the last days, are in grave peril. The Deceiver wants everyone to believe the final One World Church will be a wonderful, unified, loving **universal** organization. The Deceiver will essentially kidnap many churches to join into one counterfeit family. For the final One World Church, the Deceiver will also want to **co-opt** the denomination with the most influence, wealth, and power. So, which denomination of our current Christian family is this church? It will be the **Catholic Church. If you're Catholic, I care for you and mean no harm.**

I accept that many faithful Catholics today may initially totally dismiss that anything such as this could possibly ever happen. Of course, this has not happened yet, but, when soon-to-come world events unfold and dramatic changes rapidly occur, please do not discount this possibility as proposed.

The Catholic Church hierarchy does not believe Biblical prophecies should be taken literally. They consider them **allegorical**. This includes: **Revelation,** the **visual catching up** and Biblical **time of Jacob's distress**, which we will soon review. We **are literally seeing** God's prophecies actually happen today!

Old Testament Scriptures show us how to know when people (*false prophets*) teach incorrectly, specifically if we are told something that does not come true. These are issues that do not stand up to Biblical scrutiny:

> *Deuteronomy 18:20–22*
> [20] *["']But the prophet who speaks a word presumptuously in My name which I have not commanded him to speak, or which he speaks in the name of other gods, that prophet shall die.' [21] You may say in your heart, 'How will we know the word which the Lord has not spoken?' [22] When a prophet speaks in the name of the Lord, if the thing does not come about or come true, that is the thing which the Lord has not spoken. The prophet has spoken it presumptuously; you shall not be afraid of him.["]*

God has told us to **look for prophecies** related to His end-times scenario. When His expressed plans occur, and we *"see"* them, we must trust God's words. We have to take care not to become mesmerized or taken in by **perilous manmade doctrines**. There is great danger in doing so. We must not get angry with God when His Word does not line up with incorrect human interpretations.

In **Road Map** prophecy #15, I explained a bit about the rebuilding of the literal real city of Babylon in Iraq. Now, we'll explore this a bit more as it also relates to this coming One World Church and the establishing of this end-time church in the real city of Babylon, in current-day Iraq.

THE BABYLON MYSTERY RELIGION SETS THE MODEL FOR THE FINAL ONE WORLD CHURCH

According to Revelation 17:5, the church of the end times will similarly model the original first Babylon Mystery Religion started by Nimrod's wife, Semiramis, in current-day Iraq. Genesis 10:8–10 classified Nimrod as *"a mighty one on earth"* and ruler of the first world empire after the Flood of Noah, in the *"land of Shinar,"* the actual city of Babylon, Iraq. Nimrod was a real person listed in the Bible. Study of historical resources, independent of the Bible, is required to understand the story of this individual. Some consider Nimrod and his wife to be mythological figures; this is Biblically incorrect. There are a variety of interpretations regarding Nimrod and Semiramis and the Babylon Mystery Religion. I have provided the one that contains the most archeological support for my summary.

Semiramis, Nimrod's wife, a power-hungry individual, schemed to get her husband out of the way so she could take over power. A wild animal conveniently killed Nimrod, and his widow immediately transformed him into a god who had taken possession of the sun (a sun god). Semiramis then claimed herself to be Ishtar, the **"queen of heaven"** (*Jeremiah 44:18*) and Babylon.

A decadent harlot in her private life, she met Nimrod while running a brothel.

Soon after Nimrod's death, she claimed that Nimrod, in spirit, came and impregnated her—a quasi-virgin-like birth scenario. She gave birth to a son named **Tammuz** . . . supposedly Nimrod reincarnated (*a son of a god*). This was the beginning of **the original Babylon Mystery Religion**. All the subsequent temples built for this Mystery Religion had a prominent statue of the mother Ishtar holding in her arms her baby son, Tammuz.

Their new religion needed many priests and priestesses to explain their version of god to the people. Only their priests had access to the **mysteries** of this church; keep this thought in mind. The people could learn about god only through hearsay. As a result, with only limited knowledge of the truth, the supposedly **"enlightened"** people of that day decided to build a tower to reach the heavens to touch their **false version of god**. They built the Tower of Babel, as explained in Genesis 11:1–9. This ignorance about the true God created arrogance, and the limited false teachings of their priests angered the **true God**. As a punishment, He confused their language.

Through archeological finds, we have discovered that mankind created multiple versions of pagan **Babylon Mystery Religions**. They came into existence between 2000 and 1600 BC and, over the following centuries, developed many new cult-like rituals. Some of these included astrology, idol worship (*including the fish-god Dagon*), purgatorial purification after death, salvation by countless sacraments, priestly absolution, and the offering of round cakes to the Queen of Heaven (Jeremiah 7:18). They even created a 40-day period called **the Weeping for Tammuz** (*Ezekiel 8:14–15*) and the great **Festival of Ishtar**. The egg was sacred to Tammuz. Easter eggs today are an extension of this festival. An evergreen bush was selected to honor the birth of Tammuz at the winter solstice. We derive Christmas trees today from this origin.

God's Road Map

All of these pagan religious rituals expanded to overtake the world into what is called Babylonianism—created **2,000 years before Christ**. Babylonianism grew rampant in many formats right up to Jesus' birth. In fact, when the apostles went out to preach the gospel, Babylonianism in many forms had spread and fought the disciples on every front. At the time of Christ, Rome had already become the center of Babylonianism. Their chief priests wore mitres, hats shaped like the head and mouth of a fish honoring the fish-god Dagon. All this was created **years before Christ lived and Christianity formed**.

God tells us the church of the end times will follow this model of operation (Revelation 17:5). The Catholic Church today maintains many similarities and traditions closely related to the original Babylon Mystery Religion model. Look today at the pope's formal headwear; it resembles a fish's head and from the side an open fish's mouth.

Jesus, in the Catholic Church's mother-and-child pairing model, is, of course, not counterfeit. He is the real deal. Only He, per the Bible, has the power to save and forgive according to the Biblical Gospels (*the first four books of the New Testament*), **not His mother**. From actually reading the Bible personally, I see a major problem: God, in the 66 books of the Bible (*Appendix A*), does not place any Godly authority on the Virgin Mother. Therefore, treating Mary as a legitimate Biblical intermediary between man and God is problematic. Jesus even addresses how to look at His mother:

Luke 11:27–28
[27] While Jesus was saying these things, one of the women in the crowd raised her voice and said to Him, "Blessed is the womb that bore You and the breasts at which You nursed." [28] But He said, "<u>On the contrary,</u> blessed are those who hear the word of God and observe it."

57

From 1962 to 1965, the Catholic Church leaders held the **Second Vatican Council (Vatican II)** — a pastoral convention, convened to update and review the **doctrines**, policies, and attitudes of the Catholic Church relating to the modern world. The clergy added many new **doctrines** (*1 Timothy 4:1*) and rules to the church at that time. Even though the modern Catholic Church has chosen not to follow many of their own recorded **doctrines**, they have not revoked them, and these **doctrines** remain a part of their sacred writings and rules.

On November 21, 1964, at the end of the third session of the Vatican II, Pope Paul VI proclaimed Mary to be the **Mother of the Church** and made the following statement: *"henceforth the Blessed Virgin will be honored and invoked with this title by all Christian people."* Where might this place non-Catholic Christians who do not accept this premise?

The church of the end times, per the Bible, must have a female orientation or emphasis, and God calls it *"the Mother of Harlots"* (*Revelation 17:5*). Interestingly, this major shift in the Catholic Church regarding placing Mary in such **formal** high authority occurred only 50 years ago. **I must clarify: in no way am I suggesting that Mary, the mother of Jesus, was a harlot. God blessed her.** I simply think God's description by **gender** regarding the status and general makeup of the final One World Church in Revelation has purposeful significance.

Also, a negative transition within the Catholic Church, away from some literal Biblical teachings, occurred in the years 1545–1563 during the Protestant Reformation. The Catholic Church responded to this Reformation with their **Council of Trent**. They considered the thinking process and beliefs of this new revolutionary Protestant movement to be blasphemous and wanted to solidify their marginal positions on the Bible.

During this 18-year period, the Catholic leadership pronounced many **canons (*rules*)** and decrees as new **required doctrines** — some of which affect Christians who hold differing views from the Catholic hierarchy's newly adopted interpretations. At this same time in history, the Catholic leadership **added seven separate additional books to their Old Testament version** (*Appendix A*). The current Jewish and Protestant Bible versions do not include those seven books.

There are two types of canons. The books of the Bible are considered canons — the God-inspired books that collectively make up our current complete text. In this section, we cover the **second kind of canons** that are **rules** or **measuring sticks** representing what came out of the Council of Trent. Many of the Church's new **rules** require obedience by **all Christian people** from the Catholic leader's viewpoint.

These newly created canons are not alluded to, described, or explained anywhere in God's written Word, the Bible. Some canons totally discount the idea of simple and total instantaneous grace from Jesus. **Justification**, the subject of the **Seventh Session** of the Council of Trent, generated 33 canons and 16 decrees. These new **rules** were mandatory for Catholics. All believers in Jesus must never accept non-Biblical edicts expressed as facts or truth by **men alone**. It should be noted that if anyone does not agree with these canons, they become an **anathema**. An **anathema** by definition is *"One that is cursed or damned."*

Four examples of the 33 canons:

CANON XII. - If any one saith, that justifying faith is nothing else but confidence in the divine mercy which remits sins for Christ's sake; or, that this confidence alone is that whereby we are justified; **let him be anathema.**

CANON XV. - If any one saith, that a man, who is born again and justified, is bound of faith to believe that he is assuredly in the number of the predestinate; **let him be anathema.**

CANON XX. - If any one saith, that the man who is justified and how perfect so ever, is not bound to observe the commandments of God and of the Church, but only to believe; as if indeed the Gospel were a bare and absolute promise of eternal life, without the condition of observing the commandments; **let him be anathema.**

CANON XXIII. - If any one saith, that a man once justified can sin no more, nor lose grace, and that therefore he that falls and sins was never truly justified; or, on the other hand, that he is able, during his whole life, to avoid all sins, even those that are venial, except by a special privilege from God, as the Church holds in regard of the Blessed Virgin; **let him be anathema.**

These manmade Catholic leader's interpretations or **doctrines** have no solid basis from within the Bible itself. So, did Jesus lie to us in His Bible? **No.** Are we to assume that non-Catholic Christians are therefore, in fact, **anathemas** for disagreeing with these Catholic leader's canons? There is no other possible conclusion. We must be careful; it is highly possible the Catholic leadership does not believe someone can get to Jesus without their help. If this is true Catholic **doctrine**, it is in **serious contradiction** to what Jesus Himself says in His Bible. Because these canons were direct responses to the new Protestants' Biblical interpretations of salvation during the Reformation, this assessment makes practical sense.

Now, why am I choosing to address all of this? Because, in my opinion, these Catholic leader's canons appear to divide and separate Christians from one another, not unite us. Who ultimately benefits from this? Not the Christian family, certainly not Jesus; **the Deceiver does**! These canons and their use of the term **anathema** appear to be saying Catholics are the only true Christians. If someone does not accept their interpretation, they are *"damned"*; this is unfortunate. This interpretation of "damnation" severely marginalizes and minimizes the full unconditional grace of our Lord. Jesus tells us in the Bible, He is the only way and truth. Grace is unmerited favor from Jesus and requires nothing more than **"simple faith in His promise to us."**

Jesus Himself talks about being *"**accursed**,"* only when people seek man's approval or blessings **dispensed by human intermediaries** *(the church? NO)* and not directly from what we have *"received"* from God *"preached"* by the Lord:

Galatians 1:6–10

> *⁶ I am amazed that you are so quickly deserting Him who called you by the grace of Christ, for a different gospel; which is really not another; only there are some who are disturbing you and want to distort the gospel of Christ. But even if we, or an angel from heaven, should preach to you gospel contrary to what <u>we have preached</u> to you, he is to be accursed! ⁹ As we have said before, so I say again now, if any man is preaching to you a gospel contrary to what you <u>received,</u> he is to be accursed! ¹⁰ For am I now seeking the favor of men, or of God? Or am I striving to please men? If I were still trying to please men, I would not be a bond-servant of Christ.*

It is my serious fear that the Catholic Church is on the verge of becoming the foundation of the One World Church of the end times, **and many will not see it**. They have no idea where this is going to lead them and, to me, this is terrifying! At the Council of Trent, the Catholic leaders basically established that if people do not see things the Church's way, they are not saved.

I feel a need to clarify, emphatically, that I am not trying to pick on Catholics specifically. Many Christian churches, in the end times, will also fall away from true faith in Jesus if they do not continue to trust in the Lord alone. Again, the Catholic Church is a huge, visible, established, and wealthy organization owning more land in the world than any other entity. Right now, they have both an established figurehead *(the pope)* and a woman intermediary *(the Virgin Mary)*. Of all the Christian churches in existence at this time, I believe the Deceiver has his eyes directly on **this church model** due to its powerful position, its large worldwide wealth, and the fact again that it bears close similarities to the original **Mystery Babylonian Church model** (*Daniel 2:18, Revelation 17:5*). God tells us to both look and be watching for this **transformation** to happen. Because the Bible alone is accurate, some church will take control in the last times as the One World entity.

In the Catholic Church, the popes are the guardians and custodians of the Bible, and they say they would "**never**" change it or teach **new doctrines**. They even claim **Semper Idem** as their motto, which is "**always the same.**" The Council of Trent's doctrines and this motto seriously conflict due to inaccurate human interpretations. We need to carefully watch the spiritual warfare happening around us. I earnestly fear that Satan may soon overtake and occupy the Catholic Church in these last days. These subtle and gradual changes through **doctrines** will bring danger. Catholics should take great care not to walk on thin ice if they see this happening. Do not compromise your faith in Jesus as the only true God at any time.

The coming prophesied charismatic false prophet will appear humble; the majority of mankind will greatly respect him—very much like our current pope, who seems quite charming. Is he currently the prophesied false prophet? I don't think so, but I desire to qualify this opinion. Quite possibly, due to health issues, Pope Francis could resign into unprecedented secondary emeritus status (*Emeritus Pope Benedict XVI being still alive*), meaning the very next pope could likely be a strong candidate.

During the Council of Trent (1545), the Jesuit order came into existence. Did you know Pope Francis is the first Jesuit pope? Historically, the Jesuits' existence, since their formation in 1545, focuses on bringing all Christian religions back into the singular Catholic Church, **by any and all means possible**.

I personally believe the majority of these men today have good intentions and good hearts. The leadership—the upper hierarchy—causes the problems. The Jesuits appear loving and humble on the outside but possibly conceal something entirely different within the inner workings of their leadership.

We need to go back into history to identify the Jesuits and some past documented motives and actions. The Jesuit order, also known as the **Society of Loyola**, is renowned historically for deception, cruelty, and disruption, as one former president and one former pope attest:

> **John Adams** (1735–1826), second president of the United States:
> *"Shall we not have regular swarms of them here, in as many disguises as only a king of the gypsies can assume, dressed as painters, publishers, writers, and schoolmasters? If ever there was a body of men who merited eternal damnation on earth and in hell it is this Society of Loyola."*

> **Pope Clement XIV** (1705–1774), who had abolished the Jesuit Order, said this upon his likely poisoning (historical cover-up?) in 1773:
> *"Alas, I knew they [i.e., the Jesuits] would poison me, but I did not expect to die in so slow and cruel a manner."*

The concept that a pontiff might unilaterally **modify church doctrine** has never been more perilous than it is today, with the first Jesuit pope. The Jesuits have the power, and determination, within the church to spearhead a coming <u>universal church</u> reorganization leading to the formation of the prophesied One World Religion. This was and still is their intention, and they may soon achieve their long-desired goal.

The word **Catholic** means **universal**. Some might say the church is not a universal church but merely the **Roman Catholic Church**. Look at the two distinctions expressed in Canon XXIX (*number 29 of the 33 canons*) from the Council of Trent, under Justification:

CANON XXIX. - *If any one saith, that he, who has fallen after baptism, is not able by the grace of God to rise again; or, that he is able indeed to recover the justice which he has lost, but by faith alone without the sacrament of Penance, contrary to what the* <u>**holy Roman and universal Church**</u>*-instructed by Christ and his Apostles-has hitherto professed, observed, and taught;* **let him be anathema.**

Note: *"**holy Roman** <u>**and**</u> **universal Church**."* The Catholic Church desires to become the One Church of the world. Exactly what form this will ultimately take is still in question.

We can look at the word "**universal**" both **literally** and **figuratively.** The Catholic Church appears to believe they are to be the Universal Church in the literal sense. Jesus never used the term "**universal church**" in His Bible. **He is the Church!** Anyone who simply believes in Him and accepts Him as their Savior is saved and they **become part of Him, the Church. Period!**

<u>*John 3:16*</u>
16 *For God so loved the world, that He gave His only begotten Son, that whoever believes in Him shall not perish, but have eternal life.*

Fairly straightforward. Nowhere does this Scripture regarding Jesus require anyone to become a member of a worldly organization as a secondary prerequisite to obtain or maintain eternal life. People can personally obtain eternal life, and full salvation, from Jesus alone, directly, without intercession. For this interpretation of God's own words in John 3:16, based on Canons XII and XV above, as a Protestant, I appear to be **cursed and damned** according to existing Catholic Church **doctrine.**

Right after the completion of the Ezekiel attack, when God defeats the enemies of Israel, it will create a large spiritual chasm that will need to be quickly filled. With all the power the pope holds, we cannot totally count out a possibly infectious desire and opportunity for full religious **universal** dominance. The current or very next pope might find accepting a new fully dominant world role an enticing prospect.

In Catholicism, the pope is considered the **Vicar of Christ** or **Christ on earth**. Therefore, we should not consider a strong desire for full total religious control as out of the question. There is a saying: **total power corrupts**, so we need to carefully watch how a transition might happen as prophecy moves forward. Should this spiritual shift occur, it could bring about a Third Vatican Council (*Vatican III*) to establish how to consolidate all remaining religions into one church system for unity and perceived world peace. Please, pay careful attention, as this could get even more interesting, and dangerous, soon.

Something today called the **Ecumenical Movement** desires to create the One World Church. Many high-level Protestant church leaders will soon tell us how Jesus has always wanted all Christian religions to merge within the Catholic Church. **This has no Biblical basis.** In 1994, prominent Protestant Church leaders signed a document called *Evangelicals and Catholics Together*, basically stating that our differences are insignificant. Per the Bible, the written **doctrines** of the Catholic Church are inaccurate, so the differences are actually very significant. This document's precepts validate how apostasy is alive and well and spreading now in the Christian faith. Also, a growing **liberal theology** espouses that the Bible is flawed and filled with errors. Then, to go deeper into the Catholic Church, **magisterium** and **ex cathedra** (*papal infallibility*) tells us, unconditionally, the **doctrines** of the pope alone (*encyclicals*) in the Catholic Church are correct, no matter what God tells us directly in His Bible.

In the near future, we again need to attentively watch what happens in our churches. Please do not think the issues I am about to address could never possibly happen. If we see the church accepting behaviors and issues described in the Bible as things God specifically says displease Him, **be careful**. If we see the church indicate someone may get to heaven without Jesus, **be**

careful. If we see any Christian leaders tell us we should not use or say the name of Jesus so as not to offend anyone, **be careful**. If we see the church also accepting other religions under a proposed mantel of one-God-of-all umbrella, saying we all worship the same loving God, again **be careful**. If we see the church minimizing or trivializing Jesus in any way, to achieve harmony and lumping Him in with all other groups, we need to **be exceptionally careful**. Each of these actions would severely contradict what God has explicitly told us in His Bible.

If you put together all of what I have presented up to now in this section, it creates a recipe for the destruction of the true Christian version of the Catholic Church. Our world precariously dances on a dangerous slippery slope. When this foundational information is added to the rest of what I share from the Bible directly, the entire picture will make more sense.

For Christians, in general, when any church begins to accept all other religions as equals or decides to join or unite within one single world church unit for supposed peace, world harmony, and love, **be extremely careful**. <u>**This is apostasy!**</u> If this should occur, within any denomination or church, in the not too distant future, my suggestion and advice: **run away as fast as you can!** God even directs us to watch and then to *"come out of her"* when we see **any church** abandoning truth:

Revelation 18:4–5
⁴ I heard another voice from heaven, saying, "Come out of her, my people," so that you will not participate in her sins and receive of her plagues; ⁵ for her sins have piled up as high as heaven, and God has remembered <u>her</u> iniquities.

As previously stated, the church of the end times must be female oriented in the model of the original Babylon Mystery Religion. It must have a predominant female figurehead. The only Church today that has this now is the Catholic Church in the form of the Virgin Mary. It is important to look at Catholic viewpoints against what the Bible shares about her. This is highly important to understand as it relates to how the Catholic Church is going to severely change soon.

Per the Bible, Mary actually has no high Biblical significance other than God selecting her to give birth to His Son while still a virgin (Isaiah 7:14). She did not choose the role of Jesus' mother; God imparted this blessing on her. All Christians accept the original 66 canonical books (*Appendix A*), which do not say this blessing conveyed upon Mary provides any level of superiority or any type of power to mediate for us with God. In fact, praying to the Virgin Mary actually marginalizes what God tells us about His Son, Jesus, and tends to possibly place more emphasis and honor on the human mother than on God's Son.

1 Timothy 2:3–6

³ This is good and acceptable in the sight of God our Savior, ⁴ who desires all men to be saved and to come to the knowledge of the truth. ⁵ For there is one God, <u>and one mediator also between God and men, the man Christ Jesus</u>, ⁶ who gave Himself as a ransom for all, the testimony given at the proper time.

The Catholic Church hierarchy believes in Mary's **immaculate conception** and, therefore, she, like Jesus, was born without sin. The Bible does not say this; it is supposition. By this unsubstantiated action, God then made her perfect also as Christ. Consequently, today the Catholic Church gives her high authority. However, according to Hebrews 4:15, **<u>Jesus was the only sinless person who ever lived</u>**.

Hebrews 4:14–16

¹⁴ Therefore, since we have a great high priest who has passed through the heavens, Jesus the Son of God, let us hold fast our confession. ¹⁵ For we do not have a high priest who cannot sympathize with our weaknesses, <u>but One</u> who has been *tempted in all things as we are, <u>yet without sin</u>. [16] Therefore let us draw near with confidence to the throne of grace, so that we may receive mercy and find grace to help in time of need.*

Mary also had natural children with her husband, Joseph, so after Jesus' birth Mary no longer remained a virgin.

Matthew 1:24–25
[24] And Joseph awoke from his sleep and did as the angel of the Lord commanded him, and took Mary as his wife, [25] <u>but kept her a virgin until she gave birth to a Son</u>; and he called His name Jesus.

Acts 1:14
[14] These all with one mind were continually devoting themselves to prayer, along with the women, and Mary the mother of Jesus, and with His brothers.

Galatians 1:19
[19] But I did not see any other of the apostles except James, the Lord's brother.

Matthew 13:53–56
[53] When Jesus had finished these parables, He departed from there. [54] He came to His hometown and began teaching them in their synagogue, so that they were astonished, and said, "Where did this man get this wisdom and these miraculous powers? [55] Is not this the carpenter's son? Is not <u>His mother called Mary</u>, and <u>His brothers, James and Joseph and Simon and Judas</u>? [56] <u>And His sisters</u>, are they not all with us? Where then did this man get all these things?"

In Acts 1:14, Galatians 1:19, and Matthew 13:53–56, God describes brothers and sisters (*six at the very least*) of Jesus by both Mary and Joseph. Some people claim these people in the Bible were cousins or Joseph's children from a prior marriage, but they were actual blood half-siblings of Jesus. Here is what the Bible says in Mark 3:31–32 and Luke 8:19–20 for some added specific clarity.

Mark 3:31–32
31 Then His mother and His brothers arrived, and standing outside they sent word to Him and called Him. 32 A crowd was sitting around Him, and they said to Him, "Behold, Your mother and Your brothers are outside looking for You."

Luke 8:19–21
19 And His mother and brothers came to Him, and they were unable to get to Him because of the crowd. 20 And it was reported to Him, "Your mother and Your brothers are standing outside, wishing to see You.["]

One last **major** point on this issue: remember again, in the book of Revelation, the final Church—inside the time of Jacob's distress—is called the *"Mother of Harlots"* (*female oriented*). This makes it impossible for the Church of the end times to be Islamic. God gave it female gender to assure us.

VERY INTERESTING — CATHOLIC CHURCH'S POSSIBLE MOVE TO THE REAL BABYLON IN IRAQ?

The Church of the end times per prophecy must fully operate inside the actual real city of Babylon, in current-day Iraq. The Catholic Church, once co-opted, will actually move to the real city of Babylon in Iraq, *"the land of Shinar,"* in the not-too-distant future (*described in Zechariah 5:11, **Road Map** prophecy #15*). If something such as this does occur, and the present Catholic Church moves to Babylon, this will provide **solid proof** of what God shares in His prophecies. The move to Babylon will provide a **tremendous warning sign** for all mankind and would fit perfectly in the Biblical **Revelation** model regarding the church that will enter the **time of Jacob's distress**.

Now, what might influence the Catholic Church to literally move from Rome, in Italy, to the true city of Babylon in Iraq (*Shinar*)? What significant thing might possibly occur to make the entire Catholic Church even consider making this move?

It is my understanding that the Catholic Church fathers purposefully built the Vatican over the site that they claim houses the bones of the Apostle Peter. Peter's bones and his gravesite have profound significance. The Catholic Church considers Peter the first pope and therefore holds him in the highest regard. An interesting question: was Peter ever actually in the physical city of Rome? Are Peter's bones really buried under the Basilica?

From 1940 to 1963, multiple archeological studies took place regarding Peter's bones. A dispute arose between the Vatican archeologist, Antonio Ferrua (*1901–2003*), and Margherita Guarducci (*1902–1999*), a classical epigraphist (*essentially an inscriptions or graffiti interpreter*). Pope Pius XII commissioned Mr. Ferrua to do the first archeological study to verify that Peter's bones were actually buried under St. Peter's. After 23 years, Pope Paul VI concluded that the bones of Peter are indeed under the Basilica per some findings by Margherita — marginal at best. But Antonio, a trained archeologist, categorically, after the first 10 years of in-depth study and research, had said **no**, Peter's bones are not under St. Peter's. The tomb was empty. Antonio did find a small box of bone pieces (*no coffin*) and confirmed the bones were in no way conclusively those of Peter. But, definitely, no full-body skeleton existed . . . intriguing for a couple of major reasons:

    a.   Both Paul and Peter were apostles. It is believed that Matthias was chosen as Judas' replacement, not Paul. Matthias was selected by the apostles. Only Jesus had the authority to select His original and final 12, so He actually replaced Judas with Paul (*formally Saul*). Paul and Peter had only a few brief meetings because of a conflict in the church, in those early days, related to Grace, through faith in Jesus, and the Law. *See the book of Galatians.*

b. Paul was appointed as the apostle to the **Gentiles**, predominantly located in the actual city of Rome in Italy.

c. In Paul's letter to the Church of Rome, he greeted 27 different people by name, with no mention of Peter in the greeting; he was not likely there. Had Peter lived in Rome, they would have communicated often.

d. In all the many years Paul resided in Rome (*later part of his ministry in prison*) and in all his New Testament writings (*14 of the 27 New Testament books, if we include Hebrews*), he never indicates Peter is present with him in Rome. He does mention a brief visit with Peter in Jerusalem, in the second chapter of Galatians, but other than that, silence in 14 books.

e. Christians found it difficult to live in Rome at that time, due to persecution. In the latter part of Paul's ministry, the authorities held him in the Mamertine Prison in Rome until they put him to death. A plaque hangs there today saying both Paul and Peter were there together. Nothing in the Bible supports this. The idea that when God uses the name Babylon in relation to Peter in His Bible (*1 Peter 5:13*), He actually, symbolically, talks about Rome, is in error. **God said Babylon**, so He clearly __meant__ **Babylon**. In fact, in 2 Timothy 4:11, Paul says only Luke accompanied him in Rome. Peter never resided in the city of Rome. He lived in the city of Babylon, as God tells us in the Bible.

f. The Romans sentenced Paul to death because of his faith in Jesus, and they **beheaded** him. It was customary for Christians to be **beheaded**, at that time, __in Rome__. The Romans __did not crucify__ Christians **inside the city** in Paul and Peter's time, 30 years or more after Christ's death and resurrection. Keep this in mind, as I will address how Peter died in a moment.

g. Also, archeologists actually found Paul's true bones and full skeleton (*not just small fragments*) in a well-marked grave, outside the city boundary of Rome. The Romans considered Christians unworthy for burial inside the city walls of Rome.

h. Peter was appointed as the apostle to the **Jews**. During all of Peter's ministry years, the majority of the Jews all lived in the real **city of Babylon**, in current-day Iraq.

i. Babylon was located at the very far east of the vastly controlled Roman Empire—nowhere near the actual city of Rome, where the Vatican is currently located.

j. The Romans **crucified** Peter on a tree, but remember, they only beheaded Christians in the formal city of Rome during that period in time.

k. Also, remember, they buried Paul outside of the city walls. Why at the same time in history would they have granted Peter the right of burial inside the city walls? They would have treated him the same as Paul and buried him **outside** the city walls . . . not where the Vatican site is currently located today.

In my follow-up research, I remembered a couple of added interesting things. For many years now, the Catholic Church appears to have purchased large sections of property in the *"land of Shinar,"* the actual area of the real city of Babylon in current-day Iraq. But why?

I learned about this land purchasing about 25 years ago and, at that time, found a great deal of information online. Today when I search this topic, I find nothing. I surmise a complete planned removal from the internet. I find this highly interesting. All of this may actually come into the full light of truth soon through a possible interesting discovery in Iraq.

I have also read additional articles stipulating the Vatican City in Rome is **symbolic Babylon**. These articles talk about the geographic **Seven Hills of Rome** as proof. These Seven Hills are on the other side of the Tiber River in Rome and have no relation to the Papal State, **the Vatican itself**.

Revelation 17:9–11
⁹ Here is the mind which has wisdom. The seven heads are <u>seven mountains</u> on which the woman sits, ¹⁰ <u>and they are seven kings; five have fallen, one is, the other has not yet come</u>; and when he comes, he must remain a little while. ¹¹ The beast which was and is not, is himself also an eighth and is one of the seven, and he goes to destruction.

Revelation 17:10 tell us the *"seven mountains"* (hills) actually represent **seven kingdoms**, not geography. Five had fallen already when John wrote Revelation, and one existed in his time. And a seventh, by its description in the book of Revelation, depicts the coming One World Government of the end times. *(Give no credence to weak scholars who say this is wrong.)*

The five types of kings or governments that had already fallen by John's time were:

1. The Tarquin Kings (753 BC–509 BC)
2. Republican government (509 BC–300 BC)
3. Plebian government (300 BC–264 BC)
4. Consular government (264 BC–60 BC)
5. Triumvirate government (60 BC–27 BC)

Then, in 27 BC, the government of John's day mentioned in Revelation 17:10 as the *"one is"* came as the:

6. Caesarean Imperialism government (*A Roman "form" that is still in general practice to this day*)

The seventh listed as the *"other yet to come"*:

7. The total One World Government (*The ending of the Roman form inside the time of Jacob's distress*)

The final, seventh government version—the ending of the Roman form of government—will reside in Babylon run by the

Antichrist. We will learn more about him shortly in **Road Map** prophecy #20.

The city of Rome **cannot, and will not**, be the correct geographic location for the final World Church during the end times, or during **the time of Jacob's distress**; rather, the location will be in the *"land of Shinar,"* in the actual city of Babylon, in current-day Iraq. The final One World Church will go back to the original ungodly Babylonian model, per the book of Revelation, described as *"The Mother of Harlots,"* and must be located in Babylon in Iraq.

On a side note, why do I keep saying <u>current-day Iraq</u>? After the Ezekiel attack *(prophecy #13)*, Iraq may become a part of a new larger country. I explain this interesting concept as part of **Road Map** prophecy #22, following shortly.

So, finally, what might possibly make the Catholic Church **co-opted** in the last days to even consider moving from Rome to Babylon in Iraq? Well, the real city of Babylon is near both the Tigris and the Euphrates rivers. There will be some prophetic significance related to the Euphrates River inside **the time of Jacob's distress**, discussed later in this story. Biblically, the Antichrist must rule the world from Babylon, and the New One World Church needs to accompany him there for the first half of **the time of Jacob's distress**.

After the Ezekiel battle, we will likely witness an accelerated rebuilding process beginning in the actual city of Babylon, in Iraq, preparing for the future, **Road Map** prophecy #15. During preparations for the new construction, in the early major excavations, the construction teams may likely find something amazing. These teams will find, without any doubt, the true full **skeletal remains of Peter** in a protected, well-marked and documented grave — in the very land where the Bible says he ministered: Babylon (*the plains of Shinar*) in Iraq.

Moving the entire newly **co-opted** One World Church (*no longer in reality Christian Catholic; it will have been stolen*) to the location where their claimed first Pope Peter's bones are actually located will make perfect sense.

18. BUILDING OF THE THIRD TEMPLE IN JERUSALEM

Revelation 11:1–2
1 Then there was given me a measuring rod like a staff; and someone said, "Get up and measure the temple of God and the altar, and those who worship in it. 2 Leave out the court which is outside the temple and do not measure it, for it has been given to the nations; and they will tread under foot the holy city for forty-two months.["]

2 Thessalonians 2:3–4
3 Let no one in any way deceive you, for it will not come unless the apostasy comes first, and the man of lawlessness is revealed, the son of destruction, 4 who opposes and exalts himself above every so-called God or object of worship, so that he takes his seat in the temple of God, displaying himself as being God.

In my opinion, the construction of the new third temple in Jerusalem needs to happen soon because it will have great significance in relation to the end times. The new third Jewish temple needs to exist before **the time of Jacob's distress** starts. From my perspective as an architect, builders have the ability to construct a possibly prefabricated temple quickly, possibly as quick as 6 months with motivation. It is ready to go. The Ezekiel 38 attack would have resolved the current building site issues.

When the Antichrist signs his covenant with the Jews, this will officially start the 7-year **time of Jacob's distress** period. This covenant will also allow the Jews to immediately begin sacrificial services in the temple again. The Antichrist will allow this for only the first half of **the time of Jacob's distress** — for 42 months. With the temple in place at the start of **the time of Jacob's distress**, the sacrificial system can then immediately begin.

Sacrifices need to happen **inside the temple** . . . further verification that the building probably should exist prior to the start of **the time of Jacob's distress**.

As I was doing my research, I remembered something interesting I'd learned some years back. The new third temple must have an initial blessing before it can open, achieved only through the specific sacrifice of a **red heifer** . . . a detailed **required process**, described in the entire 19th chapter in the book of Numbers. An excerpt:

<u>Numbers 19:1-2</u>
[1] Then the Lord spoke to Moses and Aaron, saying, [2] "This is the statute of the law which the Lord has commanded, saying, 'Speak to the sons of Israel that they bring you an unblemished <u>red heifer</u> in which is <u>no defect</u> and on which a yoke has never been placed.["']

Soon after the destruction of the second temple in 70 AD, this interesting animal, the **red heifer**, went dormant (*not extinct*), no longer needed because the sacrificial system ended with the destruction of the temple. Then all of a sudden, in 1994, a miraculous event occurred. We witnessed the birth of a **red heifer** — the first sighted in 1,900 years. After 25 years, they have grown in number with some raised to be kosher — acceptable for the sacrifice to purify and cleanse the new coming third temple. An appropriate **red heifer** must be **unblemished** for this sacrifice. Does an unblemished heifer exist today? Maybe not yet. But with thousands of them in existence at this time, it will not be long until the correct specimen arrives.

Finally, according to the Bible, the **abomination of desolation** will occur, inside the temple at the midpoint of **the time of Jacob's distress,** 42 months, 1,260 days, or 3½ years into **the time of Jacob's distress**. At that time, the Antichrist ends the One World Religion and takes claim as the only god. The new temple sacrificial system will abruptly end 3½ years into the **time of Jacob's distress** at the Abomination of Desolation (*Daniel 12:11*).

19.   WORLD GOVERNMENT BREAKS INTO 10 KINGDOMS

Daniel 7:24
24 As for the ten horns, out of this kingdom ten kings will arise; and another will arise after them, and he will be different from the previous ones[.]

After the Ezekiel attack, **the entire world** will face brief bewilderment and disarray. My speculation: due to worldwide confusion, all the countries in the world (*through the United Nations*) will agree — some reluctantly — to give up all individual national sovereignty and form together into a new unified One World Government. But now what? Due to possible temporary total world economic upheaval (*not a collapse*) as a result of this attack, the people of the world may accept unification as inevitable. I also speculate that conceivably, all countries will receive a one-time **debt jubilee** (*an Old Testament event forgiving all debts every 50 years, Leviticus 25:8–13*) forgiving all national debts, and, in return, this will generate motivation to give up total individual national sovereignty. No more elections, no border walls. It will appear we will have no choice and in exchange, this will lead to world peace. **Or will it?**

Prophecies 13-18 will have arrived, so the logical next step will be breaking this new One World Government into smaller areas, controlled by kings, making local control easier. The ruling authorities at that time will decide that the number of kings will happen to be 10. Daniel 7:24 mentions that "*ten kings will arise; and another will arise after them, and he will be different from the previous ones.*" This 11th king, after the initial 10 arrive, is the Antichrist; **Road Map** prophecy #20. Remember, he needs to be present to sign the covenant with Israel. All of the One World

Government and 10 king issues must have reached full formation *before* **the time of Jacob's distress** can begin.

20. <u>RISE OF THE ANTICHRIST (after the 10 kingdoms)</u>

Daniel 9:24–27

[24] *"<u>Seventy weeks</u> have been decreed for your people and your holy city, to finish the transgression, to make an end of sin, to make atonement for iniquity, to bring in everlasting righteousness, to seal up vision and prophecy and to anoint the most holy place.* [25] *So you are to know and discern that from the issuing of a decree to restore and rebuild Jerusalem until Messiah the Prince there will be <u>seven weeks</u> and <u>sixty-two weeks;</u> it will be built again, with plaza and moat, even in times of distress.* [26] *Then <u>after the sixty-two weeks</u> the Messiah will be cut off and have nothing, and the people of the prince who is to come will destroy the city and the sanctuary. And its end will come with a flood; even to the end there will be war; desolations are determined.* [27] *And he will make a firm covenant with the many <u>for one week</u>, but in the middle of the week he will put a stop to sacrifice and grain offering; and on the wing of abominations will come one who makes desolate, even until a complete destruction, one that is decreed, is poured out on the one who makes desolate.*

In the Bible, Daniel tells us about two issues to look for that will represent timeframes indicating we are about to see the arrival of Jesus' **catching up** event—the first, **Daniel's 70th week**; the second, the *"fourth kingdom."* It's important to have a general understanding of their meanings. Although it seems as if they should tie in with the One World Government and 10 kings, these issues relate, specifically, to how we can know the impending arrival of the Antichrist just prior to the **catching up**.

Daniel 9:24–27 tells us the *"seventieth week"* refers to the 7-year **time of Jacob's distress** ruled by the Antichrist. Notice how God defines for us His word *"week"* to mean 7-year periods of time. (Daniel 9:27). The idea is that God prescribed 70 weeks (*70 × 7 = 490 years*) to complete His work to end all sin. He tells us the official start of this "70th *week*" happens when the antichrist signs a 7-year covenant with Israel. In the middle of this **week** sacrifices stop, and the abomination of desolation arrives. This seventieth week is clearly **the time of Jacob's distress**. God does not leave us confused, no guesswork needed.

69 weeks per Daniel 9:25 in God's process were completed from the time of Cyrus' decree in Isaiah 44:28 to Christ's crucifixion (*483 years*). Then the world has experienced a long time out, the Christian Age (*approximately 2,000 years*). During the **time of Jacob's distress, the 70th week,** no living Christians will enter into it; God takes us out of the way. No Christian churches were here during the first 69 weeks. Not one will be around for the final 70th week either.

Daniel 7:23–24
23 *"Thus he said: 'The fourth beast will be a <u>fourth kingdom</u> on the earth, which will be different from all the other kingdoms and <u>will devour the whole earth</u> and tread it down and crush it. 24 As for the ten horns, out of this kingdom ten kings will arise; and another will arise after them, and he will be different from the previous ones and will subdue three kings.['"]*

Daniel 7:23 talks about a *"fourth kingdom"* that *"will devour the whole earth."* Daniel chapter 2 tells us the king of Babylon, Nebuchadnezzar, had a troubling dream—one he could not understand. He searched for somebody to help him with an interpretation. Then God gave Daniel direction to provide the interpretation. This prophetic dream relates to the governments of the world that would come from the time of Nebuchadnezzar through to the second coming of Jesus.

In the dream, four different forms of government are explained using the visual of a great statue of a man of *"extraordinary splendor"* (*Daniel 2:31–33*), starting at his head and moving down to his feet. Note that the quality of these governments deteriorates based on the symbolic use of different quality of metals in this dream's explanation:

1. Head of gold
2. Breast and arms of silver
3. Belly and thighs of bronze
4a. Legs of iron
4b. Feet of iron and clay (the end of #4)

Daniel 2:36–45 lists the four **groups** of people who will control these types of governments. They sound like geographic locations, but no, they actually represent four types of governments. In *italics*, I list historically the types of governments they represent:

1. Gold, Nebuchadnezzar (*Absolute Monarchy*)
2. Silver, Medo-Persia (*Limited Monarchy*)
3. Bronze, Greece (*Democracy*)

4a. Legs of iron, Rome (*Imperialism, political Rome, still in existence today; ongoing*) (*Western and Eastern powers – two legs*)

4b. Feet of iron and clay, final form of Political Rome – the One World Government (*Evil, final political Rome – dictatorship of the Antichrist soon to come*)

A controversy occurs when we try to place **geography** into this equation. **Geography** will have nothing to do with the new coming final fourth **Roman** type actually becoming the final version of **Political Rome**. The legs of iron represent a **political Roman form of government** that started just prior to the days of Jesus and has continued in various configurations to our very day. We will soon see the conclusion of this government with the

10 toes representing the 10 divisions of the coming final One World Government, which came into being in **Road Map** prophecy #19. The Antichrist will rule this final **form of government** out of **Babylon, in the plains of Shinar**.

As earlier explained, the Antichrist comes on the scene <u>**prior**</u> to the visual **catching up**. Note the following verse:

<u>2 Thessalonians 2:1–3</u>
¹ Now we request you, brethren, with regard to the coming of our Lord Jesus Christ and our gathering together to Him, ² that you not be quickly shaken from your composure or be disturbed either by a spirit or a message or a letter as if from us, to the effect that the day of the Lord has come. ³ Let no one in any way deceive you, for it will not come <u>unless the apostasy comes first</u>, and <u>the man of lawlessness is revealed</u>, the son of destruction[.]

Paul tells us, in these verses, not to be shaken or disturbed to hear that **the day of the Lord** has come. Again, the day of the Lord is **the time of Jacob's distress**. This time cannot come until first, the *"apostasy comes,"* and second, *"the man of lawlessness,"* the Antichrist, *"is revealed."*

Only after the One World Government arrives and the 10 world divisions (*kingdoms*) are in place will the Antichrist be revealed and come on the scene. I believe the visual catching up happens on the day **the time of Jacob's distress** starts. This means Christians will get to see and know who the Antichrist is for a short time before the visual **catching up** occurs.

The majority of people in the world will have no idea of this dynamic leader's identity, but, as Christians, we should have no doubts. Others will discover his true identity at the midpoint of **the time of Jacob's distress**. Notice, I said the Antichrist comes on the scene after the 10 divisions have formed. This clearly means the entire infrastructure for the Antichrist must be physically in place before **the time of Jacob's distress** can start.

21. **TIME OF PEACE & SAFETY IN THE UNBELIEVING WORLD**

1 Thessalonians 5:1-3
¹ Now as to the times and the epochs, brethren, you have no need of anything to be written to you. ² For you yourselves know full well that the day of the Lord will come just like a thief in the night. ³ While they are saying, "Peace and safety!" then destruction will come upon them suddenly like labor pains upon a woman with child, and they will not escape.

In the last days, those who will accept the coming One World Government and Religion will feel as if they have finally come into a time of worldwide peace and safety. They will not see what actually has taken place. They will think of Christians as totally insane for not recognizing the good that appears to be happening. What appears as peace will, in reality, be just the opposite. The secular world is about to be literally, caught by surprise. Christians should find comfort in the clear knowledge God has given them. We should see and know what He is doing through prophecy and have confidence He will soon return.

22. THE APPEARANCE OF ELIJAH

Malachi 4:5-6
⁵ Behold, I am going to send you Elijah the prophet before the coming of the great and terrible day of the Lord. ⁶ He will restore the hearts of the fathers to their children and the hearts of the children to their fathers, so that I will not come and smite the land with a curse.

Before Jesus came the first time, God sent a prophet like Elijah (*John the Baptist*) into the world to announce the arrival of Jesus. He did this so many people would get an advance notice and know that Jesus was on the way. The announcement also provided a way to prepare people for who Jesus was, the Messiah, and His importance to mankind.

Elijah in the Old Testament is considered **the prophet of prophets**, a devoted man of God who did whatever was asked of him boldly with great courage. He loved God more than life itself and was a great example for us today. Elisha (*with an "s"*), Elijah's assistant (*with a "j"*), ultimately inherited his ministry.

Malachi 4:5–6 tells us that something similar to what occurred with John the Baptist at Jesus' **first coming** will happen before the **visual catching up** and **the time of Jacob's distress**. The actual Elijah will come back to provide another bold announcement that Jesus is about to return for a "**second time.**" God will send Elijah to restore the "*hearts of the fathers to their children and the hearts of the children to the fathers.*" We are told this will happen "*before the coming of the great and terrible day of the Lord*" (*the time of Jacob's distress*). Elijah will bring Hebrew *fathers (teachings of the prophets)* **and children (the Hebrews),**" together again, leading to the reestablishment of the 12 tribes of Israel. Elijah will then bring together God's special 144,000 **Jewish** men for service to God inside **the time of Jacob's distress, "before"** it begins. How is this possible? (*The answer is on page 227*).

According to Revelation 7:4–8, 144,000 Jewish converts to Jesus, the Messiah, will evangelize Jesus to the entire world through the entire **the time of Jacob's distress** — 12,000 from each of the 12 tribes of Israel. The 12 tribes need to be in place.

Presently, Israel does not control the full extent of the physical geographic land areas promised to them by God. Originally, God provided to each of Jacob's 12 sons (*the 12 tribes of Israel*) parcels of land currently outside of Israel proper, today. In order to reestablish the tribal system that God will need before He can collect the 144,000, additional land mass must return to Israel. God will reclaim this land Himself with His Ezekiel 38 attack, "*From the river of Egypt as far as the great river, the river*

Euphrates." This is the land promised to Israel in Genesis 15:18 – the Abrahamic Covenant.

Genesis 15:18
18 On that day the Lord made a covenant with Abram saying, "To your descendants I have given this land, from the river of Egypt as far as the great river, the river Euphrates."

This is educated speculation: notice something interesting on Israel's current 10 Agorot coin. This coin has a seven-candlestick menorah placed over what appears to be a map of Israel. With north assumed as up as with all maps and the Mediterranean Sea on the west or left side, we can see the map shown has a far larger land mass than the small sliver of land Israel controls today.

If we take this shape and align it with the coastline along the Mediterranean Sea, to approximate scale on the following map of the Middle East, we discover something interesting. This footprint would include almost all of the land from the river of Egypt to the river Euphrates, exactly the land promised to Israel by God Himself in Genesis 15:18.

Babylon is not shown on the following map; it is about 50 miles southeast of Baghdad in current-day Iraq (*see the tip of the arrow in the map below*). The new capital of the whole world inside **the time of Jacob's distress** will be situated in Babylon, the "*Land of Shinar*," per Zechariah 5:11, discussed earlier in **Road Map** prophecy #15. If this speculation turns out to be accurate, Babylon will actually be inside this new larger State of Israel.

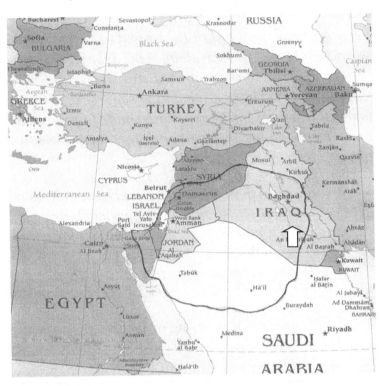

At this current time, some of Israel's enemies control this additional land mass. The Ezekiel attack discussed earlier in **Road Map** prophecy #13, with added detail shared in Chapter 5, will resolve the situation (*see Ezekiel 39:9–10, page 127*). This also needs to occur before **the time of Jacob's distress** so the 144,000 can be ready to come on the scene **on day one** of God's 7-year period of judgments.

Elijah will also help reestablish the tribal system in Israel before **the time of Jacob's distress** starts, as we head toward the end of days—vitally important as a major blessing for our Jewish family.

23. FEAR, SCOURGE, THE ANTICHRIST, AND HIS COVENANT

Isaiah 28:14-15

[14] *Therefore, hear the word of the Lord, O scoffers, who rule this people who are in Jerusalem,* [15] *Because you have said, "We have made a <u>covenant</u> with death, and with Sheol we have made a pact. The <u>overwhelming scourge</u> will not reach us when it passes by, For we have made falsehood our refuge and we have concealed ourselves with deception."*

Isaiah 28:18-19

[18] *"Your covenant with death will be canceled, and your pact with Sheol will not stand; when the <u>overwhelming scourge</u> passes through, Then you become its trampling place.* [19] *As often as it passes through, it will seize you. For morning after morning it will pass through, any time during the day or night, <u>And it will be sheer terror</u> to understand what it means."*

Just prior to the start of **the time of Jacob's distress**, the Antichrist will set demons loose on the world . . . the **overwhelming scourge**—Joel 2:1-10. Briefly, demons will march in order and devour, burn, and destroy everything in their path. They can go through windows into and over houses—terrifying to witness. The **overwhelming scourge**, a pivotal detailed warning sign just prior to the **visual catching up**, is addressed contextually in greater detail in Chapter 6.

This scourge will start to occur heading for Israel while the people of the world still live in their perceived false peace and safety. The **overwhelming scourge** will make Israel reluctantly desire to sign a covenant agreement with the Antichrist to protect them from these horrible demons. Again, the covenant signing will start the official 7-year **time of Jacob's distress**. Informed Christians have no need to fear this horrendous event.

24. SIGNS THE DAY OF THE VISUAL CATCHING UP—SUPER SIGN #3

Joel 2:30–32

30 I will display wonders in the sky and on the earth, blood, fire and columns of smoke. 31 The sun will be turned into darkness and the moon into blood <u>before the great and awesome day of the Lord comes</u>. 32 And it will come about that whoever calls on the name of the Lord will be delivered; For on Mount Zion and in Jerusalem there will be those who escape, as the Lord has said, even among the survivors whom the Lord calls.

Amos 8:9

9 "It will come about in that day," declares the Lord GOD, "That I will make the sun go down at noon and make the earth dark in broad daylight.["]

When adding the signs addressed in Joel 2:30–32 along with the **overwhelming scourge** (**Road Map** prophecy #23), on that day we get to go home with Jesus in the **visual catching up.**

The Bible explains for us (*Luke 17:26–32*) that the **visual catching up** and the start of **the time of Jacob's distress** must happen within the same 24-hour day, with no time separation (*gap*) between these two events. **God has important and profound reasons for these events to happen in this way.** Through the Grace and the promises of God, true, living believers in Jesus will escape in the **visual catching up** mere hours before the Antichrist signs his covenant with Israel, placing **the time of Jacob's distress into motion. These two events represent God's third and final "super sign."**

Matthew 24:32–34

32 Now learn the parable from the fig tree: when its branch has already become tender and puts forth its leaves, you know that summer is near; 33 so, you too, when you see all these things, recognize that He is near, right at the door. 34 Truly I say to you, this generation will not pass away until all these things take place.

CHAPTER 3

BIRTH PAINS, BIRTH, TIMELINE
PROPHECIES 1–4

We have witnessed the first set of
Biblical end-time prophecies.
God has magnificent reasons for
all these events to be witnessed.

What I am about to share in this chapter **is in no way intended to be literal predictions indicating "strict timing" or dates for future events.** For conjecture, I will use Psalm 90:10 *(page 91)* and Genesis 15:12-16 *(page 91)* along with current world events to **"postulate"** what God Himself might be showing us regarding a possible timeline for our **"season"** in history. **The actual timing of the events God has planned will occur as the Lord desires, for His glory alone**.

In Matthew 24:3-8, birth pangs and a birth will occur as the first set of end-time prophecies confirming Jesus is about to literally return. God designed two major birth "pangs" *(pains, plural)* with **specific and significant** purposes corresponding to a "birth"—the formation of the State of Israel on May 14, 1948. Let's explore the sequence of events and their true purposes.

Matthew 24:3-8

³ As He was sitting on the Mount of Olives, the disciples came to Him privately, saying, "Tell us, when will these things happen, and what will be the sign of Your coming, and of the end of the age?" ⁴ And Jesus answered and said to them, "See to it that no one misleads you. ⁵ For many will come in My name, saying, 'I am the Christ,' and will mislead many. ⁶ You will be hearing of <u>wars and rumors of wars</u>. See that you are not frightened, for those things must take place, but that is not yet the end. ⁷ For <u>nation will rise against nation</u>, and kingdom against kingdom, and in various places there will be <u>famines and earthquakes</u>. ⁸ But <u>all these things are merely the beginning of birth pangs</u>."

The Bible indicates in these Matthew verses, as we get close to His return, we are to **look for prophesied signs**. The Lord tells us of *"wars and rumors of wars,"* and that *"nation will rise against nation"* and we'll experience *"famines and earthquakes."* Well, this fairly sizes up the 20th and 21st centuries. Two major *"birth pangs"* fully set the stage for God's planned rebirth of *"His glory"* Israel. They were WWI and WWII.

Matthew 24:32–34
32 Now learn the parable from the <u>fig tree</u>: <u>when its branch has already become tender and puts forth its leaves</u>, you know that summer is near; 33 so, you too, when you see all these things, recognize that <u>He is near, right at the door</u>. 34 Truly I say to you, <u>this generation will not pass away until all these things take place.</u>

Whenever we see a parable related to a *"fig tree,"* we can know that God is talking about Israel. In these Matthew verses, God tells us when the **fig tree's** branches *"become tender,"* as a baby, and it puts forth leaves, becomes alive or born anew, *"you know that the summer is near."* Also, *"when you see all these things, recognize that He is near."* God is telling us to watch for these prophetic signs so we, as Christians, can know with certainty that Jesus is coming. Why would God tell us to **"look for something"** in the literal sense if the Lord is coming unexpectedly? **He would not.** Also notice, He is using the word *"see."*

These verses direct us **to look** for a birth, the prophesied re-birth of the land of Israel. After we witness this birth, Matthew 24:34 tells us the **generation** that will *"see"* this (*all of us today*) will not pass away until all these things (*His end time prophecies*) take place. For the speculation in this chapter, let's assume how long a **generation** might be according to the Bible. Here is what God appears to tell us Psalm 90:10 and Genesis 15:12-16:

Psalm 90:10
10 As for the days of our life, they contain seventy years, or if due to strength, eighty years[.]

Genesis 15:12-16
12 Now when the sun was going down, a deep sleep fell upon Abram; and behold terror and great darkness fell upon him. 13 God said to Abram, "Know for certain that your descendants will be strangers in a land that is not theirs, where they will be <u>enslaved and oppressed four hundred</u>

years. ¹⁴ *But I will also judge the nation whom they will serve, and afterward they will come out with many possessions.* ¹⁵ *As for you, you shall go to your fathers in peace; you will be buried at a good old age.* ¹⁶ *Then in the <u>fourth generation</u> they will return here, for the iniquity of the Amorite is not yet complete."*

God specifically indicates that a generation is between 70 and 80 years in Psalm 90:10. In Genesis 15:13 he also talks about a 400-year period of Hebrew enslavement. When we look ahead at verse 16, we see that in the *"fourth generation"* this will end. Take 400 years, divide by 4, and we get a possible 100-year generation. With this information, let's now explore some facts about the two birth pains and the rebirth of the State of Israel in 1948. God gives precise direction, so we can literally **"see"** the *"season"* we are in.

When we look at the entire chapter of Matthew 24, many believers say this is telling Christians we might need to live through the **time of Jacob's distress**. <u>This is not an accurate interpretation.</u> To avoid confusion regarding Matthew 24, we use the **hermeneutical laws** of **double reference** and **recurrence** in relation to this chapter's full context. I did not include the full text of Matthew 24 here due to its size.

The **hermeneutical laws** of **double reference** and **recurrence** are where God talks about His present day and then, for context and example, jumps into the future within the overall text. Usually, at some point, after explaining what is coming in the future, He will, in the same exact text, come back again to the present time to finish His explanation and thinking. This is done often in Scriptures. Let's apply these **hermeneutical laws** to Matthew 24.

In verse 3, the disciples ask Jesus a question regarding the "signs" of His return. In verses 4–8, Jesus tells them about certain "**signs**" that people in the distant future should look for *(all of us today)* just before the start of the **time of Jacob's distress**. He then jumps into this future time in verses 9–31. For foundation and emphasis, the Lord explains the horrors inside **the time of Jacob's distress**. Jesus then jumps back to their current time in verses 32–51. He answers the initial question asked in verse 3. In these final verses, Jesus gives us the answers as to how, today, we can know approximately when **He will be coming back** prior to **the time of Jacob's distress**.

THE TWO MAJOR BIRTH PAINS PRIOR TO A BIRTH

Here are some **significant issues** regarding two birth pains that had major influences on the rebirth of the nation of Israel.

WWI: *(1914-1919)* Well into the war, the Allies ran out of smokeless gunpowder and needed acetone in order to make the explosives required to fight and achieve victory. Up until WWI, their factories could make acetone only from wood. The English people had cut down most of their forests in the war effort. Their supplies rapidly ran low.

A young Jewish scientist named **Dr. Chaim Weizmann**, knowing the urgency of the situation, developed a way to make acetone using corn mash. This new formula allowed England and the United States to generate enough acetone to make the much-needed smokeless gunpowder to win the war.

England wanted to show their appreciation of Dr. Weizmann's discovery, so at the end of the war, they asked him what they could do to reward him. He told them he would like England (*which had control of Israel at that time*) to allow the Jewish people the ability to reestablish a country again in their former homeland, Israel. This resulted in the Balfour Declaration on November 2, 1917 (***Road Map*** prophecy #2), which allowed for, but did not form, a revived Jewish homeland, Israel, again after 1,900 years in exile.

WWI was the first major birth pain. After this war, the Jews still felt comfortable living in all the lands where God had scattered them since the destruction of their second temple in Jerusalem in 70 AD. After WWI, the Jews could not find a good reason to go home to a new and safe Israeli homeland.

WWII: *(1939–1945)* During the 1930s and through the war, anti-Semitism (*hatred of the Jews*) in Russia and Europe — particularly Germany — grew exponentially. Adolph Hitler believed the Jews needed to be exterminated from the face of the planet. During WWII, Hitler, through the efforts of one of his senior henchmen, **Adolf Eichmann**, planned for and systematically killed 50 percent of the Jews living in Europe. After this war, the Jews no longer felt safe in Europe or Russia.

Since the end of the WWII in 1945, the **Second Exodus,** Jews returning from the lands where God had scattered them, has accelerated. Jews have returned to Israel from all over the world to live in safety inside their new reestablished homeland.

WWI was the first major birth pain and made the land ready for the Jews. WWII was the second major birth pain and made the Jews ready for the land.

UNITED NATIONS AND THE BIRTH OF ISRAEL

Almost immediately after WWII came the formation of the United Nations, on October 24, 1945. One of the first acts of the United Nations: to ratify Israel as a new country on May 14, 1948, the official **rebirth** of the State of Israel. The United Nations will soon play a pivotal role in ushering in a new One World Government that will rule into **the time of Jacob's distress**. With the rebirth of Israel, the first four of God's 24 significant end-time prophecies began for us to witness.

Note that with every birth, a new *"generation"* begins. Because we have now seen two birth pains and a birth, we can equate this to a new *"generation."* Remember, Psalm 90:10 tells us our lives last about 80 years; Genesis 15:12-16 indicates 100 years as a possible period that might define **a generation**. An interesting timeline pertaining to this new generation, symbolized by the birth of the new State of Israel, has occurred.

POSSIBLE TIMELINE FOR YET-TO-COME EVENTS

In Matthew 24:34, the Bible indicates that *"this final generation will not pass away until all these things take place."* Based on Psalm 90:10, Genesis 15:12-16 and Matthew 24:34, the birth of Israel started what God intended for us to recognize as **His Biblical final generation,** one that could span between 80 to 100 years.

Let's assume for a moment that the State of Israel is a living person: Israel as a Jewish man, growing up from an infant into manhood. In Isaiah 66:7–8, God shares about the future rebirth of Israel: birth pains, symbolically the birth of a *"man child"* (*Greek "genea"* = born one) and a *"land born in one day."* We have witnessed this. Based on the life cycles of a Jewish human male, some amazing historical events and timing have occurred since Israel's May 14, 1948 rebirth.

The rebirth of the State of Israel started a **generational time clock.** It started a literal timeline that all Christians who love the study of end-time prophecies should understand. But has God provided any possible additional indications to validate this? Amazingly, **yes!**

1. Symbolically, on May 14, 1948, the date of Israel's rebirth, some of the surrounding enemy Arab countries became highly irritated. They decided to fight against Israel on day one of the new country's existence and said they would take them down quickly. They did not succeed; all of their efforts failed. This irritating action symbolically relates to a Jewish boy's circumcision.

2. A Jewish boy becomes responsible for his actions, <u>accountable</u>, at 13 years of age. He becomes a Bar Mitzvah. The Jewish people hold a Bar Mitzvah ceremony for the young

man, to **celebrate** this event. Remember from earlier, in WWII, the German **Adolf Eichmann**, the chief architect of the Holocaust? He escaped at the end of the war and was a fugitive until his capture by the Israelis in 1960. On December 11, 1961, he was tried and held <u>accountable</u> for the deaths of millions of Jews. Israel was 13 years and 7 months old when this happened, and I am sure Israel **celebrated** this event.

3. Also, a Jewish man becomes eligible to fight in wars while in his 20th year of life (*after his 19th birthday*). Adding 19 years to 5-14-1948, we get 5-14-1967. On 6-7-1967 (*Israel was 19 years and 23 days old*), Israel fought and won the Six-Day War, and the city of Jerusalem returned to the control of the Jewish people . . . after more than 1,900 years in exile — a fulfillment of prophecy.

4. Symbolically, in the life of a Jewish man, he becomes a man of peace at the age of 30. Jesus, our Rabbi Messiah, started His formal ministry at 30 years of age. Thirty years added to 5-14-1948 equals 5-14-1978. In September of 1978, when Israel was 30 years and 4 months old, the Camp David Peace Accords were negotiated. Then, in March of 1979 (*Israel was 30 years and 10 months old*), Egypt and Israel, brokered by Jimmy Carter, signed the Camp David Peace (*security*) Accords. This plan made it possible to keep the borders with Israel and its neighbors safe by agreement — another fulfillment of prophecy.

5. On 5-14-2019, the State of Israel celebrated its 71st birthday.

6. This book was updated in August of 2019. We have completed 71 years of a possible 80 to 100-year generational period. Using only the Bible as our guide, remember that the entire seven-year **time of Jacob's distress** is prophesied to occur **"before"** the completion of this final 80 to 100-year generational period.

Luke 12:54–56

[54] And He was also saying to the crowds, "When you see a cloud rising in the west, immediately you say, 'A shower is coming,' and so it turns out. [55] And when you see a south wind blowing, you say, 'It will be a hot day,' and it turns out that way. [56] You hypocrites! You know how to analyze the appearance of the earth and the sky, <u>but why do you not analyze this present time?"</u>

We are, clearly, in the **"season"** of the Lord's return. Utilizing the possible full 100 years from Genesis 15:12-16, and assuming the rebirth of Israel started the **"final generation,"** God might be telling us the following regarding this final generation:

Luke 21:32

[32] Truly I say to you, <u>this generation</u> will not pass away until all things take place. [33] Heaven and earth will pass away, but My words will not pass away.

Mathematically, using the Bible as my sole source for analysis, let's consider a couple of additional pieces of critical information related to God's possible timeline for the last days. Please note these dates are approximated, I am not dogmatic:

a. The Bible appears to indicate a generation, could last about 100 years (*Genesis 15:12-16*).

b. Again, according to the Bible, the final generation will not pass away until "*all these things take place,*" starting with a **birth** and including all 12 end-time prophecies already fulfilled as well as God's final 12 unfulfilled items in His 24-prophecy Road Map. This includes the **visual catching up** and **the time of Jacob's distress**. All these things must take place **before** the final generation has ended (*Luke 21:32*).

c. Israel's birthdate was May 14, 1948. Add 100 years, and we arrive at May 14, 2048. The end of the **time of**

Jacob's distress would then need to occur by this date. God has started the final countdown.

d. Again, in 2019, Israel will celebrate its 71st birthday. **From 2019 there are 29 years left before Israel turns 100!**

e. Subtracting 7 years from May 14, 2048, for **the time of Jacob's distress**, this would take us back to May 14, 2041. Based on the 24-prophecy Road Map, it is possible the **visual catching up** will happen at the latest by this May 14th 2041 date, **before** Israel turns 93.

f. Per God's 24-prophecy Road Map, the 13th prophecy, Ezekiel 38, must occur next. This implies that prophecies 14–24 would all need to take place prior to May 14, 2041, at the latest. How much time might be needed after Ezekiel 38 for prophecies 14–24 to be fulfilled to meet this proposed timeframe?

g. Everything for the One World Church and Government is already in place today. All that is needed is one earth-shattering event to take place, one that will alter our world. **Ezekiel 38 will be this event!**

h. From my research as an architect, a prefabricated temple structure already exists and could easily be assembled very rapidly.

i. In Ezekiel 39:9, we are told that after the Ezekiel 38 battle, *"those who inhabit the cities of Israel"* (*the vast majority at that time are unsaved individuals*) will burn the remains of the fallen enemies' weaponry in their land for 7-years. We can conclude they cannot burn things into the Millennium so it is clear that the Ezekiel 38 battle must happen, **"at an estimated minimum,"** of about three years before the start of **the time of Jacob's distress**. Using this full <u>three year</u> number as a reasonable short timeframe, we start with May 14, 2048, when Israel would be 100-years old, subtract 7-years for **the**

time of Jacob's distress, and subtract the estimated added <u>three years</u> (10-years total) for prophecies 14–24 to be fulfilled, we arrive at **November 14, 2038,** as a possible **estimated outside date** for the Ezekiel 38 attack to take place. **From 2019, this is a mere 19 years!** It is highly likely that all these things could happen much sooner, at any time. **This all in God's capable hands.**

As we see on our news each night, Israel is under severe threat of attack from many of their **surrounding enemy neighbors.** It appears today that almost every country in the world is against them, including now many in the USA. They are alone. **Coincidence? No. Part of God's Divine plan? Highly likely!**

God has given us an incredible amount of direction and actual proof of what He is doing in these last days, but how do we know this? Again, because God says He has told us the following:

John 14:29
29 *Now I have told you before it happens, so that when it happens, you may believe.*

Psalm 83:1–4

¹ O God, do not remain quiet; do not be silent and, O God, do not be still. ² For behold, Your enemies make an uproar, and those who hate You have exalted themselves. ³ They make shrewd plans against Your people, and conspire together against Your treasured ones. ⁴ They have said, "Come, and let us wipe them out as a nation, that the name of Israel be remembered no more."

CHAPTER 4

GOD'S 13TH PROPHECY
MANKIND WILL BE STUNNED!

We are currently in the final stage of God's end-time prophetical story line regarding His final generation. God's 13th prophecy is Ezekiel 38:1–39:16. **When it arrives, mankind will be STUNNED.**

We will soon witness God's inspired major attack, per Scriptures, that will come against Israel . . . His 13th prophecy, Ezekiel 38:1–39:16. When this attack happens, it will provide visual proof to mankind that God is who the Bible says He is. **Israel will be virtually unharmed, rescued from peril. This singular event will severely alter the course of human history**.

I have included the full Bible text, for both Ezekiel 38 and 39, at the end of this chapter. I quote many verses in this section from Ezekiel. Psalm 83 also included, is a prayer by Asaph, asking God to make Ezekiel 38:1–39:16 happen in his future.

The Ezekiel 38 and 39 prophecy **is highly controversial.** Some say it has already happened. Others think it must occur inside **the time of Jacob's distress** or is the battle of Armageddon. And some consider this prophecy a stand-alone event and do not apply it within the context of God's entire Biblical **Road Map**. In my estimation, this prophecy is a yet-to-come attack, a vital piece of God's larger intricate prophetic puzzle. I propose, and will share, a cohesive way of looking at this great battle. I believe, wholeheartedly, this attack will occur at any time now for us to witness, with a defined purpose.

Ezekiel 38:1–39:16 tells us how **God's inspired attack** on Israel by its neighboring enemies is a different attack than anything currently contemplated by Israel on Iran regarding their nuclear program. Historic disdain by extremist Islam for the Jews, and Jesus, *"profaning"* His name, will instigate this enemy attack on Israel. Biblically, Ezekiel 38 cannot be a world war (WWIII) or the actual final war, against the Antichrist at the end of **the time of Jacob's distress**—Armageddon.

The Bible clearly shows us how Ezekiel 38 and 39 talk about two different wars, and this creates some confusion. Ezekiel 38:1 through 39:16 talks about God's private war with Israel's surrounding enemy neighbors—only a **limited number of nations**. Ezekiel 39:17 through 39:29 talks about Armageddon . . . a different war, **including all the nations** of the world. Two distinctly different wars, in the same verses.

Ezekiel 30:1–5
¹ The word of the Lord came again to me saying, ² "Son of man, prophesy and say, 'Thus says the Lord God, "Wail, 'Alas for the day!' ³ For the day is near, <u>even the day of the Lord is near;</u> It will be a day of clouds, A time of doom for the nations. ⁴ A sword will come upon Egypt, and anguish will be in Ethiopia; when the slain fall in Egypt, they take away her wealth, and her foundations are torn down. ⁵ Ethiopia, Put, Lud, all Arabia, Libya and the people of the land that is in league will fall with them by the sword."['"]

God desires for this Ezekiel attack to occur, **for us to witness, before the time of Jacob's distress** for a couple of profound reasons. How do we know this battle occurs before the **time of Jacob's distress**? The verses in Ezekiel 30:1–5 basically refer to events, soon to follow, in all of Ezekiel 38 and 39. Please pay special attention to Ezekiel 30:3 and note the words *"even the day of the Lord is near."* It says *"near."* This battle is prophesied to happen in the future, just near and **before** the start of *"the day of the Lord."* The term *"the day of the Lord"* is **the time of Jacob's distress** period.

Having Ezekiel 38:1–39:16 occur prior to both the **visual catching up** and **the time of Jacob's distress** is the key event that will start to confirm the premise of this entire book. Some people say this attack will never happen and is symbolic. But in Ezekiel 39:8, God makes the following declaration:

Ezekiel 39:8
⁸ Behold, it is coming and <u>it shall be done</u>, declares the Lord GOD.

. . . *"it shall be done."* . . . a fairly direct statement, I would venture to say.

After the Ezekiel attack, we have only a short time left before the **visual catching up** and the start of **the time of Jacob's distress**. It is my personal belief that immediately after this Ezekiel attack, some large projects need completion quickly before the **visual catching up** occurs. We are wise to be watching what happens in the near future for God's confirmation.

1. As part of this attack, God will remove the Al-Aqsa Mosque and Dome of the Rock in Jerusalem. Construction of the new third Jewish temple must occur on this Temple Mount site. Again, I have learned from other research that plans may exist for the new third temple. From my viewpoint as an architect, with today's technology, and with an unlimited budget, a prefabricated structure won't take long to build.

2. Reconstruction of the city of Babylon will happen rapidly, and this will become the new center of the coming One World Government. The United Nations will likely relocate there as well.

3. The One World Church, led by the False Prophet, in my opinion, must be in place before **the time of Jacob's distress** starts. This will consolidate all remaining religions into an apostate unified One World Church. The new false church must operate out of Babylon, in current-day Iraq. The One World Government and economy needs to be in place, with 10 divisions or kingdoms established.

These items above are monumental projects. I do not see logistically how any projects of these magnitudes could happen during the first half of **the time of Jacob's distress**. Some Christians talk about how peace will fill the first half of **the time of Jacob's distress** until the Antichrist enters the temple at the midpoint and claims to be the only God. Then at this time, things will get bad. To put this period in some perspective: **half of all mankind remaining after the visual catching up will die** (*three billion* *people*) **in the first half of the time of Jacob's distress.** Here is how we know this:

Twenty-one judgments come upon the world inside **the time of Jacob's distress.** They occur in three groups of seven events. The first seven are the **Seal** judgments, followed by the seven **Trumpets.** The third group of seven is called the **Bowls.** The **Seals** and the **Trumpets** (*14*) happen in the first half of **the time of Jacob's distress**; the **Bowls** (*seven*) happen in the second half. (*see Chapter 7 for God's 21 judgments, not one of them for Christians*)

Seal Judgment Four (*Revelation 6:7*), the fourth of the 21 events, will kill off 25 percent of all living souls. Trumpet Judgment Six (*Revelation 9:16*), the 13th of the 14 events in the first half, will kill another 33 percent of those remaining on earth prior to the midpoint of the time of Jacob's distress. Some simple math: start with 1,000 people, kill 25 percent or 250, and you have 750 remaining. Now kill 33 percent of the remaining 750, or 250, and you end up with 500, half of the original number.

The deaths of one-half of the world's population will total a staggering, unbelievable number. When three billion people die in the first half of **the time of Jacob's distress**, which lasts 1,260 days (*Revelation 11:2*), this would equate to **2,380,000 people per day**. We can see from this that no peace of any kind could prevail inside the entire **time of Jacob's distress.** At this death rate, the same total number of people who died in all of WWII (70,000,000 +/-) will have died within the **first 30 days** of **the time of Jacob's distress.**

The second half of **the time of Jacob's distress** will also be devastating. From the analysis above, clearly the **time of Jacob's distress** will be horrendous for its entire 7-year duration. Everybody will struggle to stay alive due to all the horrible punishments God brings, inside His judgment period.

No way can any building or large-scale construction projects take place during **the time of Jacob's distress** anywhere in the world. Everything for the Antichrist must be in place first and completed *before* **the time of Jacob's distress** begins in the **pre-time of Jacob's distress**, a secular time of peace and safety. In my estimation, this is the main reason why the Ezekiel 38 attack needs to occur prior to the start of **the time of Jacob's distress**. Secular peace and safety will appear to arrive quickly after this attack. I also surmise the concept of world peace is going to be a key reason, after the Ezekiel 38 attack, for people all over the world to accept the One World Government. I believe the secular world will immediately yearn for total unification. The perception of tangible world peace will motivate everyone, even some uninformed believers. This battle against Israel and God will involve only certain regions and tribes. The Bible refers to the coming Ezekiel 38 event as the battle of **Gog and Magog**. A world war is not composed of only a limited number of nations.

It is my strong belief that Magog is actually Russia. Gog (*Russia's president at that time*) will be its leader. These limited nations (*a coalition*) will become emboldened. Did you think that as of 2014 there was any possibility that Russia would ever become aggressive again and start taking over countries for plunder? Does Crimea ring any bells? The world's nations, as a whole, put up only a mild protest. Do you think Russia might be feeling emboldened today by the apparent apathy of the global community? **Absolutely!**

Plunder will be the reason Israel is attacked, per Ezekiel 38:1–39:16. Israel recently found one of the largest and richest natural gas, and oil, discoveries in the world inside their small country, an incredible economic value. It's likely some of their enemy neighbors and Gog would like to have these for themselves. It is interesting this wealth was just recently discovered.

The specific Arab regions in this coming battle against Israel, per Ezekiel 38:1–6: *Magog, Rosh, Meshach, Tubal, Persia, Ethiopia, Put, Gomer,* **and** *Beth-togarma*. These regions and/or tribes existed in 571 BC, when the prophet Ezekiel, through God's inspiration, wrote about this, more than 2,600 years ago.

God's Thirteenth Prophecy

Ezekiel 39:7

7 My holy name I will make known in the midst of My people Israel; and I will not let My holy name be profaned anymore.

When the enemy states that surround Israel *"profane"* Jesus, it angers God. He has about had it with the name of Jesus being *"profaned"* and will not allow this to continue much longer.

Ezekiel 38:8

8 After many days you will be summoned; in the <u>latter years</u> you will come into <u>the land that is restored from the sword</u>, whose inhabitants have been gathered from many nations to the mountains of <u>Israel which had been a continual waste</u>; but its people were brought out from the nations, <u>and they are living securely</u>, all of them.

In this verse, God talks about *"after many days"* and *"in the latter years,"* which I believe is our present time. Also note *"into the land that is restored from the sword."* This occurred on May 14, 1948, with the reestablishment of the State of Israel. Also, *"whose inhabitants have been gathered from many nations to the mountains of Israel."* This has happened, largely, for the last 71 years. God is talking about the Jews who were scattered to all corners of the earth, by Him, at the destruction of the second temple, in Jerusalem, in 70 AD. Their descendants today are now, in the latter years, gathering back into Israel. This prophesied re-gathering of the Jews, from all over the world, restores them to their homeland, per Jeremiah 16:15. Also, *"Israel which had been a continual waste"* up until 1948 and mostly abandoned desert for almost 1,900 years. This was because the Jews were not in their homeland. God's land Israel was abandoned and desolate. Since Israel's rebirth in 1948, it has become economically vibrant and beautiful again. Finally, what about living in security? As discussed earlier, Israelites live in security, because they have the most powerful army in the region. They know they can defend themselves. Right now, their enemy neighbors also know this and can do nothing of any large scale against Israel on their own. But a building hatred has caused the enemies of Israel to start getting bold forming alliances.

Jeremiah 16:14–15
14 *"Therefore behold, days are coming," declares the Lord, "when it will no longer be said, 'As the Lord lives, who brought up the sons of Israel out of the land of Egypt,'* 15 *but, 'As the Lord lives, who brought up the sons of Israel from the land of the north and from all the countries where He had banished them.' For I will restore them to their own land which I gave to their fathers.["]*

In Jeremiah 16:14, during the days of Moses when God delivered Israel out of Egypt into the wilderness, the Jews knew God as *"He who brought up the sons of Israel out of the land of Egypt."* But, in our current time, He is now to be recognized as *"He who brought the sons of Israel from the land of the north and from all countries where He had banished them."* This is happening today. Israelites should accept God as **He who restores them to their own land** . . . another sign of the times.

Going back to these enemy lands: each individual surrounding country can do nothing serious against Israel, on its own, at this time. They can pester Israel with things such as missile attacks from Hamas (*Gaza*). So, Israel lives securely **internally** within **unwalled villages**. But what if these enemies, for some reason, become brazen and all decide, together with Gog of Magog as their leader, to form a coalition and come up with a plan to attack Israel as a large group? Could this happen? Yes. Let's look at Ezekiel 38:10–11.

Ezekiel 38:10–11

10 'Thus says the Lord God, "It will come about on that day, that thoughts will come into your mind and you will devise an evil plan, 11 and you will say, 'I will go up against the land of unwalled villages. I will go against those who are at rest, that live securely, all of them living without walls and having no bars or gates[.'"']

According to these verses, soon the enemy countries surrounding Israel will devise an evil plan, **a coalition** to go against Israel. When I tell you, shortly, what countries, today, match up with the prophesied regions in Ezekiel 38, you will see how they all might soon become a bit emboldened. God tells us what will happen to much of the enemy's lands and armies, in this upcoming battle:

Ezekiel 38:16

16 and you will come up against My people Israel like a cloud to cover the land. It shall come about in the last days that I will bring you against My land, so that the nations may know Me when I am sanctified through you before their eyes, O Gog.

Ezekiel 38:18–20

18 ["]It will come about on that day, when Gog comes against the land of Israel," declares the Lord God, "that My fury will mount up in My anger. 19 In My zeal and in My blazing wrath I declare that on that day there will surely be a great earthquake in the land of Israel. 20 The fish of the sea, the birds of the heavens, the beasts of the field, all the creeping things that creep on the earth, and all the men who are on the face of the earth will shake at My presence[."]

Ezekiel 38:22–23

22 With pestilence and with blood I will enter into judgment with him; and I will rain on him and on his troops, and on the

many peoples who are with him, a torrential rain, with hailstones, fire and brimstone. [23] *I will magnify Myself, sanctify Myself, and make Myself known in the sight of many nations; and they will know that I am the Lord.*

Ezekiel 39:3–6

[3] *"I will strike your bow from your left hand and dash down your arrows from your right hand.* [4] *You will fall on the mountains of Israel, you and all your troops and the peoples who are with you; I will give you as food to every kind of predatory bird and beast of the field.* [5] *You will fall on the open field; for it is I who have spoken," declares the Lord God.* [6] *"And I will send fire upon Magog and those who inhabit the coastlands in safety[."]*

God, Himself, will destroy all of the armies and governments of the enemy countries "**He causes**" to come against Israel. God, on His own, will take all the glory, so the world will know He is Lord. I think God, with this attack, also wants to give all the earth one final clear chance to accept Him before the **time of Jacob's distress** comes. Only a very few will recognize Him or even give Him credit, even after this bold and spectacular event.

Some of you probably think God is talking about this battle happening inside **the time of Jacob's distress**, but is He really? **No.** It is interesting to note that God often uses the term "*latter years.*" "*Latter years*" and "*last days*" refer to the time <u>just prior</u> to **the time of Jacob's distress**.

Ezekiel 39:9–10

[9] *"Then those who inhabit the cities of Israel will go out and make fires with the weapons and burn them, both shields and bucklers, bows and arrows, war clubs and spears, and for* <u>*seven years they will make fires of them*</u>. [10] *They will not take wood from the field or gather firewood from the forests, for they will make fires with the weapons; and* <u>*they will take the spoil*</u> *of those who despoiled them* <u>*and seize the plunder*</u> *of those who plundered them," declares the Lord GOD.*

Per Ezekiel 39:9–10, you may recall again that in Chapter 3 I explained that after the Ezekiel 38 battle those living in the cities of Israel (*the vast majority will be unsaved individuals*) will burn the remains of the fallen enemies' weaponry in their land for 7 years. We know they cannot burn things into the Millennium, so it is clear that the Ezekiel 38 battle must happen before the start of **the time of Jacob's distress**. Biblically, prophecies 14–24 along God's Road Map cannot happen until after Ezekiel 38. Prophecies 14–24 must, however, take place before **the time of Jacob's distress**.

Additionally in verse 10 God says that Israel takes "*spoils*" and "*plunder*" from their fallen surrounding enemies. This is instrumental in the formation of the coming larger physical land mass that will make up Israel after the Ezekiel 38 battle.

Earlier, I referred to nine territories or tribes God mentions will be involved in the Ezekiel 38 attack. This list represented certain countries and tribes in existence 2,500 years ago. Today, these original geographic areas include many new smaller countries, all with current contemporary names.

Over time, these tribes within their original land areas expanded and migrated in all directions, including up to Russia and to Western Europe. Descendants of the original nine tribes live in distant lands today due to this migration. Therefore, we can include outside lands at this time in the Ezekiel equation. So, which countries and tribes today fit within the original nine territories or tribes listed in Ezekiel 38?

Geographical locations where descendants of the tribes from these original areas live today or have migrated indicate the majority of the countries are *Afghanistan, Pakistan, Tajikistan, Turkmenistan, Azerbaijan, Armenia, Georgia, Turkey, Iraq, Iran, Lebanon, UAE, Syria, Jordan, Kuwait, Egypt, Bahrain, Uzbekistan, parts of India, parts of Saudi Arabia, parts of China, parts of Greece, Kyrgyzstan, parts of Eastern Europe—including Germany—also Russia and Libya, and other small countries in Northeastern Africa.*

Of course, I am not sure if all these countries will be involved, but they all fit, related to the current-day location of populations from the nine original regions listed in Ezekiel 38:5–6. Russia, Germany, and parts of Eastern Europe are outside of the original geographic areas listed in Ezekiel 38:5–6. I find it interesting that their population bases consist of the descendants of tribes traced back to Japheth, the son of Noah originally existing in Persia. Gomer and Magog, Tubal, and Meshach were the literal names of the sons of Japheth. Also, a strong Islamic influence and severe anti-Semitism exist in both Russia and Germany at this time. Russia is a strong ally of Iran and other Islamic states. They appear to be arming them now, possibly for some coming military action in the near future. Russia has a major military seaport in Syria. In addition, I think God may still have a score to settle with Germany for WWII. The Germans are descendants of Persia, and they still predominantly hate the Jews to this day. With a new German Neo-Nazi movement growing larger by the day, God may want to deal with them Himself. It is currently illegal to be a Nazi in Germany, but a large, rapidly growing, underground movement (*worldwide as well*) does exist. Because this underground group also wants to rid the world of the Jews, their destruction by God might make perfect sense.

Saudi Arabia houses the top two of the three most valued and holy locations in the Islamic faith: Mecca and Medina. The Al-Aqsa Mosque and the Dome of the Rock in Jerusalem is the third most holy Islamic site in the entire world. It currently sits right on top of the Temple Mount site. **The new third Jewish temple must be located on this mount.** An inscription on the inside of the Dome of the Rock says, specifically, **god has no son** . . . a clear example of Jesus being *"profaned"* as explained earlier in Ezekiel 39:7. This displeases God.

With all this evidence, it would appear that God intends to deal directly with the enemies of Israel that have hated and *"profaned"* His Son so severely. This seems to make sense logistically for a couple of additional reasons. God's Biblical intent, regarding the end of the Islamic influence, seems to be the basis for many factors related to the Ezekiel 38 battle. Also, I do not think the Antichrist can or will be Islamic for a specific reason: extremist Islam could never allow for peace with Israel in any form. Also, the Islamic faith would never accept a One World Church that allowed the involvement of anyone who was not Islamic, and definitely not any Jews.

This likely Islamic neutralization by God will open the door for the creation of the One World Government and One World Church so the Antichrist can come on the scene. The Ezekiel 38 attack will, most likely, remove the Al-Aqsa Mosque and Dome of the Rock in Jerusalem by God's hand alone. This will remove all obstacles, preparing the Temple Mount for the rebuilding of the new third Jewish temple. Additionally, if God were to do something to Mecca and Medina in Saudi Arabia, it would fully invalidate the entire Islamic faith system. **Important:** this will all be done by the hands of God alone. No involvement or participation by the human race will be allowed, or even possible.

The Bible tells us God will deal with the vast majority of the enemy soldiers involved against Israel. The result, the Islamic influence will not exist any longer in any viable form. Most definitely, the Bible and the Quran contradict each other regarding the outcome. They do, however, share full agreement about one thing: **both say this future battle against Israel will occur, and possibly very soon. There can be only one victor.**

Some years back, Iran's former president, Mr. Ahmadinejad, stated openly that Iran desired to *"wipe Israel off the face of the earth."* This statement by Mr. Ahmadinejad is surreal in the context of Psalm 83:4, which can be found at the end of this chapter. When the Islamic world attacks Israel, they expect this will usher in the arrival of their **final 12th Imam**, the **Mahdi**, who, in the Islamic faith, is their Savior of mankind. The God of Abraham, Isaac, and Jacob says He will *"put __hooks__ in their jaws"* (*plural*)

113

and bring them (*Islam*) against Israel. Could this idea of ushering in their Mahdi possibly be one of the many hooks God is talking about in Ezekiel 38:4?

Ezekiel 38:4
⁴ I will turn you about and put <u>hooks into your jaws</u>, and I will bring you out, and all your army, horses and horsemen, all of them splendidly attired, a great company with buckler and shield, all of them wielding swords[.]

God has told us about this; everyone needs to pay careful attention to coming events. I understand that our Islamic friends may totally disagree with this entire assessment of what is to come. Their Quran says something completely different. I know extremist Islam has stated a desire to remove Israel from this world; this should not be news to anybody. Until an attack occurs against Israel, which the Bible says *"shall happen,"* this is all merely conjecture on both sides based on diametrically opposed individual faith systems.

In Chapter 2, I mentioned that some contemporary authors have expressed some, **supposed**, newly revealed "mysteries" for the last days. Are these honestly new issues God did not want to share with us until these last moments in history? **No.**

In the Old Testament, the Bible explains about something called the "**Shemitah**" (*Shmita, Sabbatical cycles*). In the Laws of Moses, they occurred in 7-year installments. Biblically, the last year within these 7-year cycles **was a <u>blessing</u>, for Israel alone**, per Leviticus 25:1–7 and 18–22, a time for rejuvenation, **not curses**. We are told 2001, 2008, and 2015 were Sabbatical years — the Jewish years 5761, 5768 and 5775, respectively. As we all know, the United States experienced attacks on New York in 2001, and the financial crash in 2008 — both supposedly relevant **curses**, falling within Sabbatical years. But no curse hit the USA in 2015 so what are we to think. In the Bible, the United States is not mentioned related to the last days. But why? Because God's whole Biblical story regarding the last days is not about punishments on the United States for abandoning God; **the whole Bible story is all about Israel!** It's about how the Lord will use His final prophecies and **the time of Jacob's distress** period to bring Israel into a full knowledge and understanding of who Jesus the Christ is, their true Messiah.

There are a couple of additional flaws with this popular Shemitah hypothesis. These 7-year cycles, being part of the early Laws for Israel, were dealt with, and resolved, by Christ on the cross. **They are no longer relevant.** Now, if it is truly God's plan for the United States to be experiencing Biblical 7-year punishment cycles, why are we not receiving blessings instead, as God originally intended in Levitical laws for Israel? Why hasn't Israel, today, been under these blessing cycles that God originally intended for them alone in the Old Testament? The United States is not some new Israel. **Israel is Israel.** Many Biblical problems exist within this proposed so-called **"inspired"** revelation regarding the Shemitah.

Recently in 2014–2015, there was a great deal of hype regarding the four Blood Moon cycle, known as a tetrad. This was another example of how easy it is today to misinterpret Bible prophecy. God wants us to pay specific attention to the entire context of the Bible, not just selected excerpts.

The Bible talks about *"the moon turning into blood"* (*moon singular*) prior to **the time of Jacob's distress** in Joel 2:31, Acts 2:20, and Revelation 6:12. God does not use the terminology **blood moons** (*plural*) in His Bible, but certainly *"the moon turning into blood"* implies something similar.

The main flaw of these commentators who predicted the tetrad had significance is that the Bible **never references** any series of **four consecutive blood moons** happening together or as a grouping as having any literal prophetic significance. Additionally, when God talks about the *"moon turning into blood"* in the

Bible, this phenomenon must happen in conjunction with other signs at the same time. **It is not a stand-alone event**.

Acts 2:19–21

¹⁹ And I will grant wonders in the sky above, and signs on the earth beneath, blood, and fire, and vapors of smoke. ²⁰ The sun will be turned into darkness, and the <u>moon into blood</u>, before the great and glorious day of the Lord shall come. ²¹ 'And it shall be, that everyone who calls upon the name of the Lord shall be saved.'

Please be exceptionally careful in the near future. After the Ezekiel 38 battle occurs, rescuing Israel, the people who sold us this flawed blood moons concept may claim this last tetrad cycle was actually a pre-warning of God's grand Ezekiel 38 event. They may even tell us **the time of Jacob's distress** has arrived. It is even possible the Ezekiel 38 event will be called Armageddon. **Please do not accept any of these false interpretations.** The recent tetrad had **nothing** to do with any end-time events.

The Ezekiel 38 attack, when quickly completed, will also afford Christians a small bit of remaining time to evangelize. God offers a window of opportunity to share about the love of Jesus, and what He is doing in our world for us to "**see**." This Ezekiel 38 attack will be an incredible eye-opening God event for all of mankind to witness, for His glory alone.

In Chapter 2, I mentioned how God decides who world leaders will be. He places the right people in power at just the right times, for His purpose. How interesting that many of our leaders in Washington have implied that a two-state solution is the only way to peace for Israel. They see Israel as the "**occupier**," the "**invader**" in a land that Biblically was "**given to the Hebrews**," the Jews, by God Himself. This is confirmed without a doubt in Genesis 15:18–21. Palestinians say the real estate that makes up Israel is their land; the Bible does not say this anywhere. When serious problems escalate in this region, in the near future, between Israel and their surrounding enemies, it is highly likely our leaders will not support Israel wholeheartedly. As a government, our leaders will have uneducated doubts about who to support; this is unfortunate. Our current government fits in perfectly with what the Bible tells us must soon happen. When God's future inspired Ezekiel 38 attack against Israel happens, our leaders will most probably provide only a mild response. God has told us to anticipate a tepid reaction by the entire world. Fortunately, God has Israel's back.

This attack will represent our final Godly warning, not only for Christians, but for all of mankind. Christians will be around, after this attack, for only a few years—pending the completion of all of God's other final prophecies, required **before the visual catching up** and **the start of the time of Jacob's distress**.

We will see the beginning of Israel burning the destroyed weapons of the losing armies that will fall on their land. This attack will cause a worldwide financial reorganization. Back in **Road Map** prophecy #22, I explained how after Ezekiel 38 the State of Israel will become larger. This has many ramifications. The oil fields in Persia would become a part of Israel, as they will have gained back most of the real estate God gave to the 12 sons of Jacob. Babylon, the ultimate new seat of world government, will be inside the new geographic boundary of the larger Israel. Additionally, Israel with this new land and all the oil fields may become the wealthiest and most powerful country in the world, almost overnight—**the world's new mega superpower**. The Jewish tribal system can then be reestablished. The reestablishment of the 12 tribes of Israel within this newly obtained land mass will need to happen so the 144,000 (*after the catching up*) can come on the scene quickly, and must occur before **the time of Jacob's distress** starts. God will have done all this for Israel and unfortunately will get little or no credit for doing so.

After this major event, the world will miraculously desire to come together in unity to rebuild as one united global family. This will quickly usher in the prophesied One World Government, the formation of 10 world divisions (*kingdoms*), and then, following quickly, the person who is the Antichrist will come on the scene. The new capital of the world will soon be in Babylon. Babylon will become the center of commerce, politics, and religion — the new cultural center of the world.

Earlier I told you how the vast majority of the enemy army's soldiers that come against Israel will die in this battle. In fact, so many bodies will lay dead on Israel's ground that God will send predatory birds and beasts of the field to devour them, per Ezekiel 39:4–5. An interesting phenomenon is occurring in Israel today. Each season, migrating predatory birds used to fly over Israel to their intended destinations, but this has recently changed. Many of these specific predatory birds now take permanent residency inside Israel.

Also mentioned earlier, the Christian community seems confused as to when people think the Ezekiel 38:1–39:16 attack will happen. Revelation 20:7–10 mentions **Gog and Magog** one brief time. **Gog and Magog** is a generally accepted reference to the Ezekiel 38:1–39:16 battle. Some say this single mention in Revelation indicates this grand attack talked about, in great detail, in Ezekiel 38:1-39:16 (*two chapters, 39 verses*) happens during **the time of Jacob's distress** period and not before. When you read Revelation 20:7 carefully, you will notice a significant phrase: *"And when the thousand years are completed."* These Revelation 20:7–10 verses talk about something that will happen at the end of the **Millennium**, not inside the **time of Jacob's distress**. The **Millennium** is a 1,000-year period after the completion of **the time of Jacob's distress**, where Jesus will reign on the entire earth. Per the Bible, Satan is no longer on earth for the vast majority of this time period. If the idea that the **Gog and Magog** battle happens inside **the time of Jacob's distress** were true, why didn't God describe this battle inside the book of Revelation, including all its detail, instead of in Ezekiel? Because at the end of the **Millennium** it will have already happened, more than 1,000 years earlier. But how can we know this?

In Revelation 20:7–10, Jesus talks about the final defeat of Satan at the end of the **Millennium**. Satan is briefly freed for a short period of time at the end of the **1,000-year** Reign of Jesus. Remember, we are talking about Satan here, and this will become clear shortly. In the **Millennium**, Christ is with us on earth, so why would Ezekiel 38:1–39:16 need to happen when Jesus is here as the leader of the world? **It wouldn't.**

Revelation 20:10 tells of the quick final defeat of Satan, with God throwing him into the lake of fire where he *"will be tormented day and night forever and ever."* The reference to **Gog and Magog** in Revelation 20:8 is a **metaphor**. **Gog and Magog** in Revelation 20:8 is representative of how swift and decisive God's final victory over Satan will be, similar to the quick, decisive defeat by God in the Ezekiel 38:1–39:16 attack, which will have happened ages earlier.

The Ezekiel 38:1–39:16 battle is **not against Satan;** it is against the **enemy armies surrounding Israel**. The Revelation 20:8 reference is not against **the surrounding enemy armies of Israel** but, rather, **against Satan**, two distinctly different events.

For the people who still say that Ezekiel 38:1–39:16 must happen inside **the time of Jacob's distress**, here is what the Bible tells us. Let's take another look at Ezekiel 38:8 for clear understanding:

Ezekiel 38:8
8 After many days you will be summoned; in the latter years you will come into the land that is restored from the sword, whose inhabitants have been gathered from many nations to the mountains of Israel which had been a continual waste; but its people were brought out from the nations, and they are living securely, all of them.

Note five specific details mentioned in this verse:
1. *"in the latter years"*
2. *"the land that is restored from the sword"*
3. *"whose inhabitants have been gathered from many nations to the mountains of Israel"*
4. *"(Israel) which had been a continual waste"*
5. *"and they are living securely"*

All five of these items can only exist, or be in place, **prior to the time of Jacob's distress**. The Ezekiel 38 attack happens **before the start of the time of Jacob's distress**.

As secularism grows, and with the Islamic faith neutralized, all the Jesus-believing Christians will be the last people demonized. The growing group of worldwide secularists of the New One World Church and the False Prophets minions will scorn and ridicule us. I classify any supposed Christian members who join or stay within the new One World Church as secularists. Their compromises regarding Jesus will likely put them into the time of Jacob's distress.

Mohamed, the founder of the Islamic faith (*632 AD*), claimed to be an Ishmaelite, a descendant of Ishmael. Ishmael and Isaac were half-brothers, the two sons of Abraham. They have a significant place in both history and in what is happening today in the world.

Right after this next section on the Ishmaelites, I have attached the prayer by Asaph in his Psalm 83. This **imprecatory psalm** is asking God at some future time to *"bring down vengeance"* on the Ishmaelite wing of Abraham's family, Islam.

SO, WHO ARE THE ISHMAELITES?

This goes back to Abraham in the Bible. In Genesis, Abraham receives a promise from God saying he will father many nations and many peoples. But Abraham did not understand this because he had no children, and both he and his wife, Sarah, were beyond childbearing years. Because of Sarah's age, she decided to offer her maidservant, Hagar, to Abraham (*Abram*) so he could create an heir. This was not what God intended, but Abraham did have a son with Hagar. They named him Ishmael.

Genesis 16:15–16

15 So Hagar bore Abram a son; and Abram called the name of his son, whom Hagar bore, <u>Ishmael</u>. 16 Abram was eighty-six years old when Hagar bore Ishmael to him.

God wanted Abraham and Sarah to trust Him, but they decided to take things into their own hands, and "*Ishmael*" became an heir. God then **created** a fertile womb for Sarah, in her old age, and she bore Abraham a son named "*Isaac.*"

Genesis 21:1–3

1 Then the Lord took note of Sarah as He had said, and the Lord did for Sarah as He had promised. 2 So Sarah conceived and bore a son to Abraham in his old age, at the appointed time of which God had spoken to him. 3 Abraham called the name of his son who was born to him, whom Sarah bore to him, <u>Isaac</u>.

Isaac is the true heir and seed intended by God, as mentioned in Genesis 21:12–13.

Genesis 21:12–13

12 But God said to Abraham, "Do not be distressed because of the lad and your maid; whatever Sarah tells you, listen to her, <u>for through Isaac your descendants shall be named</u>. 13 And of the son of the maid I will make a nation also, because he is your descendant."

God also tells Hagar that He will make a nation (*large*) out of Ishmael in Genesis 16:10–11.

STUNNED

Genesis 16:10–11

10 Moreover, the angel of the Lord said to her, "<u>I will greatly multiply your descendants so that they will be too many to count.</u>" 11 The angel of the Lord said to her further, "Behold, you are with child, and you will bear a son and you shall call his name Ishmael, because the Lord has given heed to your affliction.["]

Jews and Christians claim relationship with Abraham through Isaac (*Jesus also came through the line of Isaac*). Genesis 21:12 also makes it clear that through Isaac, Abraham's descendants shall be named.

Those in the Islamic faith claim their lineage to Abraham through Ishmael. The Quran disputes the claim that Isaac is the legitimate heir per the Bible. The Quran also claims that Ishmael is the only true heir; thus, the controversy exists to this day. Per the Bible, one son is legitimate, in the eyes of God, and the other is legitimate in the eyes of the other god. Only one view is correct, so these deities cannot be the same entity. As a matter of fact, per the Bible, God tells us that Ishmael, as the older brother, was born into affliction, and God forced Ishmael's hand to be against everyone and everybody would be against him, per Genesis 16:11–12:

Genesis 16:11–12

11 The angel of the Lord said to her further, "Behold, you are with child, and you will bear a son; and you shall call his name Ishmael, because the Lord has given heed to your affliction. 12 He will be a wild donkey of a man, his hand will be against everyone, and everyone's hand will be against him; and he will live to the east of all his brothers."

Ishmael (*Islam*) taunted Isaac (*Jews*) from the very beginning, and this has followed right through to our current day.

God's Thirteenth Prophecy

The Ishmaelites (*Islam*) want to wipe out Israel, so their name will be remembered no more. In Psalm 83, the writer, Asaph, basically prays and asks God to destroy the Ishmaelites for His glory and their ultimate humiliation.

Some Bible commentators today erroneously tell us that Psalm 83 depicts a **prophesied** attack by Israel on its surrounding enemy nations **prior** to Ezekiel 38:1–39:16. This would make Israel a predatory conqueror, which they will never be. There are serious flaws with this thinking. But why?

What are psalms? By definition, in most instances (*not all*), they are **sacred songs**, **prayers**, or **poems**. Asaph was a skilled singer and poet. As mentioned earlier, Jesus Himself spoke about the **Tanakh** in Luke 24:44. He made a clear separation among the "*Law of Moses*," the "*Prophets*," and the "*Psalms*," all distinctly different.

Luke 24:44
44 *Now He said to them, "These are My words which I spoke to you while I was still with you, that all things which are written about Me in the <u>Law of Moses</u> and the <u>Prophets</u> and the <u>Psalms</u> must be fulfilled."*

In Psalm 83, below, please pay specific attention to the underlined items in verses 1, 9, 13, 15, and 18. Asaph cannot possibly be asking the State of Israel to do this attack. **He is asking God** to personally do this **for His glory**. Psalm 83, **specifically**, is an **imprecatory prayer, not a prophecy**, asking God to bring His future Ezekiel 38:1–39:16 battle against the Ishmaelites (*Islam*). Additionally, per Psalm 83:17, only God can fulfill the following: "*Let them be ashamed and dismayed forever, and let them be humiliated and perish.*" Israel does not have this capability; only God does. Also, if Israel's surrounding enemy countries are **dismayed** and **humiliated** "*forever*" and they "*perish*," they would no longer have the strength or even exist to come against Israel for any future secondary Ezekiel 38:1–39:16 attack. *"Forever"* is forever, and *"perish"* means no more.

Psalm 83

[1] <u>O God</u>, do not remain quiet; do not be silent and, O God, do not be still. [2] For behold, Your enemies make an uproar, And those who hate You have exalted themselves. [3] They make shrewd plans against Your people, And conspire together against Your treasured ones. [4] They have said, <u>"Come, and let us wipe them out as a nation, that the name of Israel be remembered no more."</u> [5] For they have conspired together with one mind; against You they make a covenant: [6] The tents of Edom and the Ishmaelites, Moab and the Hagrites; [7] Gebal and Ammon and Amalek, Philistia with the inhabitants of Tyre; [8] Assyria also has joined with them; They have become a help to the children of Lot. Selah. [9] <u>Deal with them</u> as with Midian, As with Sisera and Jabin at the torrent of Kishon, [10] who were destroyed at En-dor, Who became as dung for the ground. [11] Make their nobles like Oreb and Zeeb and all their princes like Zebah and Zalmunna, [12] who said, "Let us possess for ourselves the pastures of God." [13] <u>O my God</u>, make them like the whirling dust, like chaff before the wind. [14] Like fire that burns the forest and like a flame that sets the mountains on fire, [15] <u>So pursue them with Your tempest</u> and <u>terrify them with Your storm</u>. [16] Fill their faces with dishonor, that they may seek your name, O Lord. [17] Let them be ashamed and dismayed forever, and let them be humiliated and perish, [18] <u>that they may know that You alone, whose name is the Lord</u>, are the Most High over all the earth.

In this text, Asaph clearly asks God *(not the State of Israel)* to destroy the Ishmaelites for His glory. He gives multiple examples of battles that happened earlier within societies in history and resulted in great victories. They represent what Asaph is asking

God to do at some point in the future. The people of that day would have known the type of victory over the Ishmaelites that Asaph asked God to achieve in his prayer, by all the examples he listed in Psalm 83.

We live in an incredible time in history. I strongly believe we will soon witness God's Two-Minute Warning, Ezekiel 38:1–39:16, as addressed in this chapter, and will soon see all of the additional events explained in this book. God will do all of this out of love for Israel. I only hope that Christians, and maybe even some of our Jewish family, will pay attention and understand what they witness.

Ezekiel 38

PRIOR TO THE TIME OF JACOB'S DISTRESS, GOD'S BATTLE WITH ONLY A LIMITED NUMBER OF NATIONS

¹ And the word of the LORD came to me saying, ² "Son of man, set your face toward Gog of the land of Magog, the prince of Rosh, Meshech and Tubal, and prophesy against him ³ and say, 'Thus says the Lord GOD, "Behold, I am against you, O Gog, prince of Rosh, Meshech and Tubal. ⁴ I will turn you about and put hooks into your jaws, and I will bring you out, and all your army, horses and horsemen, all of them splendidly attired, a great company with buckler and shield, all of them wielding swords; ⁵ Persia, Ethiopia and Put with them, all of them with shield and helmet; ⁶ Gomer with all its troops; Beth-togarmah from the remote parts of the north with all its troops — many peoples with you. ⁷ Be prepared, and prepare yourself, you and all your companies that are assembled about you, and be a guard for them. ⁸ After many days you will be summoned; in the latter years you will come into the land that is restored from the sword, whose inhabitants have been gathered from many nations to the mountains of Israel which had been a continual waste; but its people were brought out from the nations, and they are living securely, all of them. ⁹ You will go up, you will come like a storm; you will be like a cloud covering the land, you and all your troops, and many peoples with you." [10] 'Thus says the Lord GOD, "It will come about on that day, that thoughts will come into your mind and you will devise an evil plan, [11] and you will say, 'I will go up against the land of unwalled villages. I will go against those who are at rest, that live securely, all of them living without walls and having no bars or gates, [12] to capture spoil and to seize plunder, to turn your hand against the waste places which are now inhabited, and against the people who are gathered from the nations, who have acquired cattle and goods, who live at the center of the world.' [13] Sheba and Dedan and the merchants of Tarshish with all its villages will say to you, 'Have you come to capture spoil? Have you assembled your company to seize plunder, to carry away silver and gold, to take away cattle and goods, to capture great spoil?'" [14] "Therefore prophesy, son of man, and say to Gog, 'Thus says the Lord GOD, "On that day when My people Israel are living securely, will you not know it? [15] You will come from your place out of the remote parts of the north, you and many peoples with you, all of them riding on horses, a great assembly and a mighty army; [16] and you will come up against My people Israel like a cloud to cover the land. It shall come about in the last days that I will bring you against My land, so that the nations may know Me when I am sanctified through you before their eyes, O Gog." [17] 'Thus says the Lord GOD, "Are you the one of whom I spoke in former days through My servants the prophets of Israel, who prophesied in those days for many years that I would bring you against them? [18] It will come about on that day, when Gog comes against the land of Israel," declares the Lord GOD, "that My fury will mount up in My anger. [19] In My zeal and in My blazing wrath I declare that on that day there will surely be a great earthquake in the land of Israel. [20] The fish of the sea, the birds of the heavens, the beasts of the field, all the creeping things that creep on the earth, and all the men who are on the face of the earth will shake at My presence; the mountains also will be thrown down, the steep pathways will collapse and every wall will fall to the ground. ²¹ I will call for a sword against him on all My mountains," declares the Lord GOD. "Every man's sword will be against his brother. ²² With pestilence and with blood I will enter into judgment with him; and I will rain on him and on his troops, and on the many peoples who are with him, a torrential rain, with hailstones, fire and brimstone. ²³ I will magnify Myself, sanctify Myself, and make Myself known in the sight of many nations; and they will know that I am the LORD."'["]

Ezekiel 39

¹ "And you, son of man, prophesy against Gog and say, 'Thus says the Lord GOD, "Behold, I am against you, O Gog, prince of Rosh, Meshech and Tubal; ² and I will turn you around, drive you on, take you up from the remotest parts of the north and bring you against the mountains of Israel. ³ I will strike your bow from your left hand and dash down your arrows from your right hand. ⁴ You will fall on the mountains of Israel, you and all your troops and the peoples who are with you; <u>I will give you as food to every kind of predatory bird and beast of the field.</u> ⁵ You will fall on the open field; for it is I who have spoken," declares the Lord GOD. ⁶ "And I will send fire upon Magog and those who inhabit the coastlands in safety; and they will know that I am the LORD. ⁷ My holy name I will make known in the midst of My people Israel; and I will not let My holy name be profaned anymore. And the nations will know that I am the LORD, the Holy One in Israel. ⁸ Behold, it is coming and it shall be done," declares the Lord GOD. "That is the day of which I have spoken. ⁹ Then those who inhabit the cities of Israel will go out and make fires with the weapons and burn them, both shields and bucklers, bows and arrows, war clubs and spears, and for seven years they will make fires of them. ¹⁰ They will not take wood from the field or gather firewood from the forests, for they will make fires with the weapons; and they will take the spoil of those who despoiled them and seize the plunder of those who plundered them," declares the Lord GOD. ¹¹ "On that day I will give Gog a burial ground there in Israel, the valley of those who pass by east of

the sea, and it will block off those who would pass by. So they will bury Gog there with all his horde, and they will call it the valley of Hamon-gog. ¹² For seven months the house of Israel will be burying them in order to cleanse the land. ¹³ Even all the people of the land will bury them; and it will be to their renown on the day that I glorify Myself," declares the Lord GOD.
¹⁴ *"They will set apart men who will constantly pass through the land, burying those who were passing through, even those left on the surface of the ground, in order to cleanse it. At the end of seven months they will make a search. ¹⁵ As those who pass through the land pass through and anyone sees a man's bone, then he will set up a marker by it until the buriers have buried it in the valley of Hamon-gog. ¹⁶ And even the name of the city will be Hamonah. So they will cleanse the land."'*

ARMAGEDDON AT THE END OF THE TIME OF JACOB'S TROUBLE: JESUS' FINAL BATTLE WITH ALL THE NATIONS OF THE EARTH

¹⁷ *"As for you, son of man, thus says the Lord GOD, 'Speak to every kind of bird and to every beast of the field, "Assemble and come, gather from every side to My sacrifice which I am going to sacrifice for you, as a great sacrifice on the mountains of Israel, that you may eat flesh and drink blood. ¹⁸ You will eat the flesh of mighty men and drink the blood of the princes of the earth, as though they were rams, lambs, goats and bulls, all of them fatlings of Bashan. ¹⁹ So you will eat fat until you are glutted, and drink blood until you are drunk, from My sacrifice which I have sacrificed for you. ²⁰ You will be glutted at My table with horses and charioteers, with mighty men and all the men of war," declares the Lord GOD. ²¹ "And I will set My glory among the nations; and all the nations will see My judgment which I have executed and My hand which I have laid on them. ²² And the house of Israel will know that I am the LORD their God from that day onward. ²³ The nations will know that the house of Israel went into exile for their iniquity because they acted treacherously against Me, and I hid My face from them;*

so I gave them into the hand of their adversaries, and all of them fell by the sword. [24] According to their uncleanness and according to their transgressions I dealt with them, and I hid My face from them."'" [25] Therefore thus says the Lord GOD, "Now I will restore the fortunes of Jacob and have mercy on the whole house of Israel; and I will be jealous for My holy name. [26] They will forget their disgrace and all their treachery which they perpetrated against Me, when they live securely on their own land with no one to make them afraid. [27] When I bring them back from the peoples and gather them from the lands of their enemies, then I shall be sanctified through them in the sight of the many nations. [28] Then they will know that I am the LORD their God because I made them go into exile among the nations, and then gathered them again to their own land; and I will leave none of them there any longer. [29] I will not hide My face from them any longer, for I will have poured out My Spirit on the house of Israel," declares the Lord GOD.

2 Timothy 4:3–4

3 *For the time will come when they will not endure sound doctrine; but wanting to have their ears tickled, they will accumulate for themselves teachers in accordance to their own desires,* 4 *and will turn away their ears from the truth and will turn aside to myths.*

CHAPTER 5

DECEPTIONS

The Deceiver knows we are close to the Lord's return at the visual catching up. He does not want people to recognize this, so he uses multiple, subtle deceptions and myths to fool many. God tells us to . . . take great care in these last days.

Biblical deceptions are actions or theories where the creation, or man, begins to think and believe they know more than their Creator. At this time in history, humanity—with the guidance and support of the Deceiver—rebels against the Creator more than ever. God warns about this happening in the last days. He battles against His fallen creation, the Deceiver. The Deceiver has only one goal: to keep as many people from God as possible. He knows he will not get to heaven and he knows God's supremacy has power. He also understands he will ultimately lose both the battles and the war. In spite of his awareness, he still arrogantly thinks he can change the outcome. He perceives the possibility of a victory.

Right now, one of the biggest deceptions of all faces us daily. Everything in our world regarding right and wrong is backward. What God tells us is right and moral is now ignored and discounted in the eyes of the majority. Unfortunately, the secular world now compassionately tolerates and accepts what God considers sin. The Deceiver would have us think that if we are truly intelligent, we should have no problem seeing things his way. In fact, when a Christian tries to denounce an action or theory because of Biblical teachings, many people immediately marginalize and label us as intolerant or phobic.

Isaiah 5:20–21
20 Woe to those who call evil good, and good evil; who substitute darkness for light and light for darkness; who substitute bitter for sweet and sweet for bitter! 21 Woe to those who are wise in their own eyes and clever in their own sight!

God tells us to act cautiously when we see this happening. He even says those who accept evil as good should take great care. God specifically tells us in Isaiah 5:20–21, "**Woe to those who call evil good.**"

Deceptions

So, our nemesis deceives man in many ways. He uses **indifference** and proclaims that errors and cultural myths fill the Bible. The Deceiver uses the opinions and the beliefs of alleged Bible scholars. He uses only those who agree with him as the authenticators of **his new corrupt truth** — not the truth of the all-knowing original author, God. If anyone perceives the Bible as containing only stories and myths, the Deceiver can tell them that he (*Satan*) isn't real, but rather a figment of their imaginations, and that to think he exists borders on lunacy.

<u>2 Timothy 4:3-4</u>
³ For the time will come when they will not endure sound doctrine; but wanting to have their <u>ears tickled</u>, they will accumulate for themselves teachers in accordance to their own desires, ⁴ and will turn away their ears from the truth and will turn aside to <u>myths</u>.

"*Ears tickled*," "*myths*." Secular man has great difficulty perceiving God's tremendous power. God holds the universe in the palms of His hands (*Isaiah 40:15-27*). Most of the secular world cannot accept the grandeur of God.

<u>Ephesians 4:17-18</u>
¹⁷ So this I say, and affirm together with the Lord, that you walk no longer just as the Gentiles also walk, in the futility of their mind, ¹⁸ being darkened in their understanding, excluded from the life of God because of the <u>ignorance</u> that is in them, because of the hardness of their heart[.]

To achieve his goals, the Deceiver uses "*ignorance*," which comes from a lack of true knowledge, true information, and true education. He does this with a great sense of pride. The secular world, his realm, calls Christians **ignorant** for not accepting supposedly proven scientific findings of things such as natural selection and the evolution of mankind. God, however, is supernatural, and not bound by the limited amount of natural things He has selected to allow man to discover. He has not allowed us to know everything, yet.

Luke 21:34
³⁴ *Be on guard, so that your hearts will not be weighted down with dissipation and drunkenness and the worries of life, and that day will not come on you suddenly like a trap[.]*

The Deceiver uses **infiltration** with **diversions** such as keeping us busy all day striving and searching for external pleasures in our lives. He tries to convince us that personal desires for wealth, lust, power, careers, and success will make us happy, all at the cost of lost family, relationships, joy, and time with God. Faith loses out when the Deceiver successfully makes his enticing pleasures more attractive to us than what God offers.

Ephesians 6:10–13
¹⁰ *Finally, be strong in the Lord and in the strength of His might.* ¹¹ *Put on the full armor of God, so that you will be able to stand firm against the schemes of the devil.* ¹² *For our struggle is not against flesh and blood, but against the rulers, against the powers, against the world forces of this darkness, against the spiritual forces of wickedness in the heavenly places.* ¹³ *Therefore, take up the full armor of God, so that you will be able to resist in the evil day, and having done everything, to stand firm.*

God warns us about the perpetual spiritual warfare all around us. He provides the Bible to help us know what in our world comes from Him—everything sound, good, and true. He tells us to *"Put on the full armor of God."* He also gave us His Bible to show us how to know the difference between His Holy

Bible and the Deceiver's humanistic bible. The humanistic bible is the Deceiver's plan. Individually, we all need to choose which version to accept.

Many additional issues fall into the category of deception. One highly controversial topic I explore in this chapter brings about a grand deception: man's **theory** of natural **evolution**. Non-Christians may accept evolution . . . a free will choice. I have directed the arguments made here at Christians who have accepted what I truly believe to be a flawed concept from a Biblical standpoint.

If we follow the literal genealogies in the Bible, God shows us that mankind, by His design, has lived on earth for only about 6,000 years. How can we know this? The Bible provides a full chronology of mankind from the first man, Adam, up to the birth of Christ. Genesis 5, Genesis 11:10–32, and Matthew 1:1–16 list by name the genealogies and some specific ages of Adam's descendants. A review of these Scriptures reveals that God provides actual ages for each successive individual, and, when summed up, this represents 4,000 years, from Adam to Christ's birth. Add the 2,000 years since Christ's first visit (Matthew 1:1–16), and the result is 6,000 years. This period of time relates to **only mankind**, and **not the earth itself**. This gets a bit complicated, so please follow my logic.

If we do not accept what God says about **creating** Adam and Eve but, instead, choose to think that He used some non-stated alternate path, this creates a problem, a problem related to all faith in Jesus, in general. I have looked at both sides of this evolution question and feel confident with what the Bible says, and not what man has created as their new recently accepted alternate path, **evolution** (*Charles Darwin, 1859*).

I think the time will soon come when we'll walk on dangerous ground if we even talk about the creation view. Biblical thinking will indicate to secularists that a person lacks intellect and clings to outdated fables as only a fool would do. This time has, essentially, already arrived.

I find it interesting how, today, the evolution issue — even for Christians — appears divisive . . . a topic that generates heated debates even to the point of confrontation between believers. For some reason, it seems as if some Christians have drawn battle lines on this topic. But why? Why should a controversy regarding this subject even exist within the Christian family? The Deceiver wants this to happen:

<u>Mark 3:25</u>
25 *If a house is divided against itself, that house will not be able to stand.*

Satan wants division to happen within the Christian community, causing strife and infighting. This evolution issue is but one valid sample of a divide that will grow much worse in the faith community. God expects all Christians to use the Bible alone as our sole basis for theological learning and teaching. He says not to employ speculation (*theory*) or to accept the scientific interpretations of man in this endeavor. As mankind becomes more prideful and arrogant and believes they are getting as smart as, or even possibly smarter, than some fictional God, this creates a much bigger problem. As this happens, mankind will make the very same deadly error Satan made through his pride. The need for the Bible or God's Word or any need to rely on Him alone will become more and more deluded. God becomes excluded. If a theory created by mankind, in any form, causes even one person to walk away from God due to a false perception that God may be weak, the Deceiver succeeds.

I encourage any Christian who accepts the possibility of evolution to further explore the findings of supposed archeology and scientific interpretations. If you believe God could have used evolution to achieve life from the beginning, then please take the following steps:

- Find the specific Bible text proving evolution is something God has literally shown us in His Word.
- Provide a full and complete outline of all the verses that clearly indicate God's intention to convey evolution as His desired design vehicle.

You will find this does not exist.

Some people will insist that science has proven the **theory** of evolution. We were told the big bang **theory**, for instance, help to prove the concept. Because we can see the universe expanding in deep space through our great telescopes, supposedly over billions of years — doing mathematical calculations — they even go so far as to postulate how God had nothing to do with it.

Did you know the Catholic Church diligently tries to discover extraterrestrial life? But why? It appears the Catholic Church, in this time of apostasy, has accepted a modern belief system leading to the conclusion that the solar system is one set of worlds around a single star with life on one of its planets. Because there are trillions of stars in the universe, they say **it is arrogant** for mankind to believe that a big God has created life in only one place.

It is my understanding, on May 14, 2014, during his morning mass, Pope Francis was asked a question essentially as follows:

If — for example — tomorrow an expedition of Martians came, and some of them came to us, here . . . and one says, "But I want to be baptized!" What would happen?

The pope answered and said the church does not have a closed door and would baptize them. A tongue-in-cheek answer, right? Today, possibly — but soon, maybe not. Why diligently look for extraterrestrial life? Who actually benefits from this, as God never mentions this in the Bible, anywhere? The Deceiver benefits!

This extraterrestrial search, however, seems severely flawed because of God's omnipotence. He can create anything to any

STUNNED

size, at will. The size of the universe is, in fact, daunting in scale from our small limited human perspective, but its size means nothing to God. In His scale, it is both immense and at the same time very small because He has no limits. God provides the universe to reveal His grandeur and unlimited nature.

The Catholic Jesuits operate, and the Vatican owns a majority interest in, one of the greatest telescopes in the world, located on the top of Mt. Graham, in Arizona. The Vatican scientists who run this equipment have come to the conclusion that the big bang *theory* is the most probable explanation for the formation of our world and universe. This all occurred over billions of years. So logically, we can no longer consider the six days of creation, which God talks about in Genesis, the only serious possibility; it is allegorical. I will address creation shortly.

A few interesting facts about the two Arizona telescopes: the Jesuits (*the Catholic Church*) own the VATT (*Vatican Advanced Technology Telescope*). There is also a grand second unit, the LBT (*Large Binocular Telescope*). They form a consortium. The Jesuits can use the LBT at any time. The LBT telescope and its sophisticated, deep-space camera has a rather lengthy name. It is called a **Large, Binocular Telescope with Near Infrared Utility, with Camera, and Integral, Field unit for Extragalactic Research.** Note the underlined letters in the words above create an interesting acronym. It is my understanding that the Catholic Church did not have anything to do with the naming of the LBT unit and has no responsibility for its nickname: **Lucifer.**

One of the lead institutes on board to build the LBT telescope in Arizona was the Heidelberg University in the German state of Baden-Württemberg. The governor of this state at that time, **Erwin Teufel**, was instrumental in obtaining funding for its construction. So, it is believed the telescope was nicknamed in his honor. Do you know what the German word or name **Teufel** translates to in the English language? It translates as the **Devil**, **Satan**, or **Lucifer**. The intriguing thing: Teufel is a common name in Germany right now. Nobody there understands why this might be perceived as problematic. (*Remember we talked about Germany in the Ezekiel 38 and 39 section.*) These Germans also tell us Lucifer is the **fabled** fallen angel in the Bible. They actually say **fabled**. Interestingly, the Catholic Church did not make much of a protest to this naming.

Germans with the surname Teufel tell us not to worry about this because Lucifer (*Satan*) in Latin is defined as the **bearer of light**, or the "**star of the morning**." In the Bible, the "**Morning Star**" does refer to both Satan and Jesus, but with a large separation and distinction. Satan was God's most beautiful **creation** and the highest possible cherub (*highest order of celestial beings*): the lowest are angels (*no wings*), then seraphim (*six wings*), and then the cherubim are the highest (*two wings*). Jesus, however, is God. When Satan fell, due to his arrogance and pride present in Isaiah 14:12-15, he was no longer the "**star of the morning**" in God's kingdom. After Satan's fall, all future references to the "**Morning Star**" always refer to the Messiah, the Christ, which of course, is Jesus, not the Devil. Remember, the Devil wants to be god, so he counterfeits everything and still believes he qualifies as a "**star of the morning**." It's interesting that the LBT telescope is right next door to the Catholic Church's VATT unit, and the Catholics use it often. One of the very tools they use on a regular basis to discredit what God says in His Bible is nicknamed Lucifer.

Only 400 years ago, the Catholic Church did not allow research of the heavens for truth regarding the nature of the universe. In 1592, an astronomer by the name of Giordano Bruno came up with a theory that the earth revolved around the sun. The Catholic Church did not like this and lured him to Rome under the guise of giving him a job. When he arrived in Rome, Mr. Bruno was imprisoned. He withstood 8 years of torture because he would not denounce his theory. The Catholic Hierarchy considered Mr. Bruno's theory to be heresy and put him on trial. On February 19, 1600, his judge, Cardinal Robert Bellarmine, sentenced him to death. Not a simple, kind end, but a brutal barbaric execution—all for his lack of penance related to Catholic doctrine. So how did he die? First, Mr. Bruno had his jaw clamped shut with an iron gag. Torturers drove spikes through his tongue and palate. They stripped him naked and paraded him through the streets of Rome, and then publicly burned him at the stake. In **Road Map** prophecy #17, I made reference to the possibility that the Jesuits may not be as nice and kind as they want us to believe. The horrible, cruel, sadistic death that Mr. Bruno experienced was brought about by Cardinal Bellarmine—a Jesuit.

In the years following this event, between 1616 and 1633, Cardinal Bellarmine, who died in 1621, was initially a key player in trying Galileo for heresy, due to his new astronomical observations. On July 22, 1633, the Catholic Church found Galileo **"gravely suspect of heresy"** and ordered him to indefinite imprisonment. He remained under house arrest until his death, in 1642.

Science is *"systemic knowledge of the physical or material world gained through observation and experimentation."* God has allowed us the ability to discover small pieces of the perfect design and harmony He put into existence. He did this so we can live and enjoy our daily lives productively. Let's be clear on this and not be fooled. God (*the creator*) is not bound to what we (*the creation*) have enjoyed as scientific constants regarding the universe. He established them. I will even venture to speculate that on the day of the visual **catching up** and the start of the literal **time of Jacob's distress**, all the scientific norms God has allowed mankind to discover, up to that point, will be turned upside down. How can living humans visually rise into the sky (*defying gravity*) and disappear into the clouds, never to be seen again? Remember those telescopes? After the **visual catching up**, maybe the co-opted Catholic Church (*still here?*) and the Deceiver will say they found extraterrestrials who removed all the looney dogmatic Jesus believers to cleanse the earth of a problem . . . a logical possibility, as the Deceiver will need a way to explain away to the world what they just saw happen.

After the **visual catching up**, not all people remaining on the earth will stay deceived. Many will start to realize the science they thought proved things are constant and in harmony was flawed and that man really did not get to know everything. Should this really come as a surprise to informed truth-believing Christians living today? No. I still take God's words literally, as spoken, and do not feel comfortable going down any path that deviates from His clear and simple stated concepts. I trust the literal words in the Bible.

The Bible has never changed. It has been the same since before the world existed. Intellectually, as mentioned earlier, we must decide whether or not the Bible is perfect. We cannot twist the words to make it fit our needs or our new enlightened scientific intelligence. We all know through observation that all science, in our time, constantly changes almost on a daily basis, based on new information unknown yesterday. Because man is not perfect, who is to say scientific theories discovered by man are completely correct? Issues we thought factual only 100 years ago have since been debunked and updated. I do agree the science of man has evolved because it is man's creation (*educated speculation*). The Bible, however, is a constant, created by the perfect creator and not flawed in any way.

<u>*1 Corinthians 15:12-19*</u>
12 Now if Christ is preached, that He has been raised from the dead, how do some among you say that there is no resurrection of the dead? 13 But if there is no resurrection of the dead, not even Christ has been raised; 14 and if Christ has not been raised, then our preaching is vain, your faith also is vain. 15 Moreover we are even found to be false witnesses of God, because we testified against God that He raised Christ, whom He did not raise, if in fact the dead are not raised. 16 For if the dead are not

raised, not even Christ has been raised; ¹⁷ and if Christ has not been raised, your faith is worthless; you are still in your sins. ¹⁸ Then those also who have fallen asleep in Christ have perished. ¹⁹ If we have hoped in Christ in this life only, we are of all men most to be pitied.

Romans 12:3
³ For through the grace given to me I say to everyone among you not to think more highly of himself than he ought to think; but to think so as to have sound judgment, as God has allotted to each a measure of faith.

Romans 16:17
¹⁷ Now I urge you, brethren, keep your eye on those who cause dissensions and hindrances contrary to the teaching which you learned, and turn away from them.

2 Corinthians 4:3-4
³ And even if our gospel is veiled, it is veiled to those who are perishing, ⁴ in whose case the God of this world has blinded the minds of the unbelieving so that they might not see the light of the gospel of the glory of Christ, who is the image of God.

In the preceding set of verses, notice that God tells us some things about humility, and what a world without faith can do to people. Were the people who came up with and continue to propagate evolution mainly strong believers in Jesus Christ? **No.** Is this theory now taught as fact inspired by men of God, or men of this world? **Men of this world!** The answers to these questions will determine where people place their faith, either with imperfect man, or with God the Creator.

So, does the Bible speak of **creation** or **evolution**? **Clearly creation!** If we choose to say that God is not literal in what He tells us in His Bible and that we, His creation, have discovered the truths about the world, beware. If Christians accept evolution as a fact based on new scientific assumptions and expanding levels of human enlightenment in contradiction to God's stated words, it creates a dilemma. Using this form of reasoning, we cannot accept with certainty the resurrection of Jesus as stated by God. It places all Biblical truths in doubt. The people who say evolution is now a fact provide what they think is full justification for questioning the resurrection. According to this thinking, humans would no longer need full knowledge and faith in God because the resurrection of Jesus is not scientifically plausible. Jesus, under this line of reasoning, has no real value. He was simply a nice man, and no salvation is required. Through this deception, the Deceiver has succeeded in squelching faith leading to salvation for many. **This is his goal.**

Does God have any limits? **No.** Is He limited by time, space, or dimensions? **No.** Is spiritual warfare going on in the world right now? **Yes.** This reality indicates the Deceiver actually does plan to get many things going to discredit God by offering truth as myths and fables, so he can keep as many souls as possible away from God. The idea of evolution demeans God and creates doubt in the minds of some people regarding who God really is, the resurrection of His Son, and His power over creation.

In Genesis, God talks about His six days of creation. I will soon show how He explains to us the actuality of six literal (*24-hour*) days for a "portion of creation." It sounds confusing; I will explain. If these days of creation prove to be factual, could Satan achieve any benefit for himself from this as a reality? No, because a quick partial creation process proves God's supremacy and power. If God were not powerful enough to do His specifically listed works in six literal days, as the Bible tells us in the book of Genesis, and actually needed billions of years for this process, is it possible God might appear weak to those who do not yet believe? **Yes.** Who benefits the most from this perceived weakness? The Deceiver does not want Christians to take literally God's use of the word "**day**" in the Bible. Understanding its high significance will be critical.

Revelation 22:18–19

[18] I testify to everyone who hears the words of the prophecy of this book: if anyone adds to them, God will add to him the plagues which are written in this book; [19] and if anyone takes away from the words of the book of this prophecy, God will take away his part from the tree of life and from the holy city, which are written in this book.

Although this Scripture comes from the book of Revelation, it is also true for the whole Bible. It does tell us the Word of God is precise. We are not to add to it, or subtract from it, or it will result in severe consequences.

When I have verbal disagreements with Christian friends on this evolution issue, something interesting happens. They often tell me I am narrow-minded for sticking up for what is stated, by God Himself, in His Word. Evolutionists must entirely take away God's expressed written words in Genesis for their point of view to gain any consideration. Am I wrong here? **No.** Isn't this exactly what God asks people not to do, per Revelation 22:18–19 above? **Yes.** I desire to make a strong effort to let the Bible speak for itself. What the Bible says counts—not scientists or even me, for that matter. Only what God says and means has lifesaving value.

Colossians 1:16

[16] For by Him all things were <u>created</u>, both in the heavens and on earth, visible and invisible, whether thrones or dominions or rulers or authorities <u>all things have been created</u> through Him and for Him. [17] He is before all things, and in Him all things hold together.

God created all things, with emphasis on *"created"* and *"all"*—not <u>some</u>. He did not **evolve** all things, or He would have said **evolve** using a correct Hebrew or Greek word of the day. But He purposefully did not do this.

Hebrews 1:1-2

¹ God, after He spoke long ago to the fathers in the prophets in many portions and in many ways, ² in these last days has spoken to us in His Son, whom He appointed heir of all things, through whom also He made the world.

Hebrews 11:3

³ By faith we understand that the worlds were prepared by the word of God, <u>so that what is seen was not made out of things which are visible.</u>

"So that what is seen was not made out of things which are visible." **This is an incredible statement!** *"Seeing is believing"* is for agnostics, but *"believing without seeing"* is for Christians.

As for people who still believe evolution might have occurred, versus creation by God in Genesis 1, a fabricated narrative follows that might be a way to replace portions of the basic original Genesis 1 story with basic evolution concepts in mind. How might the Genesis 1 story be rewritten to explain and justify the evolution option had God originally intended such a thing? It was difficult to attempt this, because it goes against my spirit. However, here is a pass at an alternate evolution narrative:

In the beginning, God commenced with the evolution process. After about six billion years of evolving and forming, the earth finally came to its appointed time, to a threshold point that was pleasing to God. Adam had now evolved from a lower primate to the point where man was acceptable to God in His evolutionary cycle. With man at the correct evolutionary stage, God now declared Adam ready to be called the first official man #1 (human) that had evolved to be in God's image, in the line of God's specific species. Adam now, at this correct point in God's perfect evolutionary plan, had sufficiently evolved in full wisdom, intellect, and knowledge, and had already developed the communication skills needed to proceed in

God's creation narrative. All the animals of the world have now, also, at the same exact moment in time, evolved (male and female of all like kinds) to their correct and perfect forms, to be assembled all at one time, for their naming ceremony, to be done by Adam. With Adam and all the animals now in their acceptable stages in God's evolutionary process, God was now comfortable to use one of Adam's ribs to create Eve. This, of course, is symbolic because Eve also came to being through the evolutionary process and also evolved as God had planned. Because Adam did not have a helpmate, was lonely, and did not know she existed, God decided the time had come to no longer hide Eve from him. God introduced Adam to Eve for the first time. Adam joyfully met her.

I accept the literal six-day reconstruction version exactly as God describes in Genesis. I understand what He wanted to originally convey. By reading the fabricated version provided above, assuming a way to explain the theory of evolution, it is unrealistic to assume Adam could have come to his form by any direct creation process. The theory of evolution supposedly proves that man evolved from some series of primal predecessors. So with evolution, any creation event could not be possible if God had really chosen the evolution path. So in essence, it needs to be all creation or all evolution—one or the other, but it cannot be both. Why would God do part evolution and part creation when that would make absolutely no sense at all? He didn't, and it would be improbable. God literally calls it **"*creation*"** and **"*made*"** in Genesis 1. So, is this a lie? No. Remember from Hebrews 6:18, **"*it is impossible for God to lie.*"** God requires us to trust only Him for the answers as He tells us.

When we explore Genesis 1 and look at the genealogies of the people who lived from Adam to Noah, we find the men, at that time, did not have children until they were around 120 years old *(literal years)*. According to the Bible, originally, all of these early men lived about 800 years. But, if at that time man had evolved — and evolution usually means we adapt in a positive direction to our environment and not regressively—why do we not live this long today, or even a great deal longer?

The Bible, in Genesis, indicates that until Adam and Eve sinned there was no death in the world—no physical, bodily death. According to the Bible, God's original desired plan did not include worldly death for all living creatures. This did not come into play until Adam and Eve, enticed by Satan, sinned in the Garden of Eden. They transgressed by eating fruit from the tree of the knowledge of good and evil. According to the Bible, this one action, by Adam and Eve, brought sin and death into the world. This created the entire reason and our need for the Bible. The Bible makes it possible for God to tell and show us that He would send His Son, Jesus, to correct this sin-and-death issue caused by Adam and Eve's error.

Evolution invalidates this account by God regarding death, because it would have necessitated animals and plants to evolve and die for billions of years prior to Adam and Eve's evolutionary point of acceptance. All previous iterations of early man would have died prior to Adam and Eve, as seen in fossil records, supposedly proving the long evolution period. But the very first two sentences in the Bible, in the book of Genesis, tell us the earth was void and formless and covered with water.

Genesis 1:1–2
*1 In the beginning God created the heavens and the earth.
2 The earth was formless and void, and darkness was
over the surface of the deep, and the Spirit of God was
moving over the surface of the waters.*

How could any living things exist in this stated environment? They couldn't. So logically then, using evolution would mean God must have told us about death more like a fable in Genesis 1, and only symbolically because His original plan was not to consider anything prior to Adam and Eve's sin as death. It was only evolution. Death can occur and be considered death only after God accepted Adam and Eve as the first evolutionarily acceptable humans in God's image. Does this all seem realistically logical? **Not even close!**

In the last days, the Deceiver must fully discredit the Bible by making adjustments to the smallest things God talks about in the Scripture. One example: the true understanding of the word "*day*" in Genesis. It seems small, and insignificant, but it is consequential.

What assurances has God given us to verify that He really talks about six literal (*24-hour*) days of creation and reconstruction or restoration in Genesis 1? It is my understanding that the word for "*day*" per God's original Hebrew manuscript, in Genesis, is "**yom**." I know this word "**yom**" has been made controversial, and some say this can be a variety of periods of time. If people study this word in thoughtful detail, they will discover that it has been highly overanalyzed to a point of full confusion. This has been done on purpose to discredit "**yom**" entirely. God actually gave us a variety of simple and clever ways to prove this word is meant to be "**one actual day**" within His Genesis text. God is quite brilliant.

Mankind is not perfect, but God is. So, let me postulate an idea from the Bible that I think God has provided as proof for us. God did not expect the majority of the readers of the Bible, in the last days, to be scholars. He knew the majority of us who would read the Scriptures for our current time would be regular folks. God spoke clearly in a way we could understand, even in His parables. If you have accepted Jesus as your personal Savior and have the Holy Spirit for help, amazingly the Bible and the parables become quite clear. God uses His Hebrew word for **day** "**yom**" in the original text of Genesis more than 350 times—the majority of the time with a literal number attached. Here are a couple of examples: six **days**, or 17 **days**, or one **day**, etc., all in simple, understandable language.

In the account of Noah and the flood in Genesis 7:11, God says that Noah entered the ark when he was *"six hundred years, two months, and seventeen days"* old—quite specific. And the word **days** is used with both months and years. This leaves no room for confusion as to literal days being mentioned. Why didn't God say Noah entered the ark when at an old age? God knew exactly what He was doing. He wanted the word **day** in Genesis to convey an actual calendar day.

These Noah verses and Genesis 1 use the same Hebrew words for **day**. When God used His Hebrew word "**yom**" for Noah in Genesis 7:11, along with the number 17, which represents 17 units of the word "day," could this possibly represent longer periods of time? **No.** Also, why then would the exact same words used for both Noah's age and the creation days mean different segments of time? They wouldn't.

In Genesis 1, the six days of creation and regeneration or realignment also include the attachment of the words *"evening and morning."* Two more Scriptures that reference *"morning and evening"*:

Exodus 16:8
8 Moses said, "This will happen when the Lord gives you meat to eat in the evening, and bread to the full in the morning; for the Lord hears your grumblings which you grumble against Him. And what are we? Your grumblings are not against us but against the Lord."

Exodus 18:13
13 It came about the next day that Moses sat to judge the people, and the people stood about Moses from the morning until the evening.

The clear intention is for these **day timeframes** to be **one literal 24-hour-day period**. God always chooses to be straightforward and direct with us. So my simple conclusion: God wants us to take Him literally.

STUNNED

Mark 10:15
15 Truly I say to you, whoever does not receive the kingdom of God like a child will not enter it at all.

God wants us to accept the Bible at face value, to read it with the simplicity of a child. Mankind must not try to read more into the Bible than what God provided in His text, created perfectly for the common man.

Evolution speculation has resulted in dissension and confusion. The Bible again tells us God *"created"* man and He never intended death for Adam and Eve — or any of us, for that matter. With the nudging of the evil Deceiver, Adam and Eve disobeyed God, which again brought both sin and death into the world. So, God desired to fix this serious situation. When Jesus comes **the second time**, the removal of both sin and death will soon take place. God has almost finished His process. We are the fortunate generation, for we shall see this in our time.

What about ancient fossil records as proof of evolution? This viewpoint depends on whether or not people accept God at His Word. Is the Bible literal or representative? There may be a strong correlation to fossil records and the flood of Noah. Let's explore this flood event:

Genesis 7:4–5
4 ["]For after seven more days, I will send rain on the earth forty days and forty nights; and I will <u>blot out</u> from the face of the land <u>every living thing</u> that I have made." 5 Noah did according to all that the Lord had commanded him.

Genesis 7:10–11
10 It came about after the seven days, that the water of the flood came upon the earth. 11 In the six hundredth year of Noah's life, in the second month, on the <u>seventeenth day</u> of the month, <u>on</u>

the same day all the fountains of the great deep burst open, and the floodgates of the sky were opened.

Genesis 8:3–5
³ and the water receded steadily from the earth, and at the end of one hundred and fifty days the water decreased. ⁴ In the seventh month, on the seventeenth day of the month, the ark rested upon the mountains of Ararat. ⁵ The water decreased steadily until the tenth month; in the tenth month, on the first day of the month, the tops of the mountains became visible.

Genesis 8:13–14
¹³ Now it came about in the six hundred and first year, in the first month, on the first of the month, the water was dried up from the earth. Then Noah removed the covering of the ark, and looked, and behold, the surface of the ground was dried up. ¹⁴ In the second month, on the twenty-seventh day of the month, the earth was dry.

Genesis 7:17–24
¹⁷ Then the flood came upon the earth for forty days, and the water increased and lifted up the ark, so that it rose above the earth. ¹⁸ The water prevailed and increased greatly upon the earth, and the ark floated on the surface of the water. ¹⁹ The water prevailed more and more upon the earth, so that <u>all the high mountains everywhere under the heavens were covered.</u> ²⁰ <u>The water prevailed fifteen cubits higher, and the mountains were covered.</u> ²¹ All flesh that moved on the earth perished, birds and cattle and beasts and every swarming thing that swarms upon the earth, and all mankind; ²² of all that was on the dry land, all in whose nostrils was the breath of the spirit of life, died. ²³ <u>Thus He blotted out every living thing that was upon the face of the land, from man to animals to creeping things and to birds of the sky, and they were blotted out from the earth; and only Noah was left, together with those that were with him in the ark.</u> ²⁴ The water prevailed upon the earth one hundred and fifty days.

This was not a localized flood. **It filled the entire populated world.** The entire populated earth became a giant raging sea for more than a year. Every living thing, other than those on the ark, died. The earth dried up when Noah was **601 years, 2 months, and 27 days** old . . . the second time God details a timeframe using a combination of years, months, and days. There is absolutely no confusion here regarding the word **day** being a literal 24-hour timeframe.

Can we even comprehend how much water came upon the earth from both below and above? God's flood rose higher than all the mountains . . . enough water to cover the entire earth in a mere 40 days. The quantity of water needed would have been unbelievably torrential with velocity greater than the largest known historical tsunamis. Look at the debris and death that occurred from the 30-foot tsunami waves that hit in Asia in 2004. They killed 200,000 people and buried them below a great deal of mud. This flood in Noah's time would have easily buried all destroyed life under a tremendous amount of sludge and sediment — precisely why today, all over the world, archeologists find so many animal bones, close together in groups, buried under the earth's surfaces — and also why they find whale bones in the middle of continents.

Some people still say God's flood was localized and not worldwide. Do the Bible verses we reviewed tell us this? **No.** Why would God have Noah build an ark over many years (*God gave him 120 years' advance warning*) for a small, localized flood? It took Noah a very long time to build the ark. Would this be logical for only a localized flood that would not come for **12 decades**? If localized, God could have simply had Noah migrate to some land outside of the localized flood zone. Noah, his family, and all the animals could have moved somewhere to higher ground for safety with no need for an ark. But, in reality, when the flood waters came, people continued going to higher and higher ground until no higher place existed. Logically, had the flood been localized many would have found this higher dry land. But this did not occur. The worldwide flood "**killed all land dwellers**" on earth per Genesis 7:23.

According to evolutionists, creation must be scientifically logical, or it didn't occur. This thinking does not require faith in a higher power, but rather faith in man's own science. Mankind's scientific analysis says the evolution theory cannot be wrong. The next logical step, in these last days, will entail forcing people to accept this theory as the only truth, through threats, intimidation, and fear, **demanding acquiescence**. Think this cannot happen? Well, it worked for Hitler, and the Antichrist will make Hitler look like a choir boy.

God always gives us His absolute clear intentions, and He does it for a reason. God specifically used His Hebrew word for a **day**, as previously explained in each of the six days in His creation reconstruction narrative. To nail this point home, as mentioned earlier, God also says at the end of each day in His Genesis Scriptures "*and then there was evening and morning one day, then day two . . .*" etc.

Let me try one more verse modification to see how this "*evening and morning one day*" issue might work related to evolution. Let's assume this supposed evolution view of the creation events took six billion years. Using this analogy, if God had chosen evolution, He probably should have told us the following at the end of Genesis 1:5:

<u>*Genesis 1:3–5*</u>
3 Then God said, "Let there be light"; and there was light. 4 God saw that the light was good; and God separated the light from the darkness. 5 God called the light day, and the darkness He called night. And there was evening and there was morning,
<u>one billion years.</u>

Could this one change representing an evolution long day make any sense in God's text? **No.** The problem: God did not say this, or even allude to this type of long day as an expressly desired extended period of time.

The six days of creation, talked about in Genesis 1:3–31, are actually, in reality, six literal days of **reconstruction** and **restoration**. I will address this shortly. As mentioned earlier, God talks about the conditions of the earth before His six days of reconstruction and restoration occurred. No biological life could have existed on a void, dark earth filled by water. Here again, the first two sentences of Genesis address profound issues and answer many questions:

Genesis 1:1–2
*¹ **In the beginning God created the heavens and the earth**. ² **The earth was formless and void, and darkness was over the surface of the deep, and the Spirit of God was moving over the surface of the waters**.*

In Genesis 1:1, God says, "*In the beginning God created the heavens and the earth*." So, what does God say here and why? Does Genesis 1:1 say He "*created the heavens and earth*" in the beginning, then He "*created*" it all over again in the six days explained in Genesis 1:3–31? It makes no logical sense. So, why are these first two sentences even in the Bible if they do not have great significance? They actually have great significance.

The heavens and earth existed from the beginning as God stated in Genesis 1:1. The earth was originally only a place where angels dwelt, as described in portions of the Old Testament (*Ezekiel 28:11–19*). God allowed angelic beings to freely go back and forth between heaven and earth. They had a perfect form of society until Lucifer challenged God's supremacy and brought evil into existence. Due to Satan's arrogance and pride, God needed separation. God threw Lucifer out of heaven "*down to the earth*" and, as a result, severely punished the planet. God was angry.

Isaiah 14:12
12 *"How you have fallen from heaven, O star of the morning, son of the dawn! <u>You have been cut down to the earth</u>[."]*

One-third of all the angels in heaven sided with Lucifer, and God threw them down to the earth also. God's anger, and this action, took away all the earth's original "**mineral**" beauty. In the beginning, the earth did exist as God tells us in Genesis 1:1, made up of only minerals and precious stones, quite magnificent (*Ezekiel 28:13-16*). The eternal kingdom will look similar to this after the completion of the Millennium, as described in Revelation 21:18-21. The early beautiful mineral earth *"had not yet had vegetation"* and biological life per Genesis 2:5-8 and Ezekiel 28:11-19. **This early earth had nothing to do with evolution.**

Because of Satan's arrogance and pride, God placed a full punishment on His beautiful mineral earth when He cast down Satan and the fallen angels from heaven. God made the earth *"formless"* and *"void,"* and *"darkness was over the surface of the deep"* — the consequence of Satan bringing evil and sin into existence. God put Satan and his angels on a punished earth, banished there into darkness. God tells us again the *"heavens and the earth"* existed long ago in 2 Peter 3:3-7:

2 Peter 3:3-7
3 *Know this first of all, that in the last days mockers will come with their mocking, following after their own lusts,* 4 *and saying, "Where is the promise of His coming? Forever since the fathers fell asleep, all continues just as it was from the beginning of creation."* 5 *<u>For when they maintain this, it escapes their notice that by the word of God the heavens existed long ago</u> and the earth was formed out of water and by water,* 6 *through which the world at that time was destroyed, being flooded with water.* 7 *But by His word the present heavens and earth are being reserved for fire, kept for the day of judgment and destruction of ungodly men.*

Earlier in Genesis 1:1–2, God talks about *"the surface of the deep."* What deep? What waters? God makes this absolutely clear at this point in Genesis 1:2. Also note this was not the flood of Noah; that comes later. The Scripture indicates the earth had no dry land, no light, and a full surface of water. It was severely dark, empty, without form, and completely **flooded** — completely uninhabitable, unorganized, and hostile. God then tells us He was personally *"moving over the surface of the waters."* But why? Because He was getting ready to do something wonderful. He would repair the damage He had placed on the earth because of Satan's sinful pride. The coming six days of **reconstruction** and **restoration** were about to take place. Some limited *"creation"* also occurs within this six-day timeframe.

Please note: in Genesis 1:1, God says He *"created"* the heavens and the earth, *"in the beginning."* In Genesis 1:2, the already-**created** earth was now void and formless due to sin, almost like a lump of potter's clay waiting for the artist to make something beautiful. The word *"made"* (**Hebrew, asah**) was used for all the physical attributes of the restoration process of the world itself: the reorganization of elements already created earlier, *"in the beginning."* But in the **six-day process**, the word *"create"* (**Hebrew, bara**) has new significance. During this period, God uses the word *"create"* for all the plants, animals, sea monsters, and man himself, **all new creations** to the existing world. Prior to God's six-day restoration cycle, everything created from the beginning had been seriously dismantled. This is clear from Genesis 1:2. So, even though the earth had existed from the beginning, per Genesis 1:1, mankind — including all the plants, animals, and sea creatures that God *"created"* and placed on the earth — has existed in the world for only about 6,000 years, as explained earlier.

Currently, in Christianity, a group of well-intentioned people strongly believes in a full, literal total creation of everything, including the universe, in six literal days. They believe in the **young-earth** concept, where all the heavens and the earth are only 6,000 years old. The Bible does not tell us this. These people believe that if we do not accept that God did all creation in six days, we have a theological problem, because, if the earth existed from the beginning as God tells us in Genesis 1:1, this **old-earth** thinking opens the door for the credibility of evolution.

Our all-knowing God knew from the beginning that the theory of evolution would come in our day. To dispel this future evolution concept, God boldly cleared up all this for us in the first two sentences in the Bible. I strongly believe God purposely chose these first two sentences in Genesis to clearly show us the myth of evolution. The environment God talks about in Genesis 1:2 leaves out the possibility of any biological life of any kind. God provided no logical way to justify the evolution path.

Another **"major problem"** with the theory of the literal six days for the full creation (*non-restoration view*) of all the heavens and all the earth: Where in these six literal days described in Genesis 1:3–31 are Lucifer, his fall, and his fallen angels addressed? How and when did Satan come into existence within these six days and still have time to battle with God, fall away, and be thrown down to the earth? God shows us this all happened, on earth, **long before man existed**.

Either we can accept that the world was void, formless, and covered with water, as God has specifically told us, or we can believe in evolution. Everyone, individually, must decide for themselves. I choose to take God at His literal word and believe the earth existed from the beginning, as God tells us directly.

The Bible teaches us about Satan's attributes and how the earth existed long ago only for angelic beings:

1. Ezekiel 28:1–10 talks about the arrogant, prideful King of Tyre. Then, in Ezekiel 28:11–19, God compares this King of Tyre's similarities to the characteristics of Lucifer. In verses 1–10, God clearly talks about this human king. Verses 11–19, by comparison, could in no way refer to a human, but rather to the most beautiful

fallen prideful angel: Lucifer (*or Satan the Deceiver*). How can we know this? Three excerpts of the many items talked about in Ezekiel 28:11–19 tell us the entity being referred to is not the literal human King of Tyre. These traits can be attributed only to the angelic being of Lucifer himself.

    a. Verse 12: *"You had the seal of perfection"*

    b. Verse 12: *"Full of wisdom and perfect in beauty."*

    c. Verse 14: *"You were the anointed cherub."*

2. Isaiah 14:12–15 explains about the fall of God's most beautiful angel.

As the cancer of apostasy keeps growing in our world today, many people will try to say Satan, as described in the Bible, does not exist; Satan actually does exist. **Do not be deceived!**

Here are all the verses in Genesis 1:3–31 that refer to the six days of restoration or reconstruction and the use of *"evening and morning"* for each day. God **reorganized** the earth and then added *"***created***"* new things to it in the following verses.

Genesis 1:3–31

³ *Then God said, "Let there be light"; and there was light.* ⁴ *God saw that the light was good; and God <u>separated</u> the light from the darkness.* ⁵ *God called the light day, and the darkness He called night. And there was evening and there was morning, <u>one day</u>.*
⁶ *Then God said, "Let there be an expanse in the midst of the waters, and let it <u>separate</u> the waters from the waters." ⁷ God <u>made</u> the expanse, and <u>separated</u> the waters which were below the expanse from the waters which were above the expanse; and it was so. ⁸ God called the expanse heaven. And there was evening and there was morning, a <u>second day</u>.*
⁹ *Then God said, "Let the waters below the heavens be gathered into one place, and let the dry land appear";*

and it was so. ¹⁰ God called the dry land earth, and the gathering of the waters He called seas; and God saw that it was good. ¹¹ Then God said, "Let the earth sprout vegetation, plants yielding seed, and fruit trees on the earth bearing fruit after their kind with seed in them"; and it was so. ¹² The earth brought forth vegetation, plants yielding seed after their kind, and trees bearing fruit with seed in them, after their kind; and God saw that it was good. ¹³ There was evening and there was morning, a <u>third day</u>.

¹⁴ Then God said, "Let there be lights in the expanse of the heavens to <u>separate</u> the day from the night, and let them be for signs and for seasons and for days and years; ¹⁵ and let them be for lights in the expanse of the heavens to give light on the earth"; and it was so. ¹⁶ God <u>made</u> the two great lights, the greater light to govern the day, and the lesser light to govern the night; He made the stars also. ¹⁷ God placed them in the expanse of the heavens to give light on the earth, ¹⁸ and to govern the day and the night, and to <u>separate</u> the light from the darkness; and God saw that it was good. ¹⁹ There was evening and there was morning, a <u>fourth day</u>.

²⁰ Then God said, "Let the waters teem with swarms of living creatures, and let birds fly above the earth in the open expanse of the heaven." ²¹ God <u>created</u> the great sea monsters and every living creature that moves, with which the waters swarmed after their kind, and every winged bird after its kind; and God saw that it was good. ²² God blessed them, saying, "Be fruitful and multiply, and fill the waters in the seas, and let birds multiply on the earth." ²³ There was evening and there was morning, a <u>fifth day</u>.

²⁴ Then God said, "Let the earth bring forth living creatures after their kind: cattle and creeping things and beasts of the earth after their kind"; and it was so. ²⁵ God made the beasts of the earth after their kind, and the cattle after their kind, and everything that creeps on the ground after its kind; and God saw that it was good. ²⁶ Then God said, "Let

Us make man in Our image, according to Our likeness; and let them rule over the fish of the sea and over the birds of the sky and over the cattle and over all the earth, and over every creeping thing that creeps on the earth." [27] *God* <u>*created*</u> *man in His own image, in the image of God He* <u>*created*</u> *him; male and female He* <u>*created*</u> *them.* [28] *God blessed them; and God said to them, "Be fruitful and multiply, and fill the earth, and subdue it; and rule over the fish of the sea and over the birds of the sky and over every living thing that moves on the earth."* [29] *Then God said, "Behold, I have given you every plant yielding seed that is on the surface of all the earth, and every tree which has fruit yielding seed; it shall be food for you;* [30] *and to every beast of the earth and to every bird of the sky and to everything that moves on the earth which has life, I have given every green plant for food"; and it was so.* [31] *God saw all that He had made, and behold, it was very good. And there was evening and there was morning, the* <u>*sixth day*</u>.

Earlier I mentioned that, prior to the six days of **regeneration**, no biological life existed on the earth. Without biological life, how could evolution be possible? It could not. Plants, animals, and people are all biological, and all animal life would need plants and other animals as food to sustain life within an evolutionary process. So, how can we possibly know that no biological life existed on earth prior to God's explanation about how life came to be in Genesis 1? God tells us directly:

<u>*Genesis 2:5–8*</u>
[5] *Now* <u>*no shrub*</u> *of the field was yet in the earth, and* <u>*no plant*</u> *of the field* <u>*had yet sprouted,*</u> *for the* LORD *God had not sent rain upon the earth, and* <u>*there was no man to cultivate the ground*</u>. [6] *But a mist used to rise from the earth and water the whole surface of the ground.* [7] *Then the Lord God formed man of dust from the ground, and*

breathed into his nostrils the breath of life; and man became a living being. ⁸ The Lord God planted a garden toward the east, in Eden; and there He placed the man whom He had formed.

In Genesis 1:3–31, God explains how He *"created"* animals, and then *"plants,"* and *"man"* on day six of this process. In Genesis 2:7, He tells us again, without any room for doubt, that man was *"created"* and did not evolve. Note, God shares with us that *"no shrub of the field was yet in the earth, and no plant of the field had yet sprouted,"* clear evidence that evolution did not occur. This Scripture points out the reason no plants had yet existed: *"there was no man to cultivate the ground."* Interesting: no man yet? How can this verse be explained away by Christian evolutionists? It can't.

Psalm 33:6–9
⁶ By the word of the Lord the heavens were made, and by the <u>breath of His mouth</u> all their host. ⁷ He gathers the waters of the sea together as a heap; He lays up the deeps in storehouses. ⁸ Let all the earth fear the Lord; let all the inhabitants of the world stand in awe of Him. ⁹ For He spoke, and it was done; He commanded, and it stood fast.

By His word and *"the breath of His mouth,"* the heavens and all in them were made—paraphrased, but it kind of makes my point. The precepts of man must not limit God's teachings. Human beings—part of the creation and not the creator—must not assume we are smarter than what His Word tells us.

Genesis 2:7
⁷ Then the LORD God formed man of dust from the ground, and breathed into his nostrils the breath of life; and man became a living being.

God formed man from the dust of the ground—not some single-cell creatures. He tells it like it is and will not abide with us trying to figure out some mysterious alternate path.

Genesis 2:19–23

19 Out of the ground the LORD God formed every beast of the field and every bird of the sky, and brought them to the man to see what he would call them; and whatever the man called a living creature, that was its name. 20 The man gave names to all the cattle, and to the birds of the sky, and to every beast of the field, 21 So the LORD God caused a deep sleep to fall upon the man, and he slept; then He took one of his ribs and closed up the flesh at that place. 22 The LORD God fashioned into a woman the rib which He had taken from the man, and brought her to the man. 23 The man said, "This is now bone of my bones, and flesh of my flesh; She shall be called Woman, because she was taken out of Man."

God formed all animals out of the ground, also, and had Adam name them. Then He formed Eve from one of Adam's ribs and named her *"Woman, because she was taken out of Man."* Why would God use so many details if this were all not literal? Using evolution as an answer to creation would make this account a lie, which is not possible for God.

Genesis 3:17–19

17 Then to Adam He said, "Because you have listened to the voice of your wife, and have eaten from the tree about which I commanded you, saying, 'You shall not eat from it'; Cursed is the ground because of you; In toil you will eat of it. All the days of your life. 18 Both thorns and thistles it shall grow for you; and you will eat the plants of the field; 19 By the sweat of your face. You will eat bread, Till you return to the ground, Because from it you were taken; For you are dust, and to dust you shall return."

God never intended for man to either labor or die an earthly death. Adam lived in a perfect world until sin entered him. The entire situation and fallen condition we live with now results from Adam and Eve's original sin. The good news: God corrected this through His Son, Jesus.

Exodus 31:15–17
15 ['"]For six days work may be done, but on the seventh day there is a Sabbath of complete rest, holy to the Lord; whoever does any work on the Sabbath day shall surely be put to death. 16 So the sons of Israel shall observe the Sabbath, to celebrate the Sabbath throughout their generations as a perpetual covenant.' 17 It is a sign between Me and the sons of Israel forever; for in six days the Lord made heaven and earth, but on the seventh day He ceased from labor, and was refreshed."

God *"made"* all this in six literal days and rested on the seventh. He intended this also as an example for man to do the same. Work for six days and rest on the seventh. This is also why we have seven-day weeks today. God established seven real and consistent literal 24-hour-day periods. God then enlisted 12-month years. It all goes back to God's example for us. Again, is God capable enough to do His Genesis work in six literal 24-hour days? Yes. God has special numbers that are important to him: three, seven, 12, and 24 are used all throughout the Bible.

John 1:3
3 All things came into being through Him, and apart from Him nothing came into being that has come into being.

STUNNED

Hebrews 11:3
3 By faith we understand that the worlds were prepared by the word of God, so that what is seen was not made out of things which are visible.

Romans 3:4
4 May it never be! Rather, let God be found true, though every man be found a liar.

To reiterate, some people will tell us all logic points to God creating the world through evolution over about six billion years. After all, He is God and He can do anything, right? **Yes,** I agree God can do anything. So, by using the same logic, in the other direction: His power makes it possible to have easily created everything in six-billionths of a second because, yes, He is God and, yes, He can do anything. So, we can all agree that almighty God is **all mighty**. He could have done it very slowly or incredibly fast, because He has no limits. It becomes **more logical** to accept, at face value, God's six (*24-hour*) days of restoration as He described in His own Words, in Genesis, and to accept it literally.

How can we explain the dinosaurs? For nonbelievers and even some Christians alike, when somebody tells them dinosaurs could have existed along with man, the concept is often laughed at and mocked as stupidity. Well, I still stand on my belief in God and the Genesis view of *"all animals"* being *"created"* by Him. This means the dinosaurs also. I can find nothing in God's Word that tells me otherwise. Intellectually, could a God with no limits have created and placed the dinosaurs here with man? **Absolutely He could have.** If you lived in the early days of Adam, you would have lived with what we call today the dinosaurs and would have had no need to explain them to the people of that day. God says Adam controlled *"all animals."* The Bible does not exclude the animals we refer to today as dinosaurs (*term coined by Richard Owen in 1842*). The Bible said "**all animals.**" God referred to what we call dinosaurs today as beasts; He uses the word *"Behemoth"*:

Job 40:15-18
15 *Behold now, <u>Behemoth,</u> which I made as well as you; He eats grass like an ox.* 16 *Behold now, his strength in his loins and his power in the muscles of his belly.* 17 *<u>He bends his tail like a cedar;</u> the sinews of his thighs are knit together.* 18 *His bones are tubes of bronze; His limbs are like bars of iron.*

God describes a *"Behemoth,"* a huge beast—some say a sea monster or whale. But notice something interesting in Job 40:17: *"he bends his tail like a cedar"* . . . one really big animal tail. Controversial? **Yes.** Possible? **Yes.** This illustrates that what we call dinosaurs today actually lived with man. The Bible tells us God gave Adam complete dominion over <u>**all**</u> living things, **not some**. When you get a spare moment, please take a look at Job 41; it describes an interesting creature. Myth?

So, what else does God say about living creatures?

Genesis 1:24-25
24 *Then God said, "Let the earth bring forth living creatures after their kind: cattle and creeping things and <u>beasts of the earth</u> after their kind"; and it was so.* 25 *<u>God made the beasts of the earth</u> after their kind, and the cattle after their kind, and everything that creeps on the ground after its kind; and God saw that it was good.*

Some might say, what about those massive tyrannosaurus rex teeth, and those vicious velociraptors? How could man survive living with such vicious beasts that could eat or kill them through their overpowering strength? Think about this: we still have lions, alligators, tigers, bears, and sharks, living animals right now that could both eat us or kill us for sport, but we all manage to coexist. Mankind is actually a bigger threat to mankind than any of these animals.

Whales are huge: in fact, the blue whale is still the largest animal that ever existed in this world. They are still here, and they have no desire to harm us. In reality, we are more of a potential threat to them. This whole section on the dinosaurs becomes a bit more honest when you think about it in these terms.

In 2012, a scientist, Mark Armitage, from the California State University at Northridge discovered a triceratops horn at the Hell Creek Formation in Montana. Archeologists have found many dinosaur fossils at this location. In his study of this fossil under a high-powered microscope, he found something amazing: soft tissue that had not yet fossilized. This essentially means this fossil could not be more than about 4,000 years old. This goes back to about the time of the great flood of Noah—a major surprise to paleontologists. This discovery had mixed reactions. Mr. Armitage believes in creation and that this discovery actually supported what God has told us all along. The university fired Mr. Armitage for exposing this information, and his findings have seen little light. I understand that other similar discoveries have occurred, but the secular world will not acknowledge them, as they do not fit in within a desired narrative. This reaction should not surprise Christians; rather, we should anticipate it.

The Deceiver's deceptions are rampant in our world and can easily grow within each of us. One must search out God's truth and become aware of His loving direction to avoid deception.

I have used evolution as a main example of how the Deceiver wants to do everything he can to make man speculate and change the subject away from God. Satan also wants to suppress the truth from honoring the Bible as is and to create doubt in both God's Word, as literal truth, and His supreme sovereignty. Paul tells us in Romans about those who suppress His truth:

Romans 1:18–21
18 For the wrath of God is revealed from heaven against all un-Godliness and unrighteousness of men who suppress the truth in unrighteousness, 19 because that which is

known about God is evident within them; for God made it evident to them. 20 For since the creation of the world His invisible attributes, His eternal power and divine nature, have been clearly seen, being understood through what has been made, so that they are without excuse. 21 For even though they knew God, they did not honor Him as God or give thanks, but they became futile in their speculations, and their foolish heart was darkened.

Romans 1:28–32

28 And just as they did not see fit to acknowledge God any longer, God gave them over to a depraved mind, to do those things which are not proper, 29 being filled with all unrighteousness, wickedness, greed, evil; full of envy, murder, strife, deceit, malice; they are gossips, 30 slanderers, haters of God, insolent, arrogant, boastful, inventors of evil, disobedient to parents, 31 without understanding, untrustworthy, unloving, unmerciful; 32 and although they know the ordinance of God, that those who practice such things are worthy of death, they not only do the same, but also give hearty approval to those who practice them.

I have provided the verses above, prepared for us 1,900 years ago by God Himself, so we will all know what to expect for our current time in history. The majority of the secular world considers God's views expressed in Romans 1 to be diatribe. These verses essentially explain exactly what is happening in our world today. God knew what would occur in the last days and how people would respond. God has told us what to expect.

Looking at the news each night, we can see how the world is shaping up. I think we can see from these verses that as we continue into these end times, we have a larger battle coming. Not only will mankind abandon God for full secular thinking in violation of God's Word, but they will do it arrogantly in God's face. So much so that God will not discourage them, but He Himself will give them over to their lusts. This is like God heaping hot coals on them, for their arrogance. Notice how the Apostle Paul addresses this further for us in the following verses:

Romans 2:5–8

5 But because of your stubbornness and unrepentant heart you are storing up wrath for yourself in the day of wrath and revelation of the righteous judgment of God, 6 who will render to each person according to his deeds: 7 to those who by perseverance in doing good seek for glory and honor and immortality, eternal life; 8 but to those who are selfishly ambitious and do not obey the truth, but obey unrighteousness, wrath and indignation.

Ephesians 6:10–13

10 Finally, be strong in the Lord and in the strength of His might. 11 Put on the full armor of God, so that you will be able to stand firm against the schemes of the devil. 12 For our struggle is not against flesh and blood, but against the rulers, against the powers, against the world forces of this darkness, against the spiritual forces of wickedness in the heavenly places. 13 Therefore, take up the full armor of God, so that you will be able to resist in the evil day, and having done everything, to stand firm.

For Christians who have accepted Jesus as their personal Lord and Savior and know they are truly saved, they needn't worry about their salvation, because it is secure. The Deceiver is working hard to prevent our unbelieving and doubting friends and family members from coming to a loving knowledge about Jesus.

Some people have trouble accepting the literal resurrection of Christ, because it does not fit in with the scientific created norms of secular mankind. The supernatural aspects that one must accept regarding the resurrection seem incomprehensible to people who have set, regulated, orderly, dogmatic views of how science and physics work . . . almost like some people are too smart for their own good. This is unfortunate and plays right into the Deceiver's hands.

Ephesians 6:12 explains the struggles all around us with wickedness in heavenly places. This deception causes a quandary in the minds of nonbelievers. In reality, they have only two choices. Will they place their eternal destiny in the loving hands of Jesus, or in the theories and evolving sciences of imperfect mankind? **Both of these options require faith.** It's a question of where someone chooses to place it. I understand it is a complicated choice, but this choice has severe and profound eternal consequences.

Here is a major question to think about. Is Satan truly real? Let's explore what God Himself has to say regarding this:

1 John 5:18–19
¹⁸ We know that no one who is born of God sins; but He who was born of God keeps him, and the evil one does not touch him. ¹⁹ We know that we are of God, and that the whole world lies in the power of the evil one.

Ephesians 6:11–12
¹¹ Put on the full armor of God, so that you will be able to stand firm against the schemes of the devil. ¹² For our struggle is not against flesh and blood, but against the rulers, against the powers, against the world forces of this darkness, against the spiritual forces of wickedness in the heavenly places.

Job 1:6–7
⁶ Now there was a day when the sons of God came to present themselves before the Lord, and Satan also came among them. ⁷ The Lord said to Satan, "From where do you come?" Then Satan answered the Lord and said, "From roaming about on the earth and walking around on it."

STUNNED

Matthew 4:8-11

8 Again, the devil took Him to a very high mountain and showed Him all the kingdoms of the world and their glory; 9 and he said to Him, "All these things I will give You, if You fall down and worship me." 10 Then Jesus said to him, "Go, Satan! For it is written, 'You shall worship the Lord your God and serve Him only.'" 11 Then the devil left Him; and behold, angels came and began to minister to Him.

1 Peter 5:8

8 Be of sober spirit, be on the alert. Your adversary, the devil, prowls around like a roaring lion, seeking someone to devour.

God tells us Satan (*the Deceiver*) is real, so I will let the Bible speak for itself and trust God at His own assessment.

Can you imagine what it would be like if all Bible readers could take the Word of God literally instead of trying to always read between the lines for hidden meanings? I cannot believe our God wanted to hide the truth from us. So many false ideas and theories of faith exist today. Anyone can pick whichever interpretation matches their own personal comfort zone and lifestyle. This unfortunately diminishes the greatness of our God. When the Ezekiel 38 attack happens, I sincerely hope everything will become a bit clearer. God has given us the Bible for our comfort, guidance, and protection.

I love God, and I know He loves me.

For my readers who are parents: Would you purposefully try to make life more difficult for your children, or do you try to give them sound direction and guidance? If you knew difficult times were coming, wouldn't you do your best to warn, protect, and even show them how to escape dangers? If needed, wouldn't you even die for them if the choice were either them or you? The Bible and Jesus have done all of that for us. But some try so hard to read things into the Bible that are not there and dismiss the real story. It saddens me that some Christians diminish God by accepting so many deceptions that contradict the Bible. Sadly, the Deceiver is winning this battle. The Bible tells us the Deceiver will appear to win for a short time, and to not be discouraged. The story has a good ending, and so will we.

As Christians, we need to stand with the Lord and keep our eyes keenly focused on everything that goes on in the world. In the next couple of years, things will get even more challenging for us. It will become much harder for current nonbelievers to know Jesus because their hearts will grow colder. Many will willingly choose to stay solidly with secularism right into **the time of Jacob's distress**.

Please remember, as I have continually said, after the Ezekiel 38 attack happens, and after the shock wears off, the Deceiver will go into full gear. Mankind will quickly start to look as if they are finally getting their world act together. It will begin to look as if all of us will enter into the Age of Aquarius, with harmony and understanding.

This will be the ultimate deception!

Revelation 3:10–11

[10] *Because you have kept the word of My perseverance, I also will keep you from the hour of testing, that hour which is about to come upon the whole world, to test those who dwell on the earth.* [11] *I am coming quickly; hold fast what you have, so that no one will take your crown.*

CHAPTER 6

GOD'S VISUAL CATCHING UP
MANKIND WILL BE STUNNED!

At some time in the near future, the entire world will see Christians leaving earth in what God calls the **catching up**. He shares incredible reasons for taking Christians home with Him to safety in a highly spectacular "**visual**" event.

When I discovered what God appears to tell us about the **visual catching up** of believers in the last days, it gave me a rejuvenated vigor and passion for the Lord. Understanding what must actually happen in the next couple of years has given my life new tranquility, peace, and comfort. I know many commentators have written hundreds of different ideas regarding what will happen in the end times, and most are frightening, which does a great injustice to our Lord. Some people will say the "**catching up**" explained in 1 Thessalonians 4:17 shows old thinking and that only a fool would think it is something real. If you fall into this category, please check out this entire chapter before thinking of me as antiquated. What I have learned through Biblical teaching and research represents a beautiful, spectacular, and awesome view of our magnificent, caring Lord.

The "**catching up**" explained in the Bible, and what we have described so far in this book, is what we refer to today as the **Rapture** of believers in the last days. **For the balance of this book, I will now use the term** *Rapture.*

The actual word **Rapture** does not appear in the Bible. This modern English word depicts a collective description of many scriptural references. In numerous verses, God speaks of *being caught up, taken up, redemption, raised imperishable, gathering together, escape* — all encompassed in the Greek word "*harpazo*" (*har-pad'-zo*), used in His original text, 1 Thessalonians 4:17. The word *Rapture* comes from the Latin verb "*rapiemur*," which has the same meaning as *harpazo.* God describes what we refer to today as the **Rapture** more than 300 times in the New Testament. Obviously, He considers this event to be a wonderful blessing for His family.

There is a ludicrous notion spreading today that what we refer to as the Rapture is some weak form of **wishful thinking** or **escapism.** In Joel 2:28–32 and Luke 21:36, God tells us we "*shall be delivered*" and "*escape.*" God Himself literally says "*escape.*" I personally accept this Word — **verbatim.**

This chapter provides the most beautiful and loving version of end-time prophecy I have ever discovered. Jesus is not a tyrant who wants to punish **His bride** (*Christians*) 2 Corinthians 11:2, Revelation 21:9. The **bride of Christ** is set aside from all potential harm, by her husband Jesus, at the Rapture. Then during the Tribulation, God the Father will bring His bride *(Israel)* back to Him (Jeremiah 31:31-33, Jeremiah 3, Hosea 2). **Two different brides,** one for the Son, one for the Father.

Quickly, after the initial shock of Israel's rescue due to Ezekiel 38 subsides, something far more spectacular is on the near horizon. The **24th prophecy** in God's Road Map brings the literal return of Jesus. We are told He will come in the clouds at first, not to the ground, to take born-again Christians home with Him in what the Bible tells us will be a "**visual Rapture**" of His Church, **not in secret**! God allowing both Christians and the entire world to **witness** all His specific 24 prophecies unfold appears to invalidate the doctrine of **imminence**. Some might say the notion of invalidating imminence is absurd, so let's explore what God may be telling us about His return.

I propose, with Scriptural support, that God has something **incredibly wonderful** in mind for His Rapture event. He intends to use the Rapture to **literally announce the arrival** of His **7-year** period known as **the time of Jacob's distress**, The 70th week of Daniel *(page 357)*. **There is no gap.** This 7-year period, with purposeful intent, starts within mere hours after Christians depart with the Lord in the Rapture. **The time of Jacob's distress** is also known as the **Tribulation. We will now henceforth use this terminology.**

In Luke 4:19, Jesus, during His first teaching assignment as a rabbi in a synagogue, reads from **Isaiah 61:1-2(a)** *(page 30)* and proclaims "*the favorable year of the Lord.*" He then stops, closes the Tanakh, and sits down. In Luke 4:21, Jesus makes an amazing statement: "*Today this Scripture has been fulfilled in your hearing.*" The "*year*" mentioned in this verse is God's designed long period of time from Pentecost to His literal future Rapture event. At the Rapture, Jesus will visually return, in the clouds, to announce *"the day of vengeance of our God,"* the Tribulation. This is the second of the three major time periods prophesied in Isaiah **61:2(b)**. The third, *"to comfort all that mourn,"* is the Millennium **Isaiah 61:2(c)**. This third timeframe will be announced by Jesus after His *"glorious appearing"* back on earth at the end of the Tribulation. **This is very important:** in Isaiah 61:2, God the Father **appoints Jesus** the Son to **announce all three events**! At His first coming, Jesus announced only the first **61:2(a)**, in Luke 4:19–21. He will soon personally return in the clouds announcing the arrival of the second event *(the arrival of the Tribulation)* **61:2(b)** at the Rapture. He will announce the arrival of the third event *(the Millennium)* **61:2(c)** at the end of the Tribulation after He literally comes back on the earth.

Unfortunately, some Christians at this time do not accept the idea of a literal Rapture and 7-year Tribulation. Prophecy #8, along God's Road Map, **apostasy** *(the falling away from Biblical truth)* is secretly taking root within the church today. It is so bad in fact that many churches are starting to openly say someone who believes in some **antiquated concept** that the Rapture and Tribulation are Biblically literal may not be of sound mind. Doubt me on this? Watch diligently as this wicked **sign** of the end-times **apostasy** propagates and becomes mainstream. God even tells us many individuals inside the church will literally fall away from His truth in the last days:

1 John 2:18–19
[18] Children, it is the last hour; and just as you heard that Antichrist is coming, even now many Antichrists have appeared; from this we know that it is the last hour. [19] They went out from us, but they were not really of us; for if they had been of us, they would have remained with us; but they went out, so that it would be shown that they all are not of us.

In 1 Thessalonians 5:1–11, *(page 194)* God clearly tells us the Rapture **is not intended** to come as a *"surprise"* to **informed Christians**. The Rapture **is intended** to be a *"surprise"* to the **unbelieving world**. Jesus offers informed Christians multiple clear directions how to know approximately when the Rapture will occur.

Some might say the Bible mentions in Matthew 24:36 that Jesus does not know the day or the hour of the Rapture. However, two statements in the Scriptures regarding His status as **Deity within the Trinity**, after His ascension, logically explain how Jesus does actually know today when the visual Rapture will take place, Philippians 2:5–9 and John 17:1–5 (*Appendix C*).

Some believers think the Bible tells us the Rapture will happen mysteriously in *"the twinkling of an eye"* or *"like a thief in the night."* If this is a correct interpretation, then why does Jesus tell us, in such great detail, in His Bible, to literally and **diligently watch** for His return? Why give us so many clear, vivid instructions to both **look** and **watch** for Him if we will simply secretly disappear, instantly, without any warning? He instructed us thusly because the Rapture **will not take place in secret**. On the contrary, His words depict a **spectacular monumental visual event**. The process of Jesus taking Christians home at the Rapture may actually be completely different from what many have possibly assumed or blindly accepted.

The **doctrine** called **imminence** (*Appendix C*) implies an instantaneous secret disappearing at the Rapture and has created a theological conundrum within the Christian community. Prior to the 20th century, the church had not actually seen any of God's end-time prophetic **signs** taking place as explained in the Bible. For 1,900 years after Christ's ascension, the idea of our being *"taken up"* or Raptured went beyond explanation because no visual Biblical proof of any end-time **signs** had actually happened. Due to perceived prophetic silence for such a long duration, the church developed the imminence doctrine as a way to cope with impatience and a possible lack of overall Biblical understanding. Incredibly, we are witnessing end-time prophecy **signs** happening today. Did you know the Bible tells us the Rapture does not need to be **imminent** to be a **pre-Tribulation** event? I intend to show you how this is **an accurate statement**!

Has God ever sneaked around about what He does regarding His family? **No.** So then, what do these *"twinkling of an eye"* and *"thief in the night"* ideas really mean?

By using His Biblical instructions in conjunction with both past and current historical world events and by cross-referencing between those multiple sources of knowledge and wisdom, a much brighter and glorious story has come into light, a viewpoint that magnifies God's greatness well beyond the current church's old, tired, and outdated doctrine of imminence. So, will God take us away at the Rapture quietly and with no warning? Or will He actually make this event a huge statement, allowing the entire world to hear both the first and the last trumpets and see us all leave during a **visual Rapture**? What the Bible actually shares with us about this coming event may leave many **STUNNED**. Because God always does things big for His glory alone, which of these two ideas—a secret hidden Rapture or a **miraculous visual one**—gives you goosebumps? Which one of these two options would represent God's magnificent and true nature more majestically?

The Rapture has become a somewhat contentious subject. I've read many different views of end-time eschatology. I have studied in detail a wide variety of pre-, mid-, and post-Tribulation Rapture theories. As stated at the beginning of this book, I firmly believe in a **pre-Tribulation Rapture of God's Church**. Within the majority of these differing concepts, when one examines their entire sequences, their precepts lack reasoned completion, leaving **many holes**. One example of a **hole** is from Luke 17:32, where God tells us to *"Remember Lot's wife."* This correlates to the end times and the Rapture. Almost all current end-time prophecy viewpoints seem to have skipped over this verse as irrelevant. **It holds great pertinence!**

Did you know the Bible tells us how the world will appear **normal** and **at peace** (*a secular and decadent version*) until the very **day** both the visual Rapture occurs and the Tribulation begins?

But how can this be, peaceful and **both** events linked to the same day? **This is a literal Biblical message!** Very likely, this indicates how the world probably will not experience the effects of anything severely **catastrophic** before Christians are visually Raptured. Issues such as EMP attacks (*electromagnetic pulse*) or nuclear wars (*WWIII*) or even full societal or financial collapse must happen **after Christians are removed**.

Taking all these issues into account, there is a strong likelihood of Christians not having to experience much more than the severe emotional and psychological scorn and full marginalization the world will have for any person who has truly accepted Jesus as their personal Savior. Will the world be a safe place? **No.** Crime, hate, hardened hearts, immorality, cheating, lying, deceptions, and all forms of lawlessness will prevail and worsen daily. Over time, Christians will need to be constantly on guard and praying for God's protection, which He will provide.

2 Timothy 3:12–13
[12] Indeed, all who desire to live godly in Christ Jesus will be persecuted. [13] But evil men and impostors will proceed from bad to worse, deceiving and being deceived.

The best example I can think of regarding what Christians will need to do when things get challenging relates to how we react to a coming snowstorm. When we know in advance a harsh storm is coming, and realize we will need to experience it, we put on the appropriate heavy coat, boots, warm scarf, and hat. We do exactly what is needed for the type of approaching storm. We know of the devastation to come but have thoughtfully protected ourselves in advance from the effects of the harsh elements. We cannot fight the storm but can deal with it appropriately. In the last days, we need to spiritually prepare in a similar fashion.

The second coming will take place over 7 years. Two separate Jesus events will **bookend** the Tribulation. The **visual Rapture** will **reveal** the Son of Man per Luke 17:30, but not **physically** to the earth, yet. The actual physical return-to-the-earth portion of the second coming (*the glorious appearing*) happens at the end of the Tribulation and denotes the time when Jesus comes to fix our broken world.

According to Scriptures, during the end times any believing Christian will have the opportunity to be **caught up alive** to be with the Lord in a literal visual Rapture. I have discovered God requires some **specific actions** on our part to fulfill this. Not all living Christians **will go up alive** at the final trumpet. This may sound confusing; however, I am going to elaborate.

Some Bible scholars today tell us they believe the Bible shows us the Rapture and the Tribulation occurred around the time of the second Jewish temple's destruction in the year 70 AD. This is not possible, but how can we know this? John did not write the book that prophesies this as a future event, the book of Revelation, until around 95 AD, **a full 25 years after** the temple had been destroyed.

One of the reasons God instructed John to write the book of Revelation was to help and comfort those who will enter the Tribulation period. I see Revelation as literal because it specifically mentions 1,260 days from the start of the Tribulation to the midpoint, when the Antichrist claims to be God. Then another second set of 1,260 days, until Jesus physically returns . . . the literal second coming. Why would God define specific periods of time in the Tribulation if it will not be a real event?

These future days of the Tribulation will bring horror (*outline provided in Chapter 7*), and God wants the people living during this time to know how long they must wait until the finish line. This will give them hope and strength to make it through this defined set period of time. Using these two 1,260 numbers, we can know, with specificity, when the literal second coming of the Lord to the earth (*to the ground*) will occur. It will not be an unknown event. This dispels the notion by some that the Rapture happens at the middle, or at the end of the Tribulation.

The Bible explains everything, from the time of Jesus' first visit to His second coming. God has told us a long time would pass before Christ's return and uses letters representing examples of the characteristics within seven churches of his day.

They represent snapshots of seven future time periods that explain how we will be able to know Jesus is about to return. All **seven** letters/time periods are described in Revelation 2 and 3. The **first five** took 1,793 years to complete. The **final two** church letters/time periods, Philadelphia and Laodicea (six and seven), have relevancy for our study:

Letter to the Church of Philadelphia (6th Church Time Period)

Revelation 3:7-13
7 "And to the angel of the church in Philadelphia write: He who is holy, who is true, who has the key of David, who opens and no one will shut, and who shuts and no one opens, says this: 8 'I know your deeds. Behold, I have put before you an open door which no one can shut, because you have a little power, and have kept My word, and have not denied My name. 9 Behold, I will cause those of the synagogue of Satan, who say that they are Jews and are not, but lie—I will make them come and bow down at your feet, and make them know that I have loved you. 10 Because you have kept the word of My perseverance, I also will keep you from the hour of testing, that hour which is about to come upon the whole world, to test those who dwell on the earth. 11 I am coming quickly; hold fast what you have, so that no one will take your crown. 12 He who overcomes, I will make him a pillar in the temple of My God, and he will not go out from it anymore; and I will write on him the name of My God, and the name of the city of My God, the new Jerusalem, which comes down out of heaven from My God, and My new name. 13 He who has an ear, let him hear what the Spirit says to the churches.'["]

Letter to the Church of Laodicea (7th Church Time Period)

Revelation 3:14–22

[14] "To the angel of the church in Laodicea write: The Amen, the faithful and true Witness, the Beginning of the creation of God, says this: [15] 'I know your deeds, that you are neither cold nor hot; I wish that you were cold or hot. [16] So because <u>you are lukewarm</u>, and <u>neither hot nor cold</u>, <u>I will spit you out of My mouth.</u> [17] Because you say, I am rich, and have become wealthy, and have need of nothing, and you do not know that you are wretched and miserable and poor and blind and naked, [18] I advise you to buy from Me gold refined by fire so that you may become rich, and white garments so that you may clothe yourself, and that the shame of your nakedness will not be revealed; and eye salve to anoint your eyes so that you may see. [19] Those whom I love, I reprove and discipline; therefore be zealous and repent. [20] Behold, I stand at the door and knock; if anyone hears My voice and opens the door, I will come in to him and will dine with him, and he with Me. [21] He who overcomes, I will grant to him to sit down with Me on My throne, as I also overcame and sat down with My Father on His throne. [22] He who has an ear, let him hear what the Spirit says to the churches.'"

The sixth letter to the church of Philadelphia (*Revelation 3:7–13*) represents the church/time period that started in 1793. This is when William Carey sailed to India and became the first foreign missionary. **This sixth church**, in eschatology, is referred to as **"the loving church"** because it represents the group that has a heart for the Lord and shares the truth about Jesus with others. In Revelation 3:9, God says He loves the Church of Philadelphia because it *"keeps His word."* He even says those who remain faithful will have *"the name of God written on them"* by Jesus (*sealed*). Faithful Christian believers today comprise this group.

The sixth Church of Philadelphia's time period will end at the visual Rapture.

Additional evidence in the Scriptures also indicates that believing Christians fall within the sixth church period of Philadelphia. Revelation 3:10 states that Jesus will keep this group *"from the hour of testing"* (*the Tribulation*). Also, Christ does not want anyone to take away our *"crown,"* Revelation 3:11, the *"crown of righteousness,"* 2 Timothy 4:8. We can lose this one particular **crown** if we do not remain strong and fall short in our faith during the **apostasy** we experience today. We also cannot attain this *"crown"* if we do not follow some specific instructions the Lord has for us prior to the visual Rapture. God offers **five crown** rewards for superior obedience. I will share more about **all five crowns** at the end of this chapter.

The seventh letter to the Church of Laodicea (*Revelation 3:14–22*) represents the time period that came into being in the mid- to late 1800s and **purposefully overlaps with Philadelphia**. This is the *"lukewarm"* church as God calls it in Revelation 3:16. It is neither *"hot nor cold"* and drifts away from accepting both Jesus and His Bible as the only truth. This group compromises and accepts **manmade doctrines** and morality in direct contradiction to the Bible. They do not agree to absolutes required by God; if they've decided something is right for them, it is right. They condone this as enlightenment, regardless of what God thinks. Because the *"lukewarm"* church does not believe in the Tribulation as a future reality, they will not, for the most part, recognize God's warning signs (*His prophecies*) and will dismiss them. For this reason, the final seventh church will go into the Tribulation. They will wander off God's true path, accepting concepts and doctrines that believe having faith in Jesus alone has no real specific, major defining significance.

The Antichrist will eventually take over and control the seventh church period, Laodicea. Unfortunately, again, the Deceiver will use the church of this period to steal as many people away from God as possible, before the beginning and into the Tribulation. We can see this all happening today. The Deceiver will achieve this through secular deceptions, as explained earlier in Chapter 5. In Revelation 3:17, God tells us *"the rich will say they have need for nothing,"* including God, because they are self-sufficient. What folly, dismissing God as irrelevant . . . just another example of arrogance engrained in the members of the seventh church/time period. God, due to this arrogance, will *"spit them out of His mouth"* per Revelation 3:16. This wayward seventh church group will spearhead the formation of the One World Church, led by the False Prophet, prior to the start of the Tribulation.

Within minutes after the **visual Rapture**, many people who remain will instantly know they made a serious mistake by listening to the king of all lies, the Deceiver. In Revelation 3:14–22, notice the absence of talk about the seventh church time period, Laodicea, *"being kept"* from the hour of testing. The reason: because the people who did not accept Jesus wholeheartedly before the visual Rapture, or pretended God had no absolutes, or marginalized Him, will enter the Tribulation for God's period of testing. Hope prevails, however; Jesus, though rejected before the visual Rapture, still wants all people to be with Him, per Revelation 3:20. During the Tribulation, the Lord will stand at the door knocking, hoping people will open their hearts and let Him in.

Many Christians today do not accept this time period's viewpoint of the seven churches in Revelation 2 and 3. They think of these seven churches as literally real congregations in existence, when God inspired John to write the book of Revelation. **Well, they're absolutely correct.** But yet God, in His all-knowing wisdom, knew that an enormous amount of time would pass before Jesus' second return. Many more than seven types or forms of churches existed at the time John wrote Revelation 2 and 3 by God's inspiration. But God selected only these particular seven literal churches as specific examples of the seven forms of time periods coming in the future before Jesus' second coming. God uses these time period examples as an additional clear prophetic guide for us to see and know about how history would progress leading right up to the last days.

Can we logically assume these specific, seven existing churches in John's day would have seen the second coming of Jesus? Can we logically assume the Tribulation would occur in their lifetimes? The answer to both of these questions is **NO**. So, what must we think? The answers again rest within the letter to the church of Philadelphia, Revelation 3:10–11:

Revelation 3:10–11
[10] Because you have kept the word of My perseverance, I also will keep you from the hour of testing, that hour which is about to come upon the whole world, to test those who dwell on the earth. [11] I am coming quickly; hold fast what you have, so that no one will take your crown.

If God intended the letters to the churches of Philadelphia and Laodicea for the actual literal congregations of John's day (*Revelation 1:4–3:22*), we have a dilemma. Why would God choose to keep only the people living and attending the actual real Church of Philadelphia from the *"hour of testing,"* the Tribulation? Why not also save the other five earlier mentioned churches as well? Then what about all the other churches of that day He chose not to use as examples in the Bible? **Makes no sense.**

It appears clear to me that God did indeed use the existing seven church models as examples of future time periods to come in sequence and to explain what future ages will look like. All the actual seven church periods in history have historical precedence and line up with God's church/time period models. What God has shared allows us to see, through Scriptures, how the sixth and seventh church time periods match up perfectly with the two church models in our present day: the **loving church** that trusts solely in Jesus, and the **lukewarm church**, the final church that will soon come together into the false One World Religion.

This final church/time period today, the one that accepts issues in conflict with God's laws and does not repent, will be the church that enters the Tribulation. These parallels are quite compelling and another validation of **God's Road Map** for us to see and know His season and to confirm, without doubt, that we currently live in the last days.

2 Thessalonians 2:3–7

³ Let no one in any way deceive you, for it will not come unless the apostasy comes first, and the <u>man of lawlessness is revealed</u>, the son of destruction, ⁴ who opposes and exalts himself above every so-called god or object of worship, so that <u>he takes his seat in the temple of God, displaying himself as being God.</u> ⁵ Do you not remember that while I was still with you, I was telling you these things? ⁶ And <u>you know what restrains him now</u>, so that <u>in his time he will be revealed.</u> ⁷ For the mystery of lawlessness is already at work; <u>only he who now restrains</u> will do so until he <u>is taken out of the way.</u>

2 Thessalonians 2:3–7 talks about removing the restrainer. The restrainer is not the Holy Spirit, because God will do all He can through His coming 144,000 evangelists to save as many people as possible during the entire 7-year Tribulation. But how can we know the Holy Spirit won't leave the world at the visual Rapture? The book of Mark answers this question. In the following verses, Mark 13:11 talks about the persecution of believers inside the Tribulation. God says the Spirit is still here inside the Tribulation in Mark 13:11:

Mark 13:9–11

⁹ "But be on your guard; for they will deliver you to the courts, and you will be flogged in the synagogues, and you will stand before governors and kings for My sake, as a *testimony to them. [10] The gospel must first be preached to all the nations. [11] When they arrest you and hand you over, do not worry beforehand about what you are to say, but say whatever is given you in that hour; for it is not you who speak, <u>but it is the Holy Spirit</u>.["]*

Let's refer back to the 2 Thessalonians 2:3–7 verses. Note something significant in these verses. People will not know the Antichrist is Satan (*revealed*) until he takes his seat in the temple **at the midpoint of the Tribulation**. He is restrained for the entire first half of the Tribulation. So then, who is the restrainer? Clearly, the Holy Spirit works inside the Tribulation, so it cannot be Him. Remember in the last days, 10 world divisions (*with 10 kings*) will exist at the beginning and into the first half of the Tribulation. Three of the 10 kings dislike what the Antichrist tries to do. They "**restrain**" him for a "**specific**" time from the full evil he has planned but ultimately fail and suffer defeat **at the midpoint of the Tribulation**. After this defeat, the three kings will no longer "**restrain**" the Antichrist. He then has full Satanic authority, and away he goes on his final 3½ years of sheer terror. The restrainer is also **not the church**; we left 3½ years earlier. **The restrainer** is actually the **three kings** of the defeated divisions.

As I mentioned earlier, God requires us to love Israel and do our best to help our Jewish brothers and sisters understand who Jesus is. Do you realize that, while we are still here, we have an opportunity and the great blessing to provide our Jewish family with tools they will need to discover Jesus hopefully now but definitely after the visual Rapture? Christians today might, in the end, be the catalyst for assisting the 144,000 Jewish leaders to become believers in the Messiah, Jesus, during the Tribulation. These 144,000 are the people who will ultimately help save billions of souls during the Tribulation. We are directed by God to share with our Jewish family about our Jewish Messiah Jesus. In reality, I am now, as a believer in Christ (*a Christian*), an adopted Jew. My Lord was a Jew, is a Jew, and always will be a Jew. I look forward to spending eternity with my Jewish Messiah and savior Jesus Christ as a Jew. This is what I plan to share with all my Jewish friends *(for the Messiah, see Appendix D)*.

DELIVER US FROM EVIL
Another verse similar to Revelation 3:10–11 says God does not want us to fall from grace due to current evil in the world.

Matthew 6:13
13 'And do not lead us into temptation, but deliver us from evil. For Yours is the kingdom and the power and the glory forever. Amen.'

Our God will not allow us—His current faithful church—to go into the Tribulation. Those of us who have accepted Him before the shout at the visual Rapture event get special protection from our Father through Jesus the Son.

WONDERS, DISMAY, SHOUTS, TRUMPETS: PRIOR TO THE VISUAL RAPTURE

Joel 2:30–32
30 I will display wonders in the sky and on the earth, Blood, fire and columns of smoke. 31 The sun will be turned into darkness and the moon into blood <u>before the great and awesome day of the Lord</u> comes. 32 And it will come about that whoever calls on the name of the Lord will be delivered; for on Mount Zion and in Jerusalem there will be those who escape, as the Lord has said, even among the survivors whom the Lord calls.

Luke 21:25–28
25 There will be signs in sun and moon and stars, and on the earth dismay among nations, in perplexity at the roaring of the sea and the waves, 26 men fainting from fear and the expectation of the things which are

coming upon the world; for the powers of the heavens will be shaken. ²⁷ <u>Then they will see</u> *the Son of Man coming in the cloud with power and great glory.* ²⁸ *But when these things begin to take place,* <u>straighten up and lift up your heads</u>, *because your redemption is drawing near.*

<u>1 Thessalonians 4:13–18</u>
¹³ *But we do not want you to be uninformed, brethren, about those who are asleep, so that you will not grieve as do the rest who have no hope.* ¹⁴ *For if we believe that Jesus died and rose again, even so God will bring with Him those who have fallen asleep in Jesus.* ¹⁵ *For this we say to you by the word of the Lord, that* <u>we who are alive and remain until the coming of the Lord, will not precede those who have fallen asleep</u>. ¹⁶ *For the Lord Himself will descend from heaven* <u>with a shout</u>, *with the voice of the archangel and with the trumpet of God, and* <u>the dead in Christ will rise first</u>. ¹⁷ <u>Then we who are alive and remain will be caught up together with them in the clouds to meet the Lord in the air</u>, *and so we shall always be with the Lord.* ¹⁸ <u>Therefore comfort one another with these words.</u>

<u>1 Corinthians 15:51–52</u>
⁵¹ *Behold, I tell you a mystery; we will not all sleep, but* <u>we will all be changed</u>, ⁵² <u>in a moment, in the twinkling of an eye, at the last trumpet</u>; *for the trumpet will sound, and the dead will be raised imperishable, and we will be changed.*

Now, if God had designed the entire Rapture event to happen unexpectedly, without any warning or fanfare, why would He give us so many additional explicit instructions in all these verses? God also tells us in Luke 21:25–26 how the early signs indicating the arrival of the **visual Rapture** may actually also be the beginning stages of the Tribulation. The Tribulation will start in full force the same day the Lord takes us home in the visual Rapture. Luke 21:27 tells us *"they"* (*everyone*) will *"see"* the Son of Man coming in the cloud with great power and great glory. The troubling signs God will use to show us the visual Rapture is about to begin will then continue and escalate into the Tribulation.

Many Christians claim the first Biblical reference to the Rapture occurs in 1 Corinthians 15:51–52. They say this because of the use of the word *"mystery,"* as if this is sharing something that was never revealed to us. The problem with this is that this supposed *"mystery"* is explained in 1 Thessalonians 4:13–18, which **was written at least 5 years earlier**. Also, within this chapter I share many other Old and New Testament verses that talk about what we call the Rapture. The Bible is thorough. Remember again, there are no mysteries in the Bible that are not completely and accurately answered within its full existing text.

Now, some might say that Luke 17:20 tells us **"no signs"** will precede the Rapture, and this is **partially** true:

Luke 17:20-21
[20] *Now having been questioned by the <u>Pharisees</u> as to when the kingdom of God was coming, He answered them and said, "<u>The kingdom of God is not coming with signs to be observed</u>;* [21] *nor will they say, 'Look, here it is!' or, 'There it is!' For behold, the kingdom of God is in your midst."*

In context, whom is Jesus talking too? The **Pharisees**! These were the smart **bad guys** in His time. The **"signs"** of the Lord's return are for **believers, not unbelievers**. Dozens of other verses in the Bible attest to this reality.

This is what God tells us as Christians regarding being **in the light** and **not in the darkness**. The unbelieving world has **no**

desire to look for signs, so none will be provided. The Rapture will catch them totally off guard.

The following verses provide some partial answers to our actually hearing these trumpets in the visual Rapture sequence.

Numbers 10:9

⁹ *When you go to war in your land against the adversary who attacks you, then you shall sound an alarm with the trumpets, that you may be remembered before the LORD your God, and be saved from your enemies.*

Numbers 10:3–6

³ *When both are blown, all the congregation shall gather themselves to you at the doorway of the tent of meeting.* ⁴ *Yet if only one is blown, then the leaders, the heads of the divisions of Israel, shall assemble before you.* ⁵ *But when you blow an alarm, the camps that are pitched on the east side shall set out.* ⁶ *When you blow an alarm the second time, the camps that are pitched on the south side shall set out; an alarm is to be blown for them to set out.*

God uses trumpets in the Old Testament to announce battles, wars, remembrance, and deliverance to safety. The verses above show us a precedent of how God uses trumpets as loud and **audible** announcements, in a variety of ways. At the Rapture, the whole world will hear God's trumpets. This may also serve as a loud formal announcement, by the Lord, verifying the beginning of His Tribulation is about to arrive.

The visual Rapture will likely take several minutes to complete. God seems to do almost everything in a big way, He designed **the visual Rapture** to make a grand, viewable, worldwide announcement to all of mankind. Can you imagine the statement God will make when all of mankind views the Rapture, actually seeing us all leaving up into the sky when Jesus takes us to safety, to join Him in heaven? A spectacular sight, for sure.

Earlier, I mentioned how God in His Word shares stories about specific events that also explain about His overall character and thought process. They describe the nature of Jesus. Please, keep this overall concept in mind as we proceed.

Numbers 10:9, although written for a specific event, states that at the sound of a trumpet His people are *"remembered before the Lord your God, and saved from your enemies."* At the visual Rapture, the trumpet will warn Christians and save us from our enemy, the Deceiver. Our incredible God provides us with direction. Many people remaining after the visual Rapture will realize, without a doubt, they made a grave error in judgment. By sharing with everyone we know the events explained in this book, those who scoff at all this now may come to realize, as we depart, this information was accurate, and, hopefully, many will then accept the Lord.

WE CAN KNOW THE RAPTURE TIMING BY GOD'S ADVANCE WARNING

The following verses make it clear that God does not leave His beloved people wondering about His plans. He tells us, His children, everything in advance as any loving parent does. These next verses show how He does things:

Amos 3:7
7 Surely the Lord God does nothing unless He reveals His secret counsel to His servants the prophets.

Mark 13:23
23 But take heed; behold, I have told you everything in advance.

Luke 8:16–17
16 Now no one after lighting a lamp covers it over with a container, or puts it under a bed; but he puts it on a lampstand, so that those who come in may see the light.

17 For nothing is hidden that will not become evident, nor anything secret that will not be known and come to light.

Luke 12:35–37
35 Be dressed in readiness, and keep your lamps lit. 36 Be like men who are waiting for their master when he returns from the wedding feast, so that they may immediately <u>open the door to him</u> when he comes and knocks. 37 Blessed are those slaves whom the master will find on the <u>alert</u> when he comes[.]

John 14:29:
29 Now I have told you before it happens, so that when it happens, you may believe.

God wants us to keep our lamps on and to know what the Bible tells us about the visual Rapture event, so we can stay alert in readiness to open the door for Him, so to speak, upon His return. But how can we know the process necessary to stay *"alert"* and ready to *"open the door to him"*? If God meant to hide the Rapture from us or for us not to anticipate its arrival, He wouldn't have told us to prepare. Why would He have us stay alert, if the Rapture is to be a hidden surprise event? Putting our lamps on the lampstands means God is asking us to share this light with others. This includes telling our Christian friends how to understand what will soon come upon the world.

Luke 21:34–36
34 <u>Be on guard</u>, so that your hearts will not be weighted down with dissipation and drunkenness and the <u>worries of life</u>, and that day will not come on you suddenly like a trap; 35 <u>for it will come upon all</u> those who dwell on the face of <u>all the earth</u>. 36 But keep on the alert at all times, <u>praying that you may have strength to escape all these things that are about to take place</u>, and to stand before the Son of Man.

"Be on guard." Do not let our earthly problems take our eyes off the ball. Stay alert and stand strong, because God has given us all the information "signs" we need, **to know exactly when He will return**. The Bible lights our way. God also wants us to pray for the *"strength to escape"* the horrors of the scourge and the Tribulation.

1 Thessalonians 5:1–11

¹ Now as to the times and the epochs, brethren, you have no need of anything to be written to you. ² For you yourselves know full well that the day of the Lord will come just like a thief in the night. ³ While they are saying, "Peace and safety!" Then destruction will come upon them suddenly like labor pains upon a woman with child, and they will not escape. ⁴ But you, brethren, are not in darkness, that the day would overtake you like a thief; ⁵ for you are all sons of light and sons of day. We are not of night nor of darkness; ⁶ so then let us not sleep as others do, but let us be alert and sober. ⁷ For those who sleep do their sleeping at night, and those who get drunk get drunk at night. ⁸ But since we are of the day, let us be sober, having put on the breastplate of faith and love, and as a helmet, the hope of salvation. ⁹ For God has not destined us for wrath, but for obtaining salvation through our Lord Jesus Christ, ¹⁰ who died for us, so that whether we are awake or asleep, we will live together with Him. ¹¹ Therefore encourage one another and build up one another, just as you also are doing.

The *"thief in the night"* does not refer to God taking Christians in the Rapture, but rather, specifically, to the start of the Tribulation. The visual Rapture will be part of the announcement to the world that the Tribulation has arrived. These verses tell us that, as believers, we should know, full well, the day of the Lord (*the Tribulation*) will come *"like a thief"* in the night, but only to the **unbelieving world**. 1 Thessalonians 5:3 tells us clearly while *"they"* are saying . . . well, who are these *"they"*? These *"they"* are all the **unbelievers** who will have **unexpected judgments** coming upon them. God says Christians are not of the darkness, *"but of the light."* God has given us all the **signs** we need to know as believers to understand this assessment is correct. We are not destined for wrath. God even tells us to *"encourage and build up one another"* with this information.

God specifically asks all living believers *"not to sleep,"* which means staying aware, per 1 Thessalonians 5:7–8. This word *"sleeping"* in those verses will have some major significance soon in this story.

After we see God's prophetic signs, we need to comprehend what God wants us to do and know. The visual Rapture contains **SEVEN** distinct explicit events on a grand scale:

FIRST, per Luke 21:25–26, signs and a visible display of wonders in the sky and on the earth will appear, and the unbelieving people of the world, including **uninformed Christians**, will tremble with fear. About this time, Christians who understand end-time prophecy will get a clear *"***gift***,"* a warning from God in their hearts, the *"day star,"* per 2 Peter 1:19, sharing with us, in advance, that the Rapture is about to begin.

2 Peter 1:19
19 So we have the prophetic word made more sure, to which you do well to pay attention as to a lamp shining in a dark place, until the day dawns and the ***day star* arises in your hearts.***

*The term "day star" comes from the King James Version (KJV).

Per Luke 21:27–28, when these signs *"begin,"* at this point we need to *"**look up**"* as *"our redemption is drawing near."* This is not symbolic but literal. The visual Rapture is about to begin.

Luke 21:27–28
²⁷ *Then <u>they will see</u> the Son of Man coming in the cloud with power and great glory.* ²⁸ *But when these things begin to take place, <u>straighten up and lift up your heads</u>, because <u>your redemption is drawing near</u>.*

In the **SECOND** event, the Lord descends from heaven in the clouds with a shout, announcing *"the day of vengeance of our God."* The Tribulation is about to begin. This is the second of three events Jesus is assigned to announce in **Isaiah 61:2(b).**

In the **THIRD** event, we will hear the sound of the first trumpet.

In the **FOURTH** event, the dead in Christ rise first — the reuniting of the **souls** of **those who died** between Christ's ascension and the visual Rapture. Those souls currently in heaven with the Lord will now reunite with their earthly bodies. Graves will open and empty. The sea will give up its dead. Ashes will be transformed into their original form. Additionally, certain uninformed living Christians who do not know to *"look up"* may be raptured with this group, by an **alternate path** through death. I will explain this Biblical concept shortly. At this point, all souls and their bodies have rejoined. They are still imperfect, reconstructed human bodies and are not in heavenly form **yet.**

In the **FIFTH** event, living Christians who did *"look up"* upon seeing God's warning signs (*first event*) and received the *"<u>day star</u>"* warning in their hearts, still alive, will rise into the sky *"alive"* to join those who started rising at the beginning of the <u>fourth event</u>. We will do this in our current earthly bodies also, until the <u>seventh event</u> occurs.

In the **SIXTH** event, we will hear the final trumpet, which causes the seventh event to occur.

And, in the **SEVENTH** event of the visual Rapture, at the final trumpet, we will *"all be changed, in a moment, in the twinkling of an eye"* into our new heavenly bodies (1 Corinthians

15:51b–52). **This seventh event is the only part of the Rapture that happens instantaneously.**

SIGNS JUST BEFORE THE VISUAL RAPTURE AND THE COMMAND TO LITERALLY "LOOK UP"

Earlier in this chapter, I addressed Luke 21:25–28 and Joel 2:30–31 regarding wonders and dismay. For this section, I want to review these once again, as there is additional information of great importance covered in these verses:

Luke 21:25–28
25 There will be signs in sun and moon and stars, and on the earth dismay among nations, in perplexity at the roaring of the sea and the waves, 26 men fainting from fear and the expectation of the things which are coming upon the world; for the powers of the heavens will be shaken. 27 Then <u>they will see</u> the Son of Man coming in the cloud with power and great glory. 28 But when these things begin to take place, <u>straighten up and lift up your heads</u>, because your redemption is drawing near.

Joel 2:30–31 The Day of the Lord
30 I will display wonders in the sky and on the earth, Blood, fire and columns of smoke. 31 The sun will be turned into darkness and the moon into blood before the great and awesome day of the Lord comes.

We are directed in Luke 21:25–26 to look for **actual physical signs** prior to the visual Rapture. At the time of Christ's crucifixion, the world turned dark, stormy, gloomy, and horrifying, because God showed His anger related to His Son's death on the cross. At the time of Christ's death, loud thunder roared, an earthquake came, and the world turned dark and terrifying. The people of that day realized the true Son of God had just died.

The Bible tells us a **similar situation** will occur just prior to the Tribulation because God, again, reacts in anger. When these

signs begin to happen, everyone on earth will feel terrified by what they see and sense. As informed Christians, we needn't fear, because we can know from the Bible what God is really doing.

Prior to the visual Rapture, we will *"see"* signs in the sun, moon (*not the blood moons from Chapter 4*), and stars. Those who **do not know** what is happening will feel perplexity at the roaring of the sea and the waves and men fainting with fear. In addition, we may witness the ghastly **overwhelming scourge** the Anti-christ sets loose on the world (*Joel 2:1–10*). For Christians, it's **mandatory** to understand the scourge so that when we see it, we won't feel afraid.

Luke 17:31
31 On <u>that day</u>, the one who is on the housetop and whose goods are in the house must not go down to take them out[.]

This scourge, another sign of our impending departure, will cause fearful people to attempt to leave their housetops to get their goods, and possibly save their lives due to sheer terror.

The next verses define the scourge in brilliant detail. When we, as believers in Jesus, see this scourge, our deliverance is guaranteed and nothing will harm us. The scourge:

Joel 2:1–10
1 Blow a trumpet in Zion, and sound an alarm on My holy mountain! Let all the inhabitants of the land tremble, <u>For the day of the Lord is coming; Surely it is near,</u> 2 <u>A day of darkness and gloom, a day of clouds and thick darkness. As the dawn is spread</u> over the mountains, so there is a great and mighty people; there has never been anything like it, nor will there be again after it to the years of many genera-tions. 3 A fire consumes before them and behind them a flame burns. The land is like the garden of Eden before them but a desolate wilderness behind them, And nothing at all escapes them. 4 Their appearance is like the appearance of horses; And like war horses, so they run. 5 With a noise as of

chariots they leap on the tops of the mountains, like the crackling of a flame of fire consuming the stubble, like a mighty people arranged for battle. ⁶ Before them the people are in anguish; all faces turn pale. ⁷ They run like mighty men, they climb the wall like soldiers; and they each march in line, nor do they deviate from their paths. ⁸ They do not crowd each other, they march everyone in his path; When they burst through the defenses, they do not break ranks. ⁹ They rush on the city, they run on the wall; they climb into the houses, they enter through the windows like a thief. ¹⁰ Before them the earth quakes, the heavens tremble, the sun and the moon grow dark and the stars lose their brightness.

The Antichrist places the **overwhelming scourge** on the world just prior to the start of the Tribulation. In Joel 2:1, *"for the day of the Lord is coming; surely it is near."* So, the day of the Lord, the Tribulation, has not yet started. I think the signs mentioned in Luke 21:25–26 — in the stars, the sun, the moon, and the oceans — will occur soon after the scourge arrives. The scourge will be a pivotal event prior to **the visual Rapture**.

In **Road Map** prophecies #17 and #22, I speculate that after the Ezekiel 38 attack the physical land mass of Israel will actually become much larger than its current geographic footprint. After the Ezekiel 38 battle, Israel's land mass will become its intended size, the full land area God had originally provided for Jacob's 12 sons per Genesis 13:14–15 and Genesis 15:18.

The Antichrist uses the scourge as a power of persuasion. In Joel 2:3, we can see, as the scourge marches, it destroys everything in its path and nothing behind them escapes. The whole world will hear about this happening, and the news will terrify the masses. Most of the world will not understand what is happening. Also, again, notice in Joel 2:1–2 the mention of the following:

STUNNED

Joel 2:1–2
¹ For the day of the Lord is coming; Surely it is near, ² A day of darkness and gloom, a day of clouds and thick darkness. As the dawn is spreading . . .

Please make note of the reference to *"dawn,"* as it may have an interesting correlation to the sequence of events as we proceed.

Israel will quickly surmise this scourge comes for them, with no way to stop it. Then this new charismatic leader, who recently came on the scene (*the Antichrist*), tells Israel he has a way to protect them from the impending terrors and effects of this scourge. Israel knows they cannot stop it, and they believe this new leader can. Reluctantly, Israel signs a **covenant** with the Antichrist to allow this scourge to pass over them . . . actually, a deception.

Isaiah 28:14–15
¹⁴ Therefore, hear the word of the Lord, O scoffers, who rule this people who are in Jerusalem, ¹⁵ Because you have said, "We have made a <u>covenant</u> with death, and with Sheol we have made a pact. The overwhelming scourge will not reach us when it passes by, For we have made falsehood our refuge and we have concealed ourselves with deception."

Isaiah 28:18–19
¹⁸ Your <u>covenant</u> with death <u>will be canceled</u>, and your pact with Sheol will not stand; When the overwhelming scourge passes through, Then you become its trampling place. ¹⁹ As often as it passes through, it will seize you; For morning after morning it will pass through, any time during the day or night, and it will be sheer terror to understand what it means.

The covenant signed by Israel with the Antichrist will prove to be false, and this *"covenant"* agreement *"will be canceled"* at the middle of the Tribulation. Israel will then have the scourge come upon them over and over again, causing incredible horror.

When we see the imposing signs, mentioned in Luke 21:25–26, along with the events in Joel 2:1–10, we can anticipate with certainty we will soon hear the shout from the Lord, the first trumpet, and the **visual Rapture begins**.

Many Bible commentators falsely believe the overwhelming scourge is actually the army of 200 million from the east, explained in the Sixth Trumpet Judgment inside the Tribulation, Revelation 9:13–21. The overwhelming scourge talked about in Joel 2 **is an entirely different event** and will start shortly before the Tribulation begins, as God tells us.

2 Peter 1:19–21

19 So we have the prophetic word made more sure, to which you do well to pay attention as to a lamp shining in a dark place, until the <u>day dawns</u> and the <u>day star</u>* <u>arises in your hearts</u>. 20 But know this first of all, that no prophecy of Scripture is a matter of one's own interpretation, 21 for no prophecy was ever made by an act of human will, but men moved by the Holy Spirit spoke from God.

*The term "day star" comes from the King James Version (KJV).

Luke 21:25–28

25 There will be signs in sun and moon and stars, and on the earth dismay among nations, in perplexity at the roaring of the sea and the waves, 26 men fainting from fear and the expectation of the things which are coming upon the world; for the powers of the heavens will be shaken. 27 Then they will see the Son of Man coming in the cloud with power and great glory. 28 But when these things begin to take place, <u>straighten up and lift up your heads</u>, because your redemption is drawing near.

Now again, Luke 21:28 tells us, specifically, to *"lift up your heads,"* in other words, **look up**. But can we know when to do this? How can we do this **precise command** if the Rapture is to happen without any warning? We can't. Those of us who understand end-time prophecy and truly comprehend the "**signs**" God has given us will get a **special gift** from God when the *"day dawns"* and *"the day star arises in our hearts,"* 2 Peter 1:19. But what does God tell us here? He will give us the gift, within our hearts, of a kind of **heads up** (*pardon the pun*), telling us without a doubt that He is on the way. This will alert us to have our lamps on, giving us the foreknowledge to actually know the visual Rapture is about to take place, within minutes, so we will be able to **look up with certainty**. This also answers the question many people have regarding how we can know when the **visual Rapture** comes if we are asleep in our beds. God has provided us with the answer for all those who understand what is happening. He will wake us up so we can then fully prepare and stay alert again with certainty to know when to **look up** and see Him coming for us. **I find this glorious!**

Back in Joel 2:2, God says the scourge starts *"as the dawn is spreading."* This sounds similar to the sun starting to rise in the morning. In 2 Peter 1:19, when *"the day dawns,"* or after the sun has completely risen in the morning, we will get the warning from God Himself that He is coming and *"the day star arises in your hearts."* These verses seem to tell us that, when we see the scourge starting, we won't need to worry about it because, at about the same time, we need to get ready to go home with Jesus in the visual Rapture. Note: *"As the dawn is spreading"* and then *"the day dawns"* seem to refer to the same day as events unfold. This laces all these events into a defined sequence.

We will hear about the scourge, receive the warning in our hearts by God, and begin to see the signs in the sky and on the earth, and, at this point, we **look up**. We hear the shout of the archangel, hear the first trumpet, and, while still alive, witness all the dead in Christ rise first. We all need to keep looking up, and then, prior to the final trumpet, those of us alive are also taken up. For the Biblical and spiritual obedience of knowing all this, we get **our special reward: the Crown of Righteousness**, for loving His appearing—as promised in 2 Timothy 4:8:

2 Timothy 4:8
8 in the future there is laid up for me the <u>crown of righteousness</u>, which the Lord, the righteous Judge, will award to me on that day; and not only to me, but also <u>to all who have loved His appearing</u>.

Christians who seriously understand end-time prophecies, who have longed for His "*appearing*" and are **looking up**, as God directs us to do, will get a **crown**. Do you want your crown for this action at the visual Rapture? If God wanted the Rapture unknown to us, why would He give such a wonderful blessing and reward for **looking up**? We are commanded to know about all this as God directs each of us.

We really need to understand, after 2,000 years, a great deal of prophecy has been, and is still being, fulfilled today. Because of this, it is obvious that Jesus appears to be on the way. We truly need to know what to anticipate and what the Bible does tell us. We do not want anybody to give us wrong information. We don't want to lose our crown. Time is running out. We need to choose wisely with the help of the Lord.

Revelation 3:3
3 So remember what you have received and heard; and keep it, and repent. Therefore <u>if you do not wake up</u>, I will come like a thief, <u>and you will not know at what hour I will come to you</u>.

The Lord is telling us to "**stay awake.**" Do not keep too busy with worldly things or lack the information to both see and know the signs He has graciously given us to determine when to **look up**. **Sleeping** Christians, unaware of God's signs, will not receive the *"day star."* Do not allow yourself to be afraid of these coming signs due to lack of study and understanding. Certainly, ignorance can make one terrified of these events—something God does not want Christians to experience.

TWINKLING OF AN EYE

1 Corinthians 15:51–52
⁵¹ Behold, I tell you a mystery; we will not all sleep, but <u>we will all be changed</u>, ⁵² in a moment, <u>in the twinkling of an eye, at the last trumpet</u>; for the trumpet will sound, and the dead will be raised imperishable, and we will be changed.

Verse 51 **does not tell us** the Rapture will happen in a moment, in the twinkling of an eye, but, rather, we will all change (*bodily*) *"in a moment, in the twinkling of an eye, at the last trumpet,"* not the first.

THE VISUAL RAPTURE THE SAME LITERAL DAY AS THE START OF THE TRIBULATION

Luke 17:26–27
²⁶ And just as it happened in the days of Noah, so it will be also <u>in the days of the Son of Man</u>: ²⁷ they were eating, they were drinking, they were marrying, they were being given in marriage, until <u>the day</u> that Noah entered the ark, and the flood came and destroyed them all.

God uses many different terms to describe the 7-year Tribulation. He uses *the Tribulation, the great Tribulation, the **time of Jacob's distress**, the day of wrath, **"the days of the Son of Man,"** Daniel's 70th week*, and *the day of the Lord's vengeance*. He provides a timeframe regarding Noah and the flood to make a comparison as to what will happen *"in the days of the Son of Man."* The two specific words *"the day"* (yom) in the verses above hold significance.

Luke 17:26–27 mentions a couple of profound things. People were living normally and peacefully until *"<u>the day</u>"* Noah entered the ark. On that same day (*a 24-hour period*), the flood caught **the unbelieving world** by surprise and destroyed them. But Noah expected it. God had given him, and all the people of his day, **120 years of foreknowledge** that a flood would come, so they could prepare . . . very similar to what God does for us now through His prophecies regarding the end times and visual Rapture, all intended as preparation for us to witness. Even with 120 years of warnings, the people of Noah's day scoffed at the idea of a flood happening — even as they daily looked upon Noah's huge boat. They considered Noah crazy. God delivered Noah and his family to safety on the **<u>very same day</u>** His punishing flood came upon the world.

God provides yet another example in Luke showing the complacency of mankind prior to an event that additionally happens in **one day**, with catastrophic ramifications:

Luke 17:28–29
28 It was the same as happened in the days of Lot: they were eating, they were drinking, they were buying, they were selling, they were planting, they were building;
29 but on <u>the day</u> that Lot went out from Sodom it rained fire and brimstone from heaven and destroyed them all.

Everybody in the days of Lot lived their lives in perceived peace and normalcy until *"<u>the day</u>"* Lot went out of Sodom. During the same day (*a 24-hour period*), fire and brimstone from heaven caught everyone by surprise and destroyed them. But again, God delivered Lot and his family to safety on the **<u>very same day</u>** that His punishments came upon Sodom.

Two angels forewarned Lot and his wife to take God's explicit instructions **not to look back** at what was going to take place. Lot's wife, however, upon their departure from Sodom, did not obey what God requested of them. She looked back and paid a penalty. God turned her into a pillar of salt.

Luke 17:30–36
[30] *["]It will be just the same <u>on the day</u> that the Son of Man is revealed.* [31] *On <u>that day</u>, the one who is on the housetop and whose goods are in the house must not go down to take them out; and likewise the one who is in the field must not turn back.* [32] *<u>Remember Lot's wife</u>.* [33] *Whoever seeks to keep his life will lose it, and whoever loses his life will preserve it.* [34] *I tell you, on that night there will be two in one bed; <u>one will be taken</u> and the other will be left.* [35] *There will be two women grinding at the same place; <u>one will be taken</u> and the other will be left.* [36] *Two men will be in the field; <u>one will be taken</u> and the other will be left."*

Because God specifically asks us to *"remember Lot's wife"* related to the last days, this may have a significant parallel during the visual Rapture.

Luke 17:30 says, *"It will be just the same <u>on the day</u> that the Son of Man is revealed."* The Son of Man *"revealed"* happens again at the visual Rapture just prior to the start of the Tribulation. In Luke 17:34–36, in three different examples, God talks about how *"one will be taken"* and the other left. These verses mention nothing to imply these *"takings"* will be spontaneous hidden events, in a moment or twinkling of an eye. More than likely, the three *"takings"* will be blatantly obvious.

Based on all these verses, it is implied that when Christ comes to visually Rapture believers into the clouds, taking us home, the world should expect the Tribulation to start within, literally, 24 hours of our departure. Christians are expected to know the day and the approximate hour when all of this will come upon us by God's hand alone and not by any speculation on our part. Only God knows the day and the hour. Prophecy students will know, in our hearts, when God reveals to us the approximate time of the Rapture.

We will all go to bed one night, and when we awaken the following morning, the signs will start bringing the actual day of the visual Rapture. We should know, **with certainty**, the day has come because God has provided us in advance His full, complete prophetic **Road Map** with His specific warnings.

The Bible tells us **we** cannot know the day or the hour of His return, so this all probably sounds like a contradiction when I say we can and will know the Rapture is **about to occur**. However, in reality we will not be able to say with certainty, **the day before** the visual Rapture happens, that tomorrow is the day.

THE WORLD WILL APPEAR AT PEACE UP TO THE DAY OF THE VISUAL RAPTURE

Our world will get severely crazy in the near future. It will be difficult to watch, especially for Christians. Did you pick up on something profoundly interesting in both of the **singular day** concepts in the Noah and Lot verses? From these verses, we can know the world will appear peaceful and normal to nonbelievers right up until the visual Rapture. Both Noah and Lot lived in a spiritually decadent world, yet it did not appear so to the outside secular masses. The people of the world at that time lived what they believed to be good, productive, profitable lives in counterfeit peace and harmony.

The entire world at that time had no idea that God was about to remove their so-called peace. Noah entered the ark, and Lot left Sodom on **specific individual days**. In both instances, God came suddenly and **stole everyone's false peace. He came like a**

thief! God's arrival in no way surprised either Noah or Lot, because God provided them with detailed foreknowledge of what would come. This is a model for us for our time; **be fully aware of what God is showing us.**

These Noah and Lot verses indicate to me that we will not see WWIII or any other terrible cataclysmic punishments **before the visual Rapture occurs.** Our hurt and despair as Christians come in seeing the world has basically lost Biblical morality and true faith in Jesus. We need to take caution in order to survive in a coming degenerative and unfriendly world.

Having the world seem to appear at peace and prosperous right up to the visual Rapture gives the Deceiver a great opportunity. It offers a masterful way for him to convince the secular world that when certain Christians today talk about impending gloom and doom, and survivalist-type issues, they are crazy. Satan will insist there is no need to prepare for anarchy; nothing is going to happen. The world will accept this wholeheartedly. In reality, the horrible survivalist type of events in the world **will not occur** until **after** the Tribulation begins. All of the cataclysmic happenings will touch only those who live into the Tribulation. Worried Christians today, showing fear, play right into the Deceiver's hands and make Christians in general look like frightened children. The Deceiver can then easily use this against us and say something like this to the world:

Why can't Jesus believers stop being so fearful and negative, and truly see how great and wonderful the world has become? Jesus believers are all unjustifiably fearful. Something must be wrong with them. They need my help and retraining. Pay no attention to their delusions.

Fortunately, Christians may get to benefit from this perceived peaceful world. God will remove us all in the visual Rapture right before He makes things on earth devastatingly horrible. Right after nonbelievers **see us leave,** in the visual Rapture, as I have mentioned before, many left behind will immediately figure out the deception. We need only to trust in the Lord, heed His warnings, and follow His instructions, and we will get to go home with Him just hours before God's serious judgments begin.

ADDED SUPPORT REGARDING THE VALIDITY OF BELIEVING IN A VISUAL RAPTURE

Actually, **THREE** Raptures will occur within the 7-year Tribulation period. The **FIRST** one will be on the day the Tribulation starts (*just prior to the covenant signing*). This is for all Christians who, by faith, accepted Jesus as their Savior prior to this initial visual Rapture. In the **SECOND**, God has two witnesses who minister for Him during the first half of the Tribulation, 1,260 days, a defined amount of time (*Revelation 11:1–14*). For background, these two witnesses will be sent by God to prophesy for him during the entire first half of the Tribulation. It is thought the two witnesses God sends might be Moses and Elijah (*Matthew 17:3–4*). Nobody knows for sure. Note: Elijah may already be here, per **Road Map** prophecy #22. These two men have tremendous powers and can control the entire earth's environmental systems at will. We are told they can breathe fire out of their mouths (*Revelation 11:5–6*). They are indestructible until their ministry is completed at the midpoint of the Tribulation. God, at that time, allows the Antichrist to kill them. They lay dead in the street for three and a half days. God then resurrects them, lifting them up to heaven. God literally, visually Raptures these two men. The world is terrified by this.

The **THIRD** will happen when the <u>Tribulation saints</u>, the people who accepted Jesus during the entire 7-year Tribulation and died for their faith, are reunited with their bodies (*Matthew 24:31*). This occurs at the end of the Tribulation, after another 42 months or 1,260 days, a defined period of time (*Revelation 13:5*). Events

TWO and **THREE** could not possibly happen at unspecified times: people will know when to expect them.

The visual Rapture of God's two witnesses is a Godly statement that will terrify those still living on earth at the middle of the Tribulation—another bold way God will use to try to awaken everybody, yet again, during the Tribulation.

Revelation 11:11–13

[11] *But after the three and a half days, the breath of life from God came into them, and they stood on their feet; and great fear fell upon those who were watching them.* [12] *And* <u>*they heard a loud voice*</u> *from heaven saying to them, "Come up here."* <u>*Then*</u> <u>*they went up into heaven in the cloud, and their*</u> <u>*enemies watched them.*</u> [13] *And in that hour there was a great earthquake, and a tenth of the city fell; seven thousand people were killed in the earthquake, and the rest were terrified and gave glory to the God of heaven.*

In these verses, God talks about His two witnesses and their demise at the middle of the Tribulation. Three days after their deaths, the world will hear a *"voice from heaven"* saying, *"Come up here"*—similar to how the first visual Rapture begins. Something vital is missing at this second visual Rapture event, which indicates this is not the first visual Rapture of the whole church. Did you pick up on this? **No trumpets** sound in this sequence. The first visual Rapture **with trumpets** will certainly be visible to gain the very same desired effect as this small second visual Rapture on a much grander scale, **all for God's glory alone!**

Beyond these three events that take place at the Tribulation, there is another similar event: God taking up Elijah into heaven in the Old Testament. 2 Kings 2:9–12 provides an account of Elisha witnessing Elijah going into heaven in a whirlwind and a chariot of fire. Elisha saw this as it happened:

2 Kings 2:9–12

⁹ When they had crossed over, Elijah said to Elisha, "Ask what I shall do for you before I am taken from you." And Elisha said, "Please, let a double portion of your spirit be upon me." ¹⁰ He said, "You have asked a hard thing. Nevertheless, if you see me when I am taken from you, it shall be so for you; but if not, it shall not be so." ¹¹ As they were going along and talking, behold, there appeared a chariot of fire and horses of fire which separated the two of them. <u>And Elijah went up by a whirlwind to heaven.</u> ¹² Elisha saw it and cried out, "My father, my father, the chariots of Israel and its horsemen!" <u>And he saw Elijah no more.</u>

Our majestic God truly loves showing who He is to the people of the world. I see this purposefully happening within our visual Rapture in the official Godly announcement, by Jesus Himself, that His Tribulation has arrived *(Isaiah 61:2(b))*.

God's Bible tells of yet another likely visual Rapture event just after the resurrection of Jesus:

Matthew 27:50–53

⁵⁰ And Jesus <u>cried out again with a loud voice,</u> and yielded up His spirit. ⁵¹ And behold, the veil of the temple was torn in two from top to bottom; and the earth shook and the rocks were split. ⁵² <u>The tombs were opened, and many bodies of the saints who had fallen asleep were raised;</u> ⁵³ <u>and coming out of the tombs after His resurrection they entered the holy city and appeared to many.</u>

Matthew tells how Jesus collected and resurrected many "saints" — believers — to join their souls, and they entered the holy city. God tells us they "*appeared to many.*" But to whom did they appear? Likely, the people in Jerusalem, the holy city. And did the people witness their departure to heaven with Jesus? Some speculation at this point, but highly possible.

God refers to all who accept Him as *"saints"* multiple times in the New Testament. The following verses talk about *"saints."* Notice these were all average, living believers:

Philippians 1:1–2
1 Paul and Timothy, bond-servants of Christ Jesus, to all the saints in Christ Jesus who are in Philippi, including the overseers and deacons: 2 Grace to you and peace from God our Father and the Lord Jesus Christ.

Hebrews 6:9–10
9 But, beloved, we are convinced of better things concerning you, and things that accompany salvation, though we are speaking in this way. 10 For God is not unjust so as to forget your work and the love which you have shown toward His name, in having ministered and in still ministering to the saints.

Ephesians 4:11–12
11 And He gave some as apostles, and some as prophets, and some as evangelists, and some as pastors and teachers, 12 for the equipping of the saints for the work of service, to the building up of the body of Christ[.]

It is clear this term *"saint,"* according to the Bible, refers to **every common believer**, both deceased and alive today. In the Catholic Church, **saints** are only those people selected and appointed by the **world church** (*man's concepts, not God's*) as worthy of this status, in their human opinion. Regular believers are not considered worthy of sainthood. The **world church** cannot assign or convey saint status to anyone. God has granted this status already to all believers.

ALTERNATE PATHS FOR LIVING CHRISTIANS ON THE DAY OF THE VISUAL RAPTURE

Christians who don't know about God's **signs** just prior to the visual Rapture along with the scourge will feel frightened by them. Terrified at what they see, they will try to hide, simply because they did not study the prophetic information God provided, regarding what to know and do when these signs arrive. These Christians may suffer a small penalty. Earlier in Luke 17:31, we are told that *"the ones who are on the housetops must not go down into their houses."* Also, Luke 17:33 says, *"Whoever seeks to keep his life will lose it, and whoever loses his life will preserve it."* I see a clear significance to these verses because God has shared with us everything we need to know.

1 Thessalonians 5:6–7
6 so then let us not sleep as others do, but let us be alert and sober. 7 For those who sleep do their sleeping at night, and those who get drunk get drunk at night.

1 Corinthians 15:51–52
51 Behold, I tell you a mystery; we will not all sleep, but we will all be changed[.]

Revelation 3:3
3 So remember what you have received and heard; and keep it, and repent. Therefore if you do not wake up, I will come like a thief, and you will not know at what hour I will come to you.

Luke 17:33–36
33 Whoever seeks to keep his life will lose it, and whoever loses his life will preserve it. 34 I tell you, on that night there will be two in one bed; one will be taken and the other will be left. 35 There will be two women grinding at the same place; one will be taken

213

and the other will be left. ³⁶ Two men will be in the field; one will be taken and the other will be left.

Luke 17:33 may be telling us that all living Christians, on the day of the visual Rapture, may experience the event slightly differently. Our personal obedience to God's Word and His final directions and requests through prophecy will determine how we get Raptured.

God provides something special for those of us who have loved prophecy and seek His coming. God takes those of us who trust and understand His prophecies, know about His specific "**signs**," and actually do **look up** as commanded, up alive in the visual Rapture at the **final trumpet**. All of the horrifying "**signs**" we see will look like something that would kill us. God may be requesting that we "**look up**" so we will neither see nor concentrate on the scourge, and the horror of all the "signs." Maybe as with Lot's wife, God does not want us to look upon the judgments coming on the world for our ultimate blessing. Perhaps this is why God specifically tells us to remember Lot's wife and to be **looking up**. God told Lot's wife and now possibly those of us living today **where to place our eyes** — on Him.

Christians who have not studied end-time prophecies may, basically, run and hide for their lives, down into their houses when they see these signs and the scourge. These Christians who have not learned about this prophecy regarding God's final request for us to "**look up**," but are still faithful Christians, might have to deal with something else. Due solely to the lack of end-time knowledge, these Christians who are afraid and try to hide when these terrifying "**signs**" happen, and do not "**look up**," may enter heaven by a different path. Remember Lot's wife? She died because she did not specifically follow God's required direction regarding what to do upon leaving Sodom. She immediately went to heaven, but she went the hard way, through death.

God's Visual Catching Up

The Bible appears to indicate that if a Christian does not know to "**look up**," prior to the very first trumpet blast, their bodies will die here on earth, first. God will then instantly Rapture those people with the first group, who have died on earth, from Pentecost up to the time of the Rapture. Those of us who know the "**signs**," and obey God's request, recognize them and "**look up**;" we will go up alive just prior to the final trumpet and earn our **crown** from the Lord for a job well done. We still all go together, but the paths and the rewards differ. Those of us who enter the Kingdom alive in the visual Rapture just prior to the final trumpet might get one additional wonderful blessing. This amazing blessing will occur just before God transforms us. Jesus will allow us to see the masses of the entire body of the church, rising into the sky to join Him. God will allow us to witness all the Christians' souls already with the Lord, those who died an earthly death, reunited with their bodies rising up into the sky as we join them in this event. **I hold a magnificent mental visual picture of this.**

The visual Rapture of the church will begin the second largest series of Godly events in all of human history. The first of course was Christ's birth, death, resurrection, and ascension into heaven. Why would God desire to have a secretive and hidden Rapture? Based on all Bible history and God's very nature, this would make absolutely no logical sense.

Revelation 1:7-8
7 Behold, He is coming with the clouds, <u>and every eye will see Him</u>, even those who pierced Him; and all the tribes of the earth will mourn over Him. So it is to be. Amen. 8 "I am the Alpha and the Omega," says the Lord God, "who is and who was and who is to come, the Almighty."

An interesting thought to ponder on this topic: by God allowing the whole world "*every eye*" to see us actually physically depart in the visual Rapture, something wonderful will happen.

God, in this one visual action, will have saved millions upon millions of unbelievers, still on earth, within minutes of our departure. If we simply disappeared unexpectedly, this would not happen and would be a severely wasted opportunity to save many quickly. All of our doubting friends who thought us strange and crazy, for sharing the information in this book, will understand immediately that we had provided them with the truth and had **given them the correct information**! God will not waste this opportunity and wants everybody to find Him. Therefore, it is important to offer this information to our friends for thoughtful consideration. What one event could do more for God's ultimate glory than the visual Rapture?

THE FIVE CROWNS WE CAN WIN FOR THE LORD

God has five crown rewards for excellent service during our life on earth. I didn't list them in any particular order, but start with the one we discussed in this chapter.

1. The Crown of Righteousness is for loving His appearing.

2 Timothy 4:7–8
⁷ I have fought the good fight, I have finished the course,
I have kept the faith; ⁸ in the future there is laid up for me
the crown of righteousness, which the Lord, the righteous
Judge, will award to me on that day; and not only to me,
but also to all who have loved His appearing.

Paul understood about God and loved the concept of His appearing in the second coming. He also knew he would not be living when this happened. All believers who love the study of endtime prophecies, and anticipated Jesus appearing whether living or having died prior to the visual Rapture, will receive this crown. Some Bible teachers state that God offers this crown to all people who accept Jesus as their Savior; this is incorrect.

Those of us alive who have studied Bible prophecy and love the concept of His appearing, and understand to literally look up at the Rapture, will get this crown as part of the visual Rapture.

2. The Crown of Life is the martyr's crown.

James 1:12
12 *Blessed is a man who perseveres under trial; for once he has been approved, he will receive the crown of life which the Lord has promised to those who love Him.*

Revelation 2:10
10 *Do not fear what you are about to suffer. Behold, the devil is about to cast some of you into prison, so that you will be tested, and you will have tribulation for ten days. Be faithful until death, and I will give you the crown of life.*

The 10 days listed above define a time limit for those who accept Jesus during the Tribulation. This comforting verse tells the new Christians in the Tribulation that Satan may imprison them before he puts them to death, but any suffering will last for a limited time.

3. The Crown of Glory is for Godly people who have served Christ quietly and with a good heart and pure motives.

1 Peter 5:1–5
1 *Therefore, I exhort the elders among you, as your fellow elder and witness of the sufferings of Christ, and a partaker also of the glory that is to be revealed, 2 shepherd the flock of God among you, exercising oversight not under compulsion, but voluntarily, according to the will of God; and not for sordid gain, but with eagerness; 3 nor yet as lording it over those allotted to your charge, but proving to be examples to the flock. 4 And when the Chief*

Shepherd appears, you will receive the unfading <u>crown of glory</u>. [5] *You younger men, likewise, be subject to your elders; and all of you, clothe yourselves with humility toward one another, for God is opposed to the proud, but gives grace to the humble.*

4. The Crown of Exultation (Rejoicing) is the soul winner's crown, for ministers and evangelists: those who teach the word and go out to try to help people find Jesus.

1 Thessalonians 2:19
[19] *For who is our hope or joy or <u>crown of exultation</u>? Is it not even you, in the presence of our Lord Jesus at His coming?*

5. The Incorruptible Crown is for those who have control over their lusts, which is the spirit of self-denial.

1 Corinthians 9:25 (King James Version)
[25] *And every man that striveth for the mastery is temperate in all things. Now they do it to obtain a corruptible <u>crown; but we an incorruptible</u>.*

Romans 2:5–9

5 *But because of your stubbornness and unrepentant heart you are storing up wrath for yourself in the day of wrath and revelation of the righteous judgment of God,* 6 *who will render to each person according to his deeds:* 7 *to those who by perseverance in doing good seek for glory and honor and immortality, eternal life;* 8 *but to those who are selfishly ambitious and do not obey the truth, but obey unrighteousness, wrath and indignation.* 9 *There will be tribulation[.]*

CHAPTER 7

THE TIME OF JACOB'S DISTRESS

THE TRIBULATION GOD'S 21 JUDGMENTS

Some Christians falsely believe we'll have a peaceful first
half of the Tribulation. This is categorically incorrect!
Instead, it will be 7 years of hell on earth. The Tribulation
is coming, and nobody should want to live through any
portion of this 7-year period of
God's judgments.

Some might find this chapter to be a bit disconcerting, but I feel it necessitates understanding. God loves us so much; He does not want believers to experience His coming judgments. He tells us vividly what they will be — all very horrible — and offers us a loving way to escape the Tribulation. We can achieve this by personally accepting Jesus as our personal savior.

We must look at the Tribulation period through its full accurate Biblical context, remembering that **the entire Bible story is all about Israel**.

Isaiah 26:9
[9] At night my soul longs for you, indeed, my spirit within me seeks You diligently; For when the earth experiences Your judgments the inhabitants of the world learn righteousness.

The book of Revelation (*Apokalypsis*) **reveals** God's will to put an end to evil men in the world and to **bring both true knowledge and acceptance of Jesus to Israel**. This final special book in the Bible explains the last scenes of God's great play. John the Apostle wrote the book of Revelation purposefully for God to share what must take place to fulfill and complete all the Old Testament prophecies regarding the Messiah. This will occur in the *"latter days"* . . . our time. These Biblical concepts tell us to fully understand what God requires of us and heed the warnings. The Prologue of Revelation — verses 1:1–3 — says the *"time is near."*

Revelation 1:1–3
[1] The Revelation of Jesus Christ, which God gave Him to show to His bond-servants, the things which must soon take place; and He sent and communicated it by His angel to His bond-servant John, [2] who testified to the word of God and to the testimony of Jesus Christ, even to all that he saw. [3] Blessed is he who reads and those who hear the words of the prophecy, and heed the things which are written in it; for the time is near.

The Time of Jacob's Distress

The Apostle John received inspiration from the Holy Spirit while imprisoned on the Isle of Patmos between 90 and 96 AD. Before imprisonment, John preached about Jesus as "**Lord and God.**" This infuriated Domitian, the Emperor of Rome. He demanded his subjects call him "*Dominus et Deus*," translated roughly, "**Lord and God.**" This caused Domitian to have a dilemma with John, so he imprisoned him.

Revelation contains three forms. First: a **letter** talking to the people of John's day about what will come in the distant future. Second: a **prophecy** predicting future events for us to understand in our day. This has greater importance because God makes His desires known for us to follow. He expresses issues He expects us to obey. We should not take flippantly or lightly their seriousness. Through prophecy, God tells us exactly what He wants us to know. Third: it is **apocalyptic**, enhancing prophecy by using bold, daring, vivid illustrations to drive His points home. God discusses the **Tribulation** in expressive detail. He intentionally tries to make clear points.

I will not go into tremendous detail related to the book of Revelation, but I do desire to share some interesting observations. John, after his Prologue, starts this book with a declaration of Jesus' great love for us:

Revelation 1:4–6
⁴ *John to the seven churches that are in Asia: Grace to you and peace, from Him who is and who was and who is to come, and from the seven Spirits who are before His throne, ⁵ and from Jesus Christ, the faithful witness, the firstborn of the dead, and the ruler of the kings of the earth. <u>To Him who loves us</u> and released us from our sins by His blood— ⁶ and <u>He has made us to be a kingdom, priests</u> to His God and Father—to Him be the glory and the dominion forever and ever. Amen.*

On a side note: Revelation 1:6 — "*He has made us to be a king-dom, priests.*" This tells us, in the eyes of Jesus, He considers all of His faithful believer's "*priests*" for service to Him. 1 Peter 2:4–5 and 2:9 bolster this thinking:

1 Peter 2:4–5
⁴ And coming to Him as to a living stone which has been rejected by men, but is choice and precious in the sight of God, ⁵ you also, as living stones, are being built up as a spiritual house for a <u>holy priesthood</u>, to offer up spiritual sacrifices acceptable to God through Jesus Christ.

1 Peter 2:9
⁹ <u>But you are a chosen race, a royal priesthood</u>, a Holy nation, a people for God's own possession, so that you may proclaim the excellencies of Him who has called you out of darkness into His marvelous light[.]

John wrote the book of Revelation purposefully in symbolic format. John explains some mysterious imagery, along with actual literal issues. This includes all of God's planned 21 Tribulation judgments. But why was Revelation written in such a cryptic format? In John's day, the Romans persecuted Christians for their faith in Jesus. John, being in prison on Patmos, needed to deal with Roman censors. The Romans censored anything written that was clearly related to Christianity. If John had written in a literal sense, he would not have gotten his writing past scrutiny. John, with God's help, had to be very shrewd in his approach to writing this book. He essentially wrote this book in code. God both planned and knew we would understand the book of Revelation in its final format. When placed in context along with the other books in both the Old and New Testaments, it fits perfectly in the fully completed Bible.

God had **TWO** defined reasons for the book of Revelation, both of which help current believers and, soon, nonbelievers, specifically Jews, entering the Tribulation as well.

FIRST, the subject matter provides a warning to all the people of the world today. Revelation predicts and describes a coming horrendous time. God explains for us, vividly, the defeat of sin during the Tribulation. Through the understanding of His intended severe judgments, He motivates us to consider our path wisely. By reading the Bible, we learn from God about accepting Jesus; then through the grace Jesus offers, we have nothing to fear. Jesus offers a path to safety. The judgments listed in the book of Revelation are **literal** and **not symbolic. They are coming— soon.** Not one of God's Revelation Tribulation judgments has yet occurred at any time in world history.

SECOND, the book of Revelation will guide those individuals who will live into the Tribulation. At the exact second after the visual Rapture, for a short period of time, not one Christian will remain on earth—100 percent unbelievers—a very dark moment. Right after the visual Rapture, people will begin to realize what happened.

This chapter provides an outline of the terrible judgments God has in store for those living in this 7-year period. For nonbelievers, I'm hoping this outline will help in the consideration of some options. I know some of you don't take the book of Revelation literally, thinking it is only symbolic. I personally wouldn't want to take the chance against its validity.

No peace of any kind will exist during the entire 7-year Tribulation. As mentioned earlier, some people have the false assumption about a peaceful first half. However, the entire Tribulation will have no semblance of peace.

Twenty-one major judgments occur in this 7-year period, three sets of seven judgments. Revelation chapters 6, 8, 9, and 16 describe these judgments. I am going to list the **seven Seal Judgments** and then the **seven Trumpet Judgments** that happen in the first 3½ years — **14 judgments** in the first half of the Tribulation. I then list the **final seven Bowl Judgments** that occur in the last 3½ years.

FIRST HALF OF THE 7-YEAR TRIBULATION

God's master plan includes all of the events, both good and bad, during the Tribulation. He chose the Tribulation as a time of punishment and judgment because the world treated His Son so horribly, especially the Jews. God plans to show His ire.

Day one recaps, with some added educated speculation, all we learned from Scriptural references in Chapter 6, regarding the day the visual Rapture occurs and the Tribulation begins.

DAY ONE

- Satan has, by now, brought the overwhelming scourge to earth. It will terrify the whole world, particularly Israel.
- God's **signs** in the heavens, on the earth, and on the seas will happen.
- The visual Rapture occurs hours before the signing of a covenant agreement between the Antichrist and Israel. The whole nonbelieving world will see the visual Rapture and will be deeply frightened.
- After the visual Rapture has concluded, chaos and terror will fill the entire earth. The world continues to see the scourge coming, along with all the other signs God showed us, preceding the visual Rapture. **All terrifying!**
- The peace covenant is signed between the Antichrist and Israel. This saves Israel from the effects and terror of the scourge — or so they think; **the 7-year Tribulation begins.**
- The **signs** God placed on the earth to announce the arrival of the visual Rapture will continue to grow progressively worse into the Tribulation. The **"thief"** came; peace was **"stolen away"**; it no longer exists.

- The removal by God in the visual Rapture of possibly one billion people will instantly decimate the world economy.
- The workforce will essentially be crushed. People will quickly determine they can find no way to fix this economic devastation. **Hell on earth has arrived!**

THE EARLY MONTHS OF TRIBULATION

- God's two witnesses arrive; they cannot be killed or harmed. They have incredible powers to witness for the Lord for the first half of the Tribulation.
- Israel, per previous speculation, will have already reestablished their tribal system identities through Elijah.
- **Remember Elijah from Prophecy #22** *(page 83)?* 144,000 men, 12,000 from each of Jacob's 12 tribes — will accept the Lord as their Messiah. **When? At the Rapture after seeing us leave!** They become evangelists for Jesus, for the world on day one. The 144,000 issue is controversial; some say it happens at the middle of the Tribulation? Please look at Seal Judgment #4 and Trumpet Judgment #6 below. Collectively, they tell us one half of all living beings left in the world, after the Rapture, **will die in the first half of the Tribulation**. So, why would God wait to bring these evangelists into being halfway through His period of judgments and risk losing half of the world before He can minister to them?
- The **seven Seal Judgments** and the **seven Trumpet Judgments** now start to happen.

THE SEVEN SEAL JUDGMENTS

These events happen during the early months of the Tribulation. It is possible they could all happen together rapidly.

SEAL JUDGMENT #1: *(Revelation 6:1–2)* The White Horse — with the False Christ *(Antichrist)* riding it and conquering on it. The Antichrist consolidates power and takes full control of the world right at the start of the Tribulation. We know from earlier in this book he came on the scene before the visual Rapture. This power consolidation may happen easily because of the worldwide chaos that began after Christians were taken home with Jesus in the visual Rapture.

SEAL JUDGMENT #2: (*Revelation 6:3–4*) The Red Horse — with the power to take peace from the earth, making men desire to kill each other.

SEAL JUDGMENT #3: (*Revelation 6:5–6*) The Black Horse — with the power of famines and to reduce the world's food supply.

SEAL JUDGMENT #4: (*Revelation 6:7–8*) The Ashen Horse — with the power of death and given **the authority to kill one-fourth of all mankind** with the sword, famine, and disease. If, after the visual Rapture, six billion people remain on earth, this judgment will kill one and a half billion of them. Therefore, mathematically, four and a half billion will remain.

It is possible that the first four Seal Judgments are not, literally, horses. They probably fit into categories such as government consolidation, decrees, and accelerated corruption along with famines and plagues. The world will understand about all four results related to these first four seals. And all four will likely happen almost simultaneously.

SEAL JUDGMENT #5: (*Revelation 6:9–11*) Martyrs of the Tribulation's early days cry out en masse for the Lord to judge the Antichrist. God tells them they still need to wait a bit longer because He has not yet finished with him.

SEAL JUDGMENT #6: (*Revelation 6:12–17*) Terror is unleashed, bringing earthquakes, a blackened sun, and a bloodlike moon, and the stars will be darkened . . . all much worse than the similar signs seen just prior to the visual Rapture.

We have now reached a brief interlude (*Revelation 7:1–17*) when God will place His seal of protection on the 144,000 evangelists. He will officially seal and protect them for the balance of the Tribulation. They become indestructible.

SEAL JUDGMENT #7: (*Revelation 8:1–5*) For one half-hour, only silence will prevail in heaven. This serves as the introduction of the **seven Trumpet Judgments** . . . even more severe than these first seven Seals.

THE SEVEN TRUMPET JUDGMENTS
These events happen after the Seal Judgments.

TRUMPET JUDGMENT #1: (*Revelation 8:7*) Hail and fire mixed with blood will come down on earth and will **burn up one-third** of all the green plants and trees in the entire earth.

TRUMPET JUDGMENT #2: (*Revelation 8:8–9*) **A burning mountain will fall into the sea**; one-third of all the oceans will turn to blood, one-third of all ocean life will die, and one-third of all ships will be destroyed.

TRUMPET JUDGMENT #3: (*Revelation 8:10–11*) A star will fall from the heavens (*called Wormwood*) and one-third of all the rivers and fresh water will turn rotten.

TRUMPET JUDGMENT #4: (*Revelation 8:12–13*) One-third of the sun, moon, and stars will be smitten. The earth started to get dark at the Rapture; now the world will get much darker. In Revelation 8:13, we are told *"woe, woe, woe, to those who dwell on the earth, because of the remaining blasts of the trumpet of the three angels who are about to sound!"* Trumpets 5, 6, and 7 will be even more severe.

TRUMPET JUDGMENT #5: (*Revelation 9:1–12*) Smoke, like the **smoke of a great furnace**, will come up from a bottomless pit all over the earth, bringing demon scorpion locusts. They will torment and bite those whom God has not sealed and protected. God will not allow people to die from these bites, but they will get horrendous sores all over their bodies. This torture will last for a full 5 months. People will desire to die, but God will not allow it.

TRUMPET JUDGMENT #6: (*Revelation 9:13–21*) A large army from the east (*200 million actual demons*) will be set loose on the world to kill one-third of the remaining people on earth. Remember back in Seal Judgment 4, one quarter of the world was killed, leaving four and a half billion still alive. **This Trumpet Judgment will kill one-third of the remaining four and a half billion people,** or another one and a half billion. There will then be only three billion people left in the world. Some Bible scholars say this army of 200 million comes from China, based on their great population mass. This is not accurate. Revelation tells us four angels release them. This army is not human, and it is not the scourge; they will be something entirely different.

TRUMPET JUDGMENT #7: (*Revelation 11:15–19*) It will announce to the world: Jesus is the ruler of the earth; "*He will reign forever and ever.*" But the Antichrist has another idea and will prepare a hideous reign for the second half of the Tribulation.

The Bible refers to many false Christs, and false prophets, and movements that will bring evil at different times, but Jesus also clearly talks about one exceptionally sinister individual who will come on the scene in the end times: the literal Antichrist. What can we know about this literal Antichrist? The word "**anti**" has two meanings. In the English language, it means "**against**" someone or something. However, in the **original Greek** text, the word "*anti*" when attached with the title given to Jesus "*Christ*," or "**Messiah**," means "*instead of*" or "*in place of*." Therefore, using the original Greek interpretation, the **Antichrist** does not mean

230

"**against Christ**"; it means "**in place of Christ**." This has great significance. The end goal of the Antichrist is not to merely be against Christ, but to "**completely replace Jesus,**" making Himself God. At the midpoint of the Tribulation, He will proclaim himself as the only one and true god. Pure unmitigated hubris!

I believe the Antichrist is alive today; he is a man and not Satan at this time. I would even venture to say he does not yet know who he really is. Satan is, however, grooming him now for his coming role on the world stage.

Back in Chapter 5, Ezekiel 28:12 explained that Satan was the most beautiful of all God's angels. After his fall, this did not change. I believe when he "personally" arrives, he will use his God-given attributes to his advantage. He will be attractive, charming, and cunning and will prove to be an egomaniac. According to the Bible, this "being" will have certain specific characteristics we should recognize:

- **Daniel 7:8:** He will have "*a mouth uttering great boasts*" **against Jesus**.
- **Daniel 7:25:** "*He will intend to make alterations in times and in laws,*" which could include changing our calendars away from correlation to Jesus.
- **Psalm 55:21:** "*His speech will be smoother than butter.*"
- **2 Corinthians 11:14:** "*Satan disguises himself as an angel of light.*"
- **Revelation 12:9:** "*He deceives the whole world.*"
- **Daniel 11:37:** "*He will show no regard for the gods of his fathers or for the desire of women, nor will he show regard for any other god; for he will magnify himself above them all.*"
- **2 Thessalonians 2:9:** "*He is in accord with the activity of Satan, with all the power and signs and false wonders and with all the deception of wickedness.*"
- **Luke 22:3:** As an example of what is yet to come, note that at the time of Jesus' first visit, Satan entered Judas Iscariot and

took control of him. Judas was one of the original 12 disciples of Jesus. He betrayed the Lord with a kiss (*Mark 14:44–45*), leading to His crucifixion. Judas later committed suicide when he realized what he had done. Satan essentially guided Jesus to the cross, through Judas. Satan will reside within the Antichrist in a similar fashion at the midpoint of the Tribulation for the remaining 42 months.

- **Daniel 8:23–26:** Finally, paraphrased, *"he is insolent, skilled in intrigue, powerful but not by his own power; he destroys mighty men and devastates the holy people. Shrewd, a master of deception, he destroys many, and will become arrogant and magnify himself. He will even oppose the 'Prince of princes,'"* Jesus, as we see in Daniel 8:25.

The Antichrist will be a wicked individual. Satan will pull all the strings within this man. It will appear the Antichrist is killed at the middle of the Tribulation, but he is not really dead, only severely wounded. He cannot be dead because Satan has no power over life and death, only God does, so the Deceiver intends to do a "**counterfeit resurrection**" from supposed death. The Antichrist appears dead for three days. Satan, at this point, enters him with "**a miraculous false resurrection,**" similar to **the true resurrection** of Jesus. Then he claims to be god, the only god for the balance of the Tribulation. The last half of the Tribulation will be exceedingly severe.

As discussed in an earlier chapter, at the beginning of the Tribulation, 10 kings have power over 10 kingdoms—three of them in strong disagreement with the Antichrist's doings. A battle at the midpoint of the Tribulation appears to kill the Antichrist by the hands of these three kings. It is the three kings who will "**restrain him**" during the first half of the Tribulation. After three days, the Antichrist "**miraculously**" appears to come back to life; he then kills these three kings.

232

Now, with the three **restraining kings** dead, the fully Satan-indwelled Antichrist has no restraint or restrictions, and he unleashes incredible demonic terror on the whole world for the next 3½ years.

HALFWAY INTO THE TRIBULATION

- Revelation 11:3 tells us those still alive inside the Tribulation have survived 1,260 days into the total 2,520-day process.
- At the start of the Tribulation, six billion people likely remained on earth after the visual Rapture. At this halfway point, the world population has been reduced to three billion people. Only half of the world's population that remained on the earth after the Rapture has survived.
- God allows the death of His two witnesses, and their bodies lay in the street for three and a half days. The people rejoice at their deaths. But after three and a half days, God brings them back to life and takes them up into heaven in a second visual Rapture. This sight terrifies the world (*Revelation 11:11–13*).
- As explained above, at this halfway point the Antichrist goes from being an evil man to Satan incarnate. All hell literally has broken loose. The three kings—the *"restrainer"*—have been removed. Satan is unrestrained, and his rule will be terrifying.
- The Antichrist now enters the temple and declares himself the only god. He demands that everyone shall worship him alone. Per Daniel 12:11, this is the *"Abomination of Desolation."*
- Per Revelation 13:17–18, the Antichrist's mark, the number of man, is 666, and all people will now be required to take this mark on their right hand or forehead. Without this mark, they cannot buy or sell things. Without this mark, death is mandatory.

- At this point, all saved Jews flee from Israel for protection. They now know the Antichrist is pure evil, and they run for their very lives.

SECOND HALF OF THE TRIBULATION

THE SEVEN BOWL JUDGMENTS

These events occur during the last half of the Tribulation. They are set into motion by seven angels.

BOWL JUDGMENT #1: (*Revelation 16:2*) The first angel will set loose loathsome and malignant sores on those who have taken the mark of the beast, 666, on their right hand or foreheads, those who worship the beast, the Satan-indwelled Antichrist.

BOWL JUDGMENT #2: (*Revelation 16:3*) The second angel turns the sea into blood. This is the second time this is done. This time, the entire sea turns to blood, and everything in it dies. This is much more severe than Trumpet Judgment #2.

BOWL JUDGMENT #3: (*Revelation 16:4–7*) The third angel will turn all the freshwater lakes and rivers into blood and praise Jesus for His judgments.

BOWL JUDGMENT #4: (*Revelation 16:8–9*) The fourth angel will **make the sun hot enough to scorch men fiercely, with fire**. The people still will not repent after this and will continue to blaspheme His name.

BOWL JUDGMENT #5: (*Revelation 16:10–11*) The fifth angel will darken the planet almost completely. God will be terribly angry. He will add more pains and sores to the people, also. The people still will not repent after this and will continue to blaspheme His name.

BOWL JUDGMENT #6: (*Revelation 16:12–16*) The sixth angel will dry up the blood in the Euphrates River in preparation for the army from the east (*demons, not the Chinese*) to come for the final battle of Armageddon against Jesus alone.

BOWL JUDGMENT #7: (*Revelation 16:17–21*) A seventh angel will send flashes of lightning, peals of thunder, and a great worldwide earthquake — greater than ever in history. It will be so great an earthquake that Babylon will split into three parts and the cities of all the sinful nations will fall. All the islands in the world will disappear, and no more mountains in the world will remain standing. Huge hailstones, 100 pounds each, will come down from heaven. The remaining people still will not repent and will continue to blaspheme God's name.

Satan will be defeated at the end of the Tribulation when Jesus comes back with His great multitude (*us*) for His final battle of Armageddon. He will win this battle on His own; we get to watch. This multitude will be made up of all the pre-visual Rapture Christians. **What a glorious day this will be!**

★★★★★★★★★★★★★★★★

When anyone looks at all of this and realizes this "*shall*" happen, would any rational person want to consider going through something like this? The choice and corresponding consequences are purely individual.

When God offers all of us a lifeboat to safety in the form of Jesus, please, consider your decision wisely.

Revelation 1:3

[3] *Blessed is he who reads and those who hear the words of the prophecy, and heed the things which are written in it; for the time is near.*

CLOSING THOUGHTS

It is my hope you have found this fresh concept of Biblical prophetic interpretation both informative and interesting. Here are some closing thoughts for your prayerful consideration.

If any of this interpretation as presented is ultimately wrong and the Rapture happens without warning, then **PRAISE THE LORD!** We are home with Jesus — end of story.

But what if we do live to see the Ezekiel 38 attack as I've described in this book? And then, shortly after the battle, we begin to see the onset of additional prophecies expounded in the Bible? Our knowledge will help us deal with these events.

We need to fully prepare to evangelize for a short period of time after the Ezekiel 38 attack. Remember after 9/11 how people filled the churches for about a month? The horrors of that day resulted in a short time of great harvesting for the Lord. The Ezekiel 38 attack will have an even stronger overall impact.

For me, Pascal's wager comes to mind. Blaise Pascal (1623– 1661) — a French philosopher, scientist, mathematician, and probability theorist — offered a profoundly simplistic viewpoint. I have paraphrased his thoughts:

If there is no God and we believed in Him, we have lost nothing. But if there truly is a God and we do not choose to believe in Him, we have a great deal to lose.

Many people in the world are beginning to say Christians are ignorant, hateful, judgmental, intolerant, and phobic because we love Jesus and accept His written Word, verbatim. Christians will discover that actually, the nonbelievers who discount the Bible and Jesus, and then us by association, through "projection," say and do all the things listed in the sentence above to us, not the other way around. This should come as no surprise because Jesus tells us we will be hated on His account.

Matthew 10:22
22 You will be hated by all because of My name, but it is the one who has endured to the end who will be saved.

Closing Thoughts

Luke 6:22
²² *Blessed are you when men hate you, and ostracize you, and insult you, and scorn your name as evil, for the sake of the Son of Man.*

It may actually be a blessing for Christians to live through some adversity in the last days. We've learned how Jesus has shown us the right way to deal with the coming travail. He has given us the blessing of knowledge, and time, to help some of our unbelieving friends and family to find and accept Jesus as their personal Savior up until the very day the visual Rapture arrives.

The Ezekiel 38 attack will shake the very roots of faith for millions of Christians who have yet to hear about this version of events. Some people, after this attack, might live in fear because, due only to a lack of Biblical knowledge, it may appear that Jesus is not coming to save us. Doubters might think the Ezekiel 38 attack is actually Armageddon—which, with Biblical understanding, cannot be the case. Others will believe the attack proves the Rapture will happen after all the wars and difficult times in the Tribulation. And no doubt, more will feel the attack begins the Tribulation. But we know otherwise.

I have made many references to the Catholic Church, specifically, regarding coming events. I choose only to bring attention to what the Deceiver might do to all Christian organizations—particularly Catholics, but Protestants as well. Although no Christians will be safe, I think I have clearly expressed my belief that the Deceiver specifically wants to use the Catholic Church to achieve his final plans. When unchristian things start to happen in any church system, I want to have everybody aware and alert with a good feel for what is actually happening.

If Satan is indeed seeping into the Catholic Church, changing **doctrines** in opposition to the Bible, we have a serious problem. Believing and accepting only what our church leaders espouse could result in some serious personal consequences. Blindly accepting bad information humans express, instead of placing our trust in the inerrant Bible, would lead us down a path to destruction.

Jesus uses sheep in the Bible as an example to represent His flock who have desperate need for a Good Shepherd to guide us. Of all the animals in the world God could have chosen for this analogy, He selected one with low intelligence. It's not mean-spirited, but rather truthful. God knows our weaknesses.

Lack of awareness regarding the actual real truths inside the Bible, independent of all manmade Church doctrines, prevents us from having the ability to protect ourselves from cunning deceptions. Please be careful. I, sincerely—with all my heart—do not want anyone to be fooled, and I give thanks to our loving Lord Jesus for giving us instruction and protection.

God provides us with some added instructions in the book of Jude related to the last days:

Jude 1:17–25

17 But you, beloved, ought to remember the words that were spoken beforehand by the apostles of our Lord Jesus Christ, 18 that they were saying to you, "In the last time there will be mockers, following after their own ungodly lusts." 19 These are the ones who cause divisions, worldly-minded, devoid of the Spirit. 20 But you, beloved, building yourselves up on your most holy faith, praying in the Holy Spirit, 21 keep yourselves in the love of God, waiting anxiously for the mercy of our Lord Jesus Christ to eternal life. 22 And have mercy on some, who are doubting; 23 save others, snatching them out of the fire; and on some have mercy with fear, hating even the garment polluted by the flesh. 24 Now to Him who is able to keep you from stumbling, and to make you stand in the presence of His glory blameless with great joy, 25 to the only God our Savior, through Jesus Christ our Lord, be glory, majesty, dominion and authority, before all time and now and forever. Amen.

Closing Thoughts

During Christ's crucifixion, one of the two criminals on each side of Him scoffed at Jesus, saying He was not the Christ. He even got to the point of mocking Jesus, saying, *"Save yourself"* sarcastically, implying, **"Then prove it!"**

Luke 23:39–43
[39] One of the criminals who were hanged there was hurling abuse at Him, saying, "Are You not the Christ? Save Yourself and us!" [40] But the other answered, and rebuking him said, "Do you not even fear God, since you are under the same sentence of condemnation? [41] And we indeed are suffering justly, for we are receiving what we deserve for our deeds; but this man has done nothing wrong." [42] And he was saying, "Jesus, remember me when You come in Your kingdom!" [43] And He said to him, "Truly I say to you, today you shall be with Me in Paradise."

The second criminal recognized Jesus as his Savior, and, although under condemnation, he felt the Lord's power to forgive him. He rebukes the first criminal for not recognizing who Jesus really was. The second criminal realized he deserved his own sentence and recognized Jesus' innocence. In his last minutes of life, he realized he needed and wanted Jesus and humbly asked the Lord to remember him when He gets to His Kingdom. He accepted Jesus at that very moment, and what did Jesus then tell him in Luke 23:43? *"Truly I say to you, today you shall be with Me in Paradise."* This man believed for mere minutes in our gracious and loving Jesus, and for this **brief faith**, the Lord gave him **a full share of eternity**, with Him, in paradise.

Please remember this: if the majority of the remaining prophecies listed in this book start happening, watch carefully for the final signs. The world appears to look as if achievement of peace and harmony has arrived; strange things are happening in the sun, moon, stars, and oceans—the scourge—mankind fearful of what they sense and see. This is the moment in time the Bible tells

Christians to literally watch for. **The visual Rapture is about to occur!**

Please think of this book as an invitation to truly get to know and accept Jesus before His shout to come up (*1 Thessalonians 4:16*) at the visual Rapture. God has given mankind all the necessary verifiable information to know Him and to accept Him, right up to the absolute last moments, before the Tribulation begins. God shows us how to achieve salvation and escape His judgments that will soon come upon the world (*Appendix B*).

However, the people who do enter the Tribulation can still be saved by accepting Jesus as their Savior. Heed His Word now and avoid the horrific Tribulation.

At the end of Chapter 6, I referred to where the Bible offers five crowns to good and faithful servants. Remember, we can win the **Crown of Righteousness** by **looking up** at the visual Rapture. God has blessed today's population, giving us the chance to win this one particular crown for Jesus, visually, and not simply in our hearts . . . **a tremendous honor and gift as long as we understand how to achieve it!**

Even though we may have some challenges ahead, we still need to remember to enjoy each day—to stop and take the time to see all the wonderful things God places around us: family, friends, and the natural beauty of the earth the Lord graciously provided. Embrace and appreciate all these gifts for peace of mind as we rapidly move toward our glorious future destiny. Always trust our loving God; He knows everything and has already perfected all of His plans.

I hope to have helped make the end times a bit more understandable. I wrote this book in anticipation of showing you how to know when to take God's final directed action at the start of the visual Rapture. May you **look up**, as a believer with joyful open arms, and welcome our magnificent Lord back in the clouds at the **visual Rapture**.

All praise and glory be given to Jesus Christ our Lord. Amen.

Closing Thoughts

John 16:33

[33] *These things I have spoken to you, so that in Me you may have peace. In the world you have tribulation, but take courage; "I have overcome the world."*

2 Timothy 3:16–17

16 All Scripture is inspired by God and profitable for teaching, for reproof, for correction, for training in righteousness; 17 so that the man of God may be adequate, equipped for every good work.

APPENDIX A

BIBLE CREDIBILITY

God has provided us evidence in the Bible proving the inerrancy of His Word. This provides validation regarding the visual Rapture.

The Bible is an amazing piece of historical and prophetic literature. It is a highly organized, detailed, compact library of 66 divine books broken into three distinct segments. Christians actually have what we refer to as the Old Testament (*the Tanakh, 60 percent of the total library*), the New Testament (*the first 26 of 27 books, 38 percent of the library*), and then the final, 27th book — Revelation (*2 percent*). The Old Testament shares about the history of mankind, the origin of sin, and how God promises He will send **"somebody"** to fix this sin epidemic. The New Testament tells us **"who came once"** and resolved this sin problem on the cross. Revelation explains how **"this Man will come a second time"** and how both Testaments integrally fit together seamlessly, explaining how God will finally conquer sin, saving Israel for all eternity in the process.

As Christians, we are to accept the credibility of the Bible's passages as the singular, Divine, inspired, inerrant, and infallible Word of the single triune God. This is important because, if the Bible's sacred writings are not reliable and perfect, then the idea of using the Bible to substantiate its own claims creates the problem of **circular logic**. Any Biblical imperfection would doom our whole interpretation, basing our faith on lies. In the following verses, Paul addresses what would happen if Jesus is not who He claims to be:

1 Corinthians 15:12–19
[12] Now if Christ is preached, that He has been raised from the dead, how do some among you say that there is no resurrection of the dead? [13] But if there is no resurrection of the dead, not even Christ has been raised; [14] and if Christ has not been raised, then our preaching is vain, your faith also is vain. [15] Moreover we are even found to be false witnesses of God, because we testified against God that He raised Christ, whom He did not raise, if in fact the dead are not raised. [16] For if the dead are not raised, not even Christ has been raised; [17] and if Christ has not been raised,

your faith is worthless; you are still in your sins. ¹⁸ Then those also who have fallen asleep in Christ have perished. ¹⁹ If we have hoped in Christ in this life only, we are of all men most to be pitied.

John 1:1–5
¹ In the beginning was the Word, and the Word was with God, and the Word was God. ² He was in the beginning with God. ³ All things came into being through Him, and apart from Him nothing came into being that has come into being. ⁴ In Him was life, and the life was the Light of men. ⁵ The Light shines in the darkness, and the darkness did not comprehend it.

The preceding verses explain how God has known everything from before the beginning and through eternity because time has never bound Him. The words we have in our Bible today **existed from the beginning**, before God created the universe, long before God had men scribe them for use in our Bible today. They were in full force long before God created any physical matter, and long before any possible concept of any proposed evolutionary process.

These truthful words include exactly what will happen in our current day and in the near future. God is the author.

Up until this century, the Bible has predicted or prophesied more than 2,500 events, all of which have come true with 100 percent accuracy. Jesus Himself fulfilled more than 300 prophecies at His first coming. Here are two prophetic examples regarding Jesus scribed many years prior to His birth:

Isaiah 53:4–6
⁴ Surely our griefs He Himself bore, and our sorrows He carried; Yet we ourselves esteemed Him stricken, smitten of God, and afflicted. ⁵ But He was pierced through for our transgressions, He was crushed for our iniquities; the chastening for our well-being fell upon Him, and by His

scourging we are healed. ⁶ All of us like sheep have gone astray, each of us has turned to his own way; but the LORD has caused the iniquity of us all to fall on Him.

Isaiah 9:6–7
⁶ For a child will be born to us, a son will be given to us; and the government will rest on His shoulders; and His name will be called Wonderful Counselor, Mighty God, Eternal Father, Prince of Peace. ⁷ There will be no end to the increase of His government or of peace, On the throne of David and over his kingdom, to establish it and to uphold it with justice and righteousness From then on and forevermore. The zeal of the Lord of hosts will accomplish this.

Both of these Old Testament passages describe Jesus *(not the land of Israel)* and what He will do for us in the future. The first set of verses talks about the cross and the second set about His reign. The prophet Isaiah wrote both sets of verses around 680 BC. The fulfillment of the first verses occurred at the cross. The second group of verses is yet to be fulfilled as His second coming.

The Bible predicts the birth, death, and resurrection of Christ numerous times. Many witnessed His death when it occurred in real time, and, after His death, historically, at least 500 people saw Him alive, 1 Corinthians 15:6.

Acts 1:9–11
⁹ And after He had said these things, <u>He was lifted up while they were looking on,</u> and <u>a cloud received Him</u> out of their sight. ¹⁰ And as they were gazing intently into the sky while He was going, behold, two men in white clothing stood beside them. ¹¹ They also said, "Men of Galilee, why do you stand looking into the sky? <u>This Jesus, who has been taken up from you into heaven, will come in just the same way as you have watched Him go into heaven.</u>"

He ascended to heaven per Acts 1:9–11. He *"lifted up"* off the ground, *"while they were looking on,"* and *"a cloud received Him."* They literally watched Jesus leave, and *"This Jesus, who has been taken up from you into heaven, will come in just the same way as you have watched Him go into heaven."* The witnessing of the ascension is in Acts 1:9, and the coming back is shown in the same way in Acts 1:11. One tells of an event actually viewed and the second of a promise of a future viewing.

What about archeology? Numerous archeological finds in the world have related to the Bible. Everything found to correlate with the Bible, or a Bible event, continues to prove the accuracy of God's book. In fact, back in **Road Map** prophecy #17, I explained that Peter's bones may soon be found, in the true city of Babylon (*in current-day Iraq*) after the Ezekiel 38 attack.

God, in His Scriptures, presented certain aspects of the true configuration of the universe a long time before mankind could actually prove or anticipate these things:

Isaiah 40:22
22 It is He who sits above the <u>circle of the earth</u>, and its inhabitants are like grasshoppers, Who stretches out the heavens like a curtain and spreads them out like a tent to dwell in.

God talks about the fact that *"He sits above the circle of the earth,"* indicating the earth is round. The Bible made it clear that the earth was not flat long before Columbus' discovery.

Ecclesiastes 1:7
7 All the <u>rivers flow into the sea</u>, <u>yet the sea is not full</u>. To the place where the rivers flow, there they flow again.

God describes how rivers work in a cycle. They *"flow into the sea,"* and *"yet the sea is not full,"* and then *"there they flow again."* A mystery related to where this continuous water supply is coming from — a mystery that God understood, but man could not contemplate, written in 935 BC.

<u>*Jeremiah 33:22*</u>
[22] ["']As <u>*the host of heaven cannot be counted*</u> and <u>*the sand of the sea cannot be measured,*</u> <u>*so I will multiply the descendants of David*</u> *My servant and the Levites who minister to Me.'"*

Here Jeremiah relates to an infinite number of stars in the heavens. Man could see stars but had no idea of the infinite number because mankind at that time had no concept about deep space. God compared the number of stars to the number of grains of sand on a beach, a totally incomprehensible yet accurate number.

<u>*Job 26:7*</u>
[7] <u>*He stretches out the north over empty space and hangs the earth on nothing.*</u>

Job states that the earth exists in *"empty space"* and God *"hangs the earth on nothing"* in 1800 BC. How could these men, at the verifiable times these Scriptures were written, know all this? They didn't, but God did . . . more proof that a higher power inspired Bible Scripture.

The Bible is a compilation of 66 canonical (*Canon*) books (*73 for Catholics*) written by 40 authors over 2,000 years, with a completed library of 66 books fully written by around 95 AD. Many of the Old Testament writers did not know each other or live at the same time, yet their writings were collected into one cohesive library of books, through God's inspired direction. The Scriptures flow in perfect unity and consistency with remarkable structure and symmetry. Everything works together in perfect mathematical harmony. In no way could this be chance, but rather Divine authorship. Obviously, our Lord perfectly planned and spread the Word out over time, and as a result we can read His Divinely inspired library with confidence today.

In the New Testament, when we look at the Gospels (**Matthew, Mark, Luke,** and **John**), we know these four authors knew each other. They lived with Jesus and witnessed, personally, almost everything He did during His earthly ministry. These disciples wrote the gospel books between 55 AD/CE and 95 AD/CE. Note: the suffix CE (*Common Era*) has replaced AD (*Anno Domini = day of our Lord*). I will stay with AD; I like it better. Also interesting: BC (*Before Christ*), used for the time periods prior to Jesus, has also been changed to BCE (*Before Common Era*). Our calendar years today totally revolve around the birth of Jesus because of His importance.

At the time the four apostles scribed the Gospels, many other people who witnessed Jesus, personally, could have easily disputed anything they wrote through God's inspiration. But this did not occur. People at that time knew of Jesus and accepted the interpretations of these four men, without dispute, because of the accuracy of their written accounts. This adds yet another level of credibility to the foundations of the New Testament.

Why do we have so many translations of the Bible? The original writings of the books of the Bible were in Hebrew, Aramaic, and Greek. The Pentateuch — the first five books of the Old Testament (**Genesis, Exodus, Leviticus, Numbers,** and **Deuteronomy**), written by Moses — were transcribed from clay tablets. From the time of Adam until the time of Moses, tablets provided preservation for their accurate content and genealogies. During the time of Moses, these earlier tablet document writings were rewritten onto parchments.

For 1,400 years from the time Christ lived on the earth, only the clergy had copies of the Bible. They informed the masses about God and did a less-than-accurate job with their interpretations. Then, around 1450 AD, Johannes Gutenberg invented the first working printing press, and things soon changed. The printing press now made it possible to make quality copies of the Bible for royalty and the wealthy. In 1455, using this new technology, Gutenberg printed 200 Bibles.

As time went on, other people wanted Bibles in their languages and needed translators. These translators made every effort to keep consistent to the actual written meaning or intent of the original written languages (*Hebrew, Aramaic, and Greek*). They converted the original text into different languages using the current words and phrases customary to each new language group.

The reason we even needed to translate the Bible at all is a consequence of the Tower of Babel, which is discussed in Genesis 11:1-10. Mankind built the tower to reach God, which showed arrogance. Because of this Tower (*built in Babylon*), God confused languages, and this has resulted in our current-day translation problems—a curse we need to deal with today due to man's earlier sins. This makes our understanding of God's Word in our day more challenging than it ever should have been. All sin has lasting consequences.

In 1384, John Wycliffe created the first English Bible translation. In the English language today, we have two major widely accepted versions of the Bible. The King James (1611) Bible contains 66 books. This is made up of 39 total books in the Old Testament. Judaism combines these 39 books into 24 books . . . an arrangement issue. The Old Testament in both the Protestant and the Hebrew Bibles are virtually identical. There are 27 books in the New Testament. All Christian versions have 27 books in the New Testament; Protestant faiths consider the 66-book version (*39 + 27 = 66*) to be the true, complete, official canon. The canon is the accepted, God-inspired collection (*library*) of books that makes up our current Bibles.

The Catholic Church uses the Douay-Rheims Bible. This contains the original 66 books translated from the Latin Vulgate translation (*which contains many errors*), completed around 400 AD. Today, this Bible version has **73 books**, which include the 66 mentioned above and seven main additional sections: Deutero-canonical books, also referred to as Apocryphal books. Today, the Catholic Church has 46 books in their Old Testament and 27 in their New Testament (*46 + 27 = 73*).

The Apocryphal books, written before and during Christ's time here on earth, have some controversial writings. These seven books were added into the Catholic Bible by the Catholic hierarchy at the Council of Trent in 1546 AD, **Road Map** prophecy #17, Chapter 2. These books all intertwine within their Old Testament. They include the books of *Tobit, Judith, Wisdom, Sirach, Baruch, 1 Maccabees*, and *2 Maccabees*. Protestants do not acknowledge these added seven books, because they believe they contain some concepts contradicting the mutually accepted 66 canonical books. With these books added in 1546, this violates **what God tells us not to do** in Revelation 22:18. Additionally, at some point within its text, the New Testament references the majority of the original 39 universally accepted Old Testament books. The New Testament never refers to these specific seven additional Catholic books.

In Luke 24:44, Jesus indicates He, as a rabbi, used the **24-book Tanakh** during His earthly ministry. The Tanakh is, to this day, the Holy Scriptures of Judaism. The Tanakh includes *"the Law of Moses and the Prophets and the Psalms,"* from the book of *Genesis* through the book of *Malachi*:

Luke 24:44
⁴⁴Now He said to them, "These are My words which I spoke to you while I was still with you, that all things which are written about Me in the <u>Law of Moses and the Prophets and the Psalms must be fulfilled</u>."

Malachi, written by the prophet Malachi, is the youngest of the books in the Tanakh, completed around 450 BC. The seven Apocryphal books were written between 350 BC and 90 AD. Jesus, per Luke 24:44, gave them no mention and, therefore, no credibility. He states clearly that He recognizes *"the Law of Moses and the Prophets and the Psalms."* The Apocryphal books do not fit within these specific defined categories.

We know there were only handwritten copies of all the Biblical verses up until the time of the printing press. Moses wrote the first books around 1,450 BC (*3,460+ years ago*). The onset of the printing press made Bibles attainable in quantity a mere 565 years ago, but plentiful and affordable to the masses for only the last 100 years. God wanted to warn, prepare, and protect His family for what will soon come. More importantly, He has chosen to provide us all with peace regarding His coming judgments against nonbelievers. God desires for everybody, in our current time, to have access to a personal Bible — a tool and guide to warn us, prepare us, and comfort us in these last days.

Some history: the Old Testament contains some of the oldest known books in the world — between 2,450 and 3,500 years old. Throughout history, over time, archeologists have discovered more than 5,800 copies or portions of the Old Testament, and many more original and partial-manuscript copies of the New Testament. Our current Bible today is identical to the original manuscripts scribed and completed about 95 years after the birth of Christ.

The greatest archeological find of Bible parchments was the Dead Sea Scrolls, first discovered in 1947. They date back to between 200 BC and approximately 68 AD. After the initial find in one cave, archeologists found 10 additional caves in the area that contained additional scrolls. Collectively, these scrolls contained multiple copies of the entire Old Testament. However, the book of Esther is missing. Also, interestingly, many of the seven Apocryphal books the Catholic Church added to their Old Testament in 1546 AD are missing. They found other items explaining a link to the new faith, belief in Jesus Christ as Messiah, which came out of Judaism. God has protected His Word perfectly for our accurate use today. We have everything absolutely correct as originally written—**this in itself is a miracle!**

Accelerated major attacks on the Bible's credibility have occurred now for about 200 years. These attacks have grown in intensity with the purpose of completely discrediting God's Word—also part of the Divine plan. Mankind has become extremely arrogant.

2 Timothy 4:1–5

1 I solemnly charge you in the presence of God and of Christ Jesus, who is to judge the living and the dead, and by His appearing and His kingdom: 2 preach the word; be ready in season and out of season; reprove, rebuke, exhort, with great patience and instruction. 3 For the time will come when they will not endure <u>sound doctrine</u>; but wanting to have their ears tickled, they will accumulate for themselves teachers in accordance to their own desires, 4 and will turn away their ears from the truth and will <u>turn aside to myths</u>. 5 But you, <u>be sober in all things</u>, endure hardship, do the work of an evangelist, fulfill your ministry.

Titus 1:8–9

8 be hospitable, loving what is good, sensible, just, devout, self-controlled, 9 holding fast the faithful word which is in accordance with the teaching, so that he will be able both to exhort in <u>sound doctrine</u> and to refute those who contradict.

God tells us to preach the Word using "*sound doctrine.*" This refers to the literal Bible itself. The complete text tells us everything we need to know. Jesus and His Word are perfect. Therefore, when anybody has beliefs or theories they attach to God, they need to back them up using actual Scripture as their sole proof for any alternate points of view. This is called being "*sober in all things,*" per 2 Timothy 4:5. God says not to subscribe to **beliefs** without heeding verification found in Scriptures. He tells us not to stray away from truth by listening or *"turning aside to myths."* We need to take care not to speculate about anything that differentiates from His stated Word. We are not allowed to read between the lines. We have to provide and share the solid Word of God as He has given it to us.

In the near future, many will accept the sweet talk by evil leaders promising the nearness of achieving final peace on earth. This mistake will lead to ultimate peril for the unbelieving masses. Deception will persuade the majority, and we need to help share the truth with as many people as possible by introducing them to Jesus and what will soon come. God will do the rest.

John 1:1–5

¹ In the beginning was the Word, and the Word was with God, and the Word was God. ² He was in the beginning with God. ³ All things came into being through Him, and apart from Him nothing came into being that has come into being. ⁴ In Him was life, and the life was the Light of men. ⁵ The Light shines in the darkness, and the darkness did not comprehend it.

Genesis 1:26

²⁶ Then God said, "Let Us make man in <u>Our image</u>, according to Our likeness[."]

God has told us His Word existed, and was in place, and perfect from before creation. God knew, when He created man, that Adam and Eve would choose the sin option. Fortunately, He had everything prepared in advance to fix sin through His Son. Jesus existed from the beginning. Note the words *"Our image."* God pre-designated Jesus to become the perfect God/man to save us at the correct moments in history. He came once and will soon return a second time, forever.

Hebrews 6:18

¹⁸ so that by two unchangeable things in which <u>it is</u>

256

impossible for God to lie, we who have taken refuge
would have strong encouragement to take hold
of the hope set before us.

As previously mentioned multiple times, the Scriptures tell us *"it is impossible for God to lie."* We should expect this of a perfect God. We can feel confident that what He shares with us will actually occur.

Ephesians 5:13–17

13 But all things become visible when they are exposed by the light, for everything that becomes visible is light. 14 For this reason it says, awake, sleeper, and arise from the dead, and Christ will shine on you. 15 Therefore be careful how you walk, not as unwise men but as wise, 16 making the most of your time, because the days are evil. 17 So then do not be foolish, but understand what the will of the Lord is.

As Christians, we are to walk in *"wisdom,"* because *"the days are evil."* We cannot merely coast through life, especially at this late hour. God expects us to be good representatives for Him, countering evil in the world. Through Christ and with Christ, we represent the introduction of His hope for many.

1 Timothy 4:11–16

11 Prescribe and teach these things. 12 Let no one look down on your youthfulness, but rather in speech, conduct, love, faith and purity, show yourself an example of those who believe. 13 Until I come, give attention to the public reading of Scripture, to exhortation and teaching. 14 Do not neglect the spiritual gift within you, which was bestowed on you through prophetic utterance with the laying on of hands by the presbytery. 15 Take pains with these things; be absorbed in them, so that your progress will be evident to all. 16 Pay close attention to yourself and to your teaching; persevere in these things, for as you

*do this you will ensure salvation both for yourself and
for those who hear you.*

I desire to live as **a good and faithful servant** for Jesus. I feel strongly that the story I have shared with you is what God intends for us to know in these last days. I encourage you, again, to research my comments for yourselves to determine if they are right for you. Can I answer all possible questions regarding God's plans? **No.** That would be impossible and also not my job. Everybody has a responsibility to discover their own path with God and to do research on their own. Test everything for yourself against the Bible provided to you from our Lord for your benefit. My intention has been to open a thought process and contribute a viable option of coming events. Hopefully, this information has enhanced your levels of joy, peace, understanding, and personal relationship with the Lord for His ultimate glory. To recap:

2 Timothy 3:16–17
*16 All Scripture is inspired by God and profitable for
teaching, for reproof, for correction, for training in
righteousness; 17 so that the man of God may be adequate,
equipped for every good work.*

2 Peter 1:20–21
*20 But know this first of all, that no prophecy of Scripture
is a matter of one's own interpretation, 21 for no prophecy
was ever made by an act of human will, but men moved by
the Holy Spirit spoke from God.*

Man did not create the Bible. They scribed the books through the inspiration of God through the Holy Spirit, and it is therefore 100 percent reliable.

James 1:22–25
*22 But prove yourselves doers of the word, and not merely
hearers who delude themselves. 23 For if anyone is a hearer*

of the word and not a doer, he is like a man who looks at his natural face in a mirror; 24 for once he has looked at himself and gone away, he has immediately forgotten what kind of person he was. 25 But one who looks intently at the perfect law, the law of liberty, and abides by it, not having become a forgetful hearer but an effectual doer, this man will be blessed in what he does.

Christians are not to simply listen to the Word; we are to do what it says.

Psalm 33:4
4 For the word of the Lord is upright and all His work is done in faithfulness.

The Lord is faithful in all He does.

Psalm 119:97–104
*97 Oh, how I love your law! I meditate on it all day long.
98 Your commands are always with me and make me wiser than my enemies.
99 I have more insight than all my teachers, for Your testimonies are my meditation.
100 I understand more than the aged, because I have observed your precepts.
101 I have restrained my feet from every evil way that I may keep Your word.
102 I have not turned aside from Your ordinances, for You Yourself have taught me.
103 How sweet are Your words to my taste, yes, sweeter than honey to my mouth!
104 From Your precepts I get understanding; Therefore I hate every false way.*

These Old Testament Psalm verses refer to the "*law*." The law represents 613 moral commandments contained in the first five books of the Old Testament (*the Pentateuch*) and, specifically, Leviticus. God required mankind to adhere to them.

Because God knew we could never follow the *law* perfectly, He provided us with a pardon through the sacrifice of His Son, Jesus, on the cross. This gave us **"grace"** for all our sins, no longer subject to the *law*. Christians may substitute *law* in these verses with the word **gospel**. The first four books of the New Testament contain the four Gospels. When you meditate on the **Gospels**, God provides joy, peace, wisdom, understanding, protection, perseverance, appreciation, forgiveness and grace. The **Gospels** teach us about the **full forgiveness and grace** of God.

Hebrews 4:12–13

12 For the word of God is living and active and sharper than any two-edged sword, and piercing as far as the division of soul and spirit, of both joints and marrow, and able to judge the thoughts and intentions of the heart. 13 And there is no creature hidden from His sight, but all things are open and laid bare to the eyes of Him with whom we have to do.

These verses tell us how the Bible is alive, precise, and powerful.

Remember: all through the Bible, Jesus tells us stories. He talks about history—the present and the future. He tells of His desires and explains how to live and act in life. His instruction and oratory often reveal something specific about His personality, makeup, abilities, and overall character. Even though He uses these characteristics in designated verses in a particular context, they also have deeper overall meanings. In Matthew 10, Jesus provides instructions to His disciples on how to serve. They yield a couple of clear examples:

Matthew 10:26–31

26 *"Therefore do not fear them, <u>for there is nothing concealed that will not be revealed, or hidden that will not be known.</u> 27 What I tell you in the darkness, speak in the light; and what you hear whispered in your ear, proclaim upon the housetops. 28 Do not fear those who kill the body but are unable to kill the soul; but rather fear Him who is able to destroy both soul and body in hell. 29Are not two sparrows sold for a cent? And yet not one of them will fall to the ground apart from your Father. 30 <u>But the very hairs of your head are all numbered.</u> 31 So do not fear; you are more valuable than many sparrows.["]*

In verse 26, Jesus says *"for there is nothing concealed that will not be revealed, or hidden that will not be known."* In verse 30, *"But the very hairs of your head are all numbered."*

Even though in context He is talking to His disciples, we can derive comfort from these two representations of His nature. Example 1: Jesus tells us God does *"nothing in secret that will not be revealed."* This is why we have the Bible. God has no plans in the last days to be secretive about telling us what is happening. God's full disclosure is evident in His Scriptures. Example 2: *"But the very hairs on our heads are numbered."* God is precise and has everything well planned out. Both examples 1 and 2 yield intentions and attributes of Jesus. They build upon themselves through the entire text to create a full picture of His grandeur.

Revelation 1:3

3 *Blessed is he who reads and those who hear the words of the prophecy, and heed the things which are written in it; for the time is near.*

Please remember, all the individual books of the Bible, completed more than 1,900 years ago and then combined into the official Canonical Bible (*God's 66 book library*), were by Divine intervention. The Bible has predicted things that are actually happening today right before our eyes. The mathematical odds that this could be happening in an expressed sequence for us to see at this time, as predicted between 4,000 and 2,000 years ago, are astronomical.

As an architect, when I design buildings, I draw detailed plans showing how to construct them — right down to the multiple different types and sizes of nails to use to put them together. Of course, God is a whole lot smarter than I am. From my perspective, His 66-volume library of writings provides us with an incredibly detailed set of blueprints for our current time in history — flawlessly designed and extremely precise — and absolutely in no way a matter of random chance.

The Bible's **credibly** shows us we are truly in the end times. The world has hit the iceberg and now spirals down. The only question remaining: how many people will be able or even willing to get into the lifeboats? I thought this an appropriate analogy as we just passed the after the 107th anniversary of the sinking of the Titanic. Its sinking makes a fitting metaphor. The only difference: God has provided enough lifeboats for everybody on this earth, but individuals need to enter of their own free will. Sadly, few will choose to enter a boat.

John 3:3

[3] *Jesus answered and said to him, "Truly, truly, I say to you, unless one is born again he cannot see the kingdom of God."*

APPENDIX B

WHO ARE CHRISTIANS?

By God's Biblical standards, how can we know with certainty that we are truly believers in Christ?

What is God's simple process for nonbelievers to become believers in Christ?

Who are Christians? The Bible gives us answers. God provides a great deal of information so we can make a decision either to accept His Son, Jesus, as our Savior, our Messiah, or not to accept Him. Choosing Jesus allows someone eternal life with God. Not accepting Him will send someone somewhere else, a place that is extremely horrible, a real location. All human souls will live forever, so a right choice in this life is critical.

A Christian is a person who has accepted that Jesus Christ is the Jewish God/man who was prophesied in the Old Testament (*the Tanakh*), **the Jewish Messiah!** This man was a rabbi, He was a Jew, is still a Jew today sitting at the right hand of God the Father and will always be a Jew both inside the Millennium and forever into the Eternal Order. What this means today is that, "in reality," **as a Christian, I am an adopted Jew**, one who has accepted Jesus as my promised Jewish Messiah. **Jesus is my Lord and my God.** This fact holds great significance.

C. S. Lewis (*1898–1963*), a noted author, scholar, and Christian apologist, wrote about Jesus:

> "*I am trying here to prevent anyone saying the really foolish thing that people often say about Him: 'I'm ready to accept Jesus as a great moral teacher, but I don't accept His claim to be God. That is the one thing we must not say.' A man who was merely a man and said the sort of things Jesus said would not be a great moral teacher. He would either be a lunatic — on the level with the man who says he is a poached egg — or else he would be the Devil of Hell. You must make your choice. Either this man was, and is, the Son of God, or else a madman or something worse. You can shut him up for a fool, you can spit at him and kill him as a demon or you can fall at His feet and call Him Lord and God, but let us not come with any patronizing nonsense about His being a great human teacher. He has not left that open to us. He did not intend to.*"

Appendix B: Who are Christians?

Many people think of Jesus as simply a good and kind man and believe that acknowledging Him as a **great moral teacher** classifies them as **Christians**. They find no need to accept Christ as God. This represents a grave error in thinking.

Others think of the title **Christian** as generic, referring to a good person who believes in any god . . . a totally inaccurate assessment. To become a true Christian, per the Bible, Jesus requires specific acknowledgments and concessions. Jesus requires some simple actions from us to become a true *"born again"* believer. To be saved, a person must be *"born again."*

Apostasy has marginalized and demeaned the term *"born again."* Some so-called Christians have told me the term *"born again"* bothers them. If you feel this way, please consider what **Jesus Himself** says regarding being *"born again."*

<u>John 3:3</u>
³ Jesus answered and said to him, "Truly, truly, I say to you, unless one is <u>born again</u> he cannot see the kingdom of God."

<u>John 3:7</u>
⁷ ["]Do not be amazed that I said to you, 'You must be <u>born again</u>.'["]

<u>1 Peter 1:3</u>
³ Blessed be the God and Father of our Lord Jesus Christ, who according to His great mercy has caused us to be <u>born again</u> to a living hope through the resurrection of Jesus Christ from the dead.

<u>1 Peter 1:23</u>
²³ for you have been <u>born again</u> not of seed which is perishable but imperishable, that is, through the living and enduring word of God.

Being *"born again"* has a specific spiritual meaning and significance. But first, we need to fully understand who Jesus is and His great importance related to our ultimate eternal salvation. The Bible is all about Jesus, so let's look at a sampling from the Scriptures describing who Jesus is:

Matthew 1:21
21 She will bear a Son; and you shall call His name Jesus, for He will save His people from their sins.

John 3:35-36
35 The Father loves the Son and has given all things into His hand. 36 He who believes in the Son has eternal life; but he who does not obey the Son will not see life, but the wrath of God abides on him.

John 8:23-24
23 And He was saying to them, "You are from below, I am from above; you are of this world, I am not of this world. 24 Therefore I said to you that you will die in your sins; for unless you believe that I am He, you will die in your sins."

John 10:25-30
25 Jesus answered them, "I told you, and you do not believe; the works that I do in My Father's name, these testify of Me. 26 But you do not believe because you are not of My sheep. 27 My sheep hear My voice, and I know them, and they follow Me; 28 and I give eternal life to them, and they will never perish; and no one will snatch them out of My hand. 29 My Father, who has given them to Me, is greater than all; and no one is able to snatch them out of the Father's hand. 30 I and the Father are one."

John 11:25-27
25 Jesus said to her, "I am the resurrection and the life; he who believes in Me will live even if he dies, 26 and everyone who lives and believes in Me will never die. Do you believe this?"

[27]She said to Him, "Yes, Lord; I have believed that You are the Christ, the Son of God, even He who comes into the world."

John 14:6

[6] Jesus said to him, "I am the way, and the truth, and the life; no one comes to the Father but through Me.["]

John 20:29

[29] Jesus said to him, "Because you have seen Me, have you believed? Blessed are they who did not see, and yet believed."

Acts 4:12

[12] And there is salvation in no one else; for there is no other name under heaven that has been given among men by which we must be saved.

1 Corinthians 12:3

[3] Therefore I make known to you that no one speaking by the Spirit of God says, "Jesus is accursed"; and no one can say, "Jesus is Lord," except by the Holy Spirit.

1 John 5:9–12

[9] If we receive the testimony of men, the testimony of God is greater; for the testimony of God is this, that He has testified concerning His Son. [10] The one who believes in the Son of God has the testimony in Himself; the one who does not believe God has made Him a liar, because he has not believed in the testimony that God has given concerning His Son. [11] And the testimony is this, that God has given us eternal life, and this life is in His Son. [12] He who has the Son has the life; he who does not have the Son of God does not have the life.

1 Timothy 2:3–6

[3] This is good and acceptable in the sight of God our Savior, [4] who desires all men to be saved and to come to the knowledge of the truth. [5] For there is one God, and one mediator also between God and men, the man Christ

Jesus, ⁶ who gave Himself as a ransom for all, the testimony given at the proper time.

John 3:16
¹⁶ For God so loved the world, that He gave His only begotten Son, that whoever believes in Him shall not perish, but have eternal life.

These verses speak for themselves. Let's, however, review a couple of repeated categorical statements. 1 Timothy 2:5 says that *"there is one God, and one mediator also between God and men, the man Christ Jesus,"* His Son. Acts 4:12 tells us *"there is salvation in no one else"*; Jesus is the only way. The majority of these verses make it clear that judgment will come to those who do not accept Jesus. The good news: grace, salvation, and forgiveness await all those who truly accept Him. To get to know Jesus a bit better, I recommend reading the four Gospels, the first four books of the New Testament: *Matthew, Mark, Luke,* and *John.*

Why do we need a Savior, a mediator, somebody to intercede for our sins with the Father in the form of Jesus? Due to sin, we need grace, forgiveness, and salvation leading to eternal life, attainable only through Jesus. This sin problem goes back to the original transgression by Adam and Eve, prompted by Satan in the Garden of Eden. The process of atonement for sins in the Old Testament is quite detailed, so I will try to simply explain the overall concept of why Jesus holds such great importance.

Because of sin, God provided the Law for all people to obey. Per the Old Testament—specifically, the first seven chapters of *Leviticus*—when somebody sinned, God required a blood sacrifice to atone for each specific sin activity. God required sacrifice to make things **right and whole** again . . . usually the sacrifice of a **pure, unblemished lamb**.

Shedding the lamb's blood, an act of obedience, washed away the sin committed and made things right again with God. He never intended sin for mankind. When Adam and Eve sinned in the garden, they essentially let the genie out of the bottle. Both sin and death entered the world. This necessitated the sacrificial system to be established. God would have preferred not to go the sacrifice route, but man—His creation—gave Him no choice.

But why did God require such a severe atonement for sin? The killing of an animal, the shedding of its blood, the taking of its life for correcting sin, seems so Draconian . . . exceedingly drastic and purposefully so. God is perfect—sinless; to Him, sin of any size is a serious thing. So serious, in fact, that He cannot even look upon it. What better way to show His creation the seriousness of sin than by requiring a blood sacrifice as the only way to atone for it . . . a highly **visual** way to show us all how severe sin actually is in the eyes of God. **Sin is death!** God knew all along, from the beginning of time, that man would choose the sin option. But He requires perfection. He knew the very minute when Adam and Eve opened sin's door that no created human could cure this disease. So out of pure love, God intervened. He gave mankind a feasible remedy for the entire sin problem through His Old Testament sacrificial system, explained in *Leviticus*. But it turned out futile. Mankind had no way to put the genie back in the bottle. Again, fortunately, for us, God had, from the beginning, designed a way to fix this problem once and for all. The solution came through His only begotten Son, Jesus the Christ, **the Lamb of God**.

God sent His one and only **perfect Son, Jesus,** into the world to die on the cross, and to become the **final, perfect, unblemished sacrifice** for us all. Jesus is the only human who lived a **perfect** life on earth, ever. By the shedding of His blood on the cross for us, Jesus fulfilled the Law (*Scriptural prophecy*) and became the final pure sacrifice. Jesus did it once, and for all time, through the shedding of His own blood, and His death. Then God resurrected Him, and today He sits at the right hand of the Father in heaven.

By accepting Jesus as our personal Savior, we have essentially fulfilled the Law through His blood sacrifice for us. By accepting Jesus as our Savior, we are indeed saved by His perfect grace. God forgives us for all our sins, and we have accepted salvation and eternal life through Him. **Through the faith of Jesus**, and our **placing our faith in Him**, God sees us as perfect — washed by the blood of the **Lamb of God**. **We have been purified <u>through the love of Jesus</u>**. God always desires to make things right . . . precisely why Jesus holds so much importance for us all individually.

When the Bible talks about sin, it specifically points out actions that **<u>God considers unacceptable</u>**. However, the only unforgivable sin today comes with non-acceptance of Jesus as our Savior. Even after salvation we will all still sin, but **<u>through the love of Jesus</u>** God forgives all transgressions. He requires us to acknowledge and confess to Him when we sin and always faithfully forgives us through **grace . . . free, unmerited favor.**

All sins as "**<u>defined by God,</u>**" big or small — are the same to Him with no distinction. God gives both heavenly and worldly consequences for sins. Some sins have a much larger range of human consequences, but God sees only black or white, right or wrong. Sin, of any size, is sin. Note a few of God's issues:

1 Corinthians 6:9–11
⁹ Or do you not know that the unrighteous will not inherit the kingdom of God? Do not be deceived; neither <u>fornicators</u>, nor <u>idolaters</u>, nor <u>adulterers</u>, nor <u>effeminate</u>, nor <u>homosexuals</u>, ¹⁰ nor <u>thieves</u>, nor <u>the covetous</u>, nor <u>drunkards</u>, nor <u>revilers</u>, nor <u>swindlers</u>, will inherit the kingdom of God. ¹¹ Such were some of you; but you were washed, but you were sanctified, but you were justified in the name of the Lord Jesus Christ and in the Spirit of our God.

God does not condone "**anything <u>He</u> qualifies as sin.**" In the verses above, **there are 10 specific traits listed** that, **without**

Jesus, will keep someone from *"inheriting the Kingdom of God."* Note something profound mentioned here: *"Such were some of you."* If we accept Jesus as our Savior, God gives grace and full forgiveness for all our transgressions, **including the 10 traits listed above**. None of the activities listed in 1 Corinthians 6:9–11 is more hideous to God than any of the others. All of them have a listed consequence. He cannot even look upon them. **To God, sin is sin — period!** Also, **when we accept Jesus** we instantly change from **spiritual death** into **spiritual life** through Christ. This is becoming *"born again,"* as explained earlier. In this earthly life, and in our worldly bodies, we will all struggle with sin, yes, **even after salvation**. We do however, all need to work out our sinful imperfections and traits, individually, on a personal level with God alone, through prayer.

How does God tell Christians to relate to people in this life? He tells us how He judges, and what He requires of us regarding judgment and association with others. We also learn about different ways to relate and associate with believers and nonbelievers:

Matthew 7:1–5
[1] *"Do not judge so that you will not be judged.* [2] *For in the way you judge, you will be judged; and by your standard of measure, it will be measured to you.* [3] *Why do you look at the speck that is in your brother's eye, but do not notice the log that is in your own eye?* [4] *Or how can you say to your brother, 'Let me take the speck out of your eye,' and behold, the log is in your own eye?* [5] *You hypocrite, first take the log out of your own eye, and then you will see clearly to take the speck out of your brother's eye.["]*

1 Corinthians 5:9–13
[9] *I wrote you in my letter not to associate with immoral people;* [10] *I did not at all mean with the immoral people of this world, or with the covetous and swindlers, or with idolaters, for then you would have to go out of the*

> *world.* ¹¹ *But actually, I wrote to you not to associate with any so-called brother if he is an immoral person, or covetous, or an idolater, or a reviler, or a drunkard, or a swindler—not even to eat with such a one.* ¹² *For what have I to do with judging outsiders? Do you not judge those who are within the church?* ¹³ *But those who are outside, God judges.* <u>*Remove the wicked man from among yourselves*</u>*.*

In Matthew 7:1-5, God tells us how not to judge others, because we also will receive judgment. These verses also tell us how we should look at fellow believers or *"brothers."*

In 1 Corinthians 5:12, the Lord asks a question: *"Do you not judge those who are within the church?"* Yes, we are to judge only those inside the church; those outside the church God will deal with. This is not a judgment of condemnation and guilt, but one of compassion and guidance. God wants us to lovingly reprove wayward professed Christians *"within the church,"* to compassionately help our friends when they are possibly walking down a dangerous path. God wants us to help and support each other. But we must never be dogmatic.

In 1 Corinthians 5:9-12, the Lord explains how we are to deal with *"immoral people."* He talks here about only *"brothers"* — people who proclaim to be Christians—believers not following what God expects of us in His Word. The Bible even tells us *"not even to eat with such a one."* This refers to so-called believers who justify certain activities in their lives—issues God considers sinful. These believers wholeheartedly feel that a loving God accepts alternate ways of looking at things, even when in full contradiction to the Bible. They consider those who believe in God's written Word, literally, to be intolerant, unloving, and ungodly—for not accepting their flawed, alternate views, attached to God, in error. Worse yet, when disagreements escalate into confrontation, they willfully take their family, fellow Christians, who disagree with their flawed Biblical interpretations, into the **secular court system,** a court system that, by honest analytical review of case outcomes over the last 50 years, has attacked and sided almost totally against all true Biblical standards.

The government, as a whole, has taken God out of schools, public parks, government buildings, and institutions. We have blatantly endured a flawed version of "**separation of church and state**," against God . . . in His face. The original concept of the founding fathers was to keep the **government** out of the **church**, but today we live under the corrupted opposite viewpoint. In the last days, rebellious **quasi-Christians** may obtain shallow human court victories against the true Bible. God is not happy when this occurs. All of this happens today, as God has told us it would. One cannot truly love God and blatantly deny what He says in His Word. This is utter folly and self-serving rebellion.

If, after accepting Jesus, a Christian sins, does this mean he will lose his salvation? **May it never be!** God asks us not to associate with "*brothers*" who persistently sin; otherwise, others will see us as validating inappropriate behaviors. God wants us, as believers, to represent Him accurately, by His expressed Biblical standards.

Now, on the other hand, if we have non-Christian friends, our allowable relationships with them are entirely different. By their own validation, they do not accept Jesus, and per 1 Corinthians 5:10, we are allowed to freely associate with them. We do not need to try to address their life's sinful activities in any way. God will do this, personally, per 1 Corinthians 5:13. We are not to join in any inappropriate sin activities with them, but God wants us near them so we can be ambassadors for the Lord, 2 Corinthians 5:20. Hopefully, they will see something about us, the light of Jesus within our spirit, and we may gain the opportunity, by their own invitation, to share about Jesus. When we are given this opportunity, our sharing must be done with patience, love, and kindness.

In 1 Corinthians 5:13, God tells us to "*Remove the wicked man from among yourselves.*" So, who is the wicked man? A practicing Christian who wholeheartedly embraces any sin nature and also the unbeliever, so far lost he could impose a threat to a Christian spiritually or physically.

Matthew 7:21–23 and 1 John 2:18–19 teach us that God tells us not everyone who professes to be a Christian truly qualifies. Some are in the church today and do not realize "*they were not really of us.*" Just because some people think of themselves as Christians and talk the talk doesn't guarantee salvation. Jesus tells us many people who profess His name openly will not receive salvation—specifically, because they have taken His words in the Bible and from a human perspective have changed them into something He never intended. When anyone departs from or **modifies** God's specific "*laws*" in His Bible, this is "*lawlessness*":

Matthew 7:21–23
21 "Not everyone who says to Me, 'Lord, Lord,' will enter the kingdom of heaven, but he who does the will of My Father who is in heaven will enter. 22 Many will say to Me on that day, 'Lord, Lord, did we not prophesy in Your name, and in Your name cast out demons, and in Your name perform many miracles?' 23And then I will declare to them, 'I never knew you: depart from Me, you who practice lawlessness.'["]

1 John 2:18–19
18 Children, it is the last hour; and just as you heard that Antichrist is coming, even now many Antichrists have appeared; from this we know that it is the last hour. 19 They went out from us, but <u>they were not really of us</u>; for if they had been of us, they would have remained with us; but they went out, so that it would be shown that they all are not of us.

Appendix B: Who are Christians?

Every individual needs to assess for themselves if they do truly abide in God's Word. We need to be wise, not foolish.

Ecclesiastes 10:2

² A wise man's heart directs him toward the <u>right</u>, but the foolish man's heart directs him toward the <u>left</u>.

Matthew 25:31–34

[The Judgment] ³¹ "But when the Son of Man comes in His glory, and all the angels with Him, then He will sit on His glorious throne. ³² All the nations will be gathered before Him; and He will separate them from one another, as the shepherd separates the sheep from the goats; ³³ and He will put the <u>sheep on His right</u>, and the <u>goats on the left</u>. ³⁴ "Then the King will say to <u>those on His right</u>, 'Come, you who are blessed of My Father, inherit the kingdom prepared for you from the foundation of the world.['"]

Matthew 25:41 and 46

⁴¹ "Then He will also say to <u>those on His left</u>, 'Depart from Me, accursed ones, into the eternal fire which has been prepared for the devil and his angels;['] . . . ⁴⁶ These will go away into eternal punishment, but the righteous into eternal life."

God defines wisdom and foolishness from His perspective. Note: God defines wisdom in Ecclesiastes 10:2. Then, in His final Judgment period, Matthew 25:31–34, 41, and 46, He tells us about blessings and punishments based on the direction in which we guide our hearts. Finally, He tells us of certain consequences we will endure based on our decisions.

Because of Adam and Eve's original sin in the Garden of Eden, we now come into the world as sinners at birth. Due to original sin, we are currently spiritual beings inside an earthly, imperfect body. God has set all souls (*all our spirits*) to live on forever into eternity. The question: which eternity will we choose?

In John 14:2–3, God tells us about heaven, a place in the presence of God. He also tells us vividly in Matthew 13:49–50 and 2 Thessalonians 1:6–9 about a place of darkness . . . eternal separation from God. For Christians, eternal separation from God would be **Hell**, so let's call it that. We get to choose our own eternal destiny by the choice of free will. This means **the only person in this world who can place us into Hell is ourselves!**

Jesus talks a great deal in the Bible about **Hell** as **a real and horrible place**. Hell has many pseudonyms. In the Old Testament, it is *Sheol, the grave, death and destruction,* and *the pit.* In the New Testament, it is *Hell, Hades, eternal fire, furnace of fire, lake of fire, the second death,* and, most horrible of all, *separation from God.* God tells us **Hell** is both eternal and torments *"forever and ever"* in the following verse:

Matthew 25:41
[41] *"Then He will also say to those on His left, 'Depart from Me, accursed ones, into the eternal fire which has been prepared for the devil and his angels[.'"]*

Revelation 20:9–11
[9] *And they came up on the broad plain of the earth and surrounded the camp of the saints and the beloved city, and fire came down from heaven and devoured them.* [10] *And the devil who deceived them was thrown into the lake of fire and brimstone, where the beast and the false prophet are also;* <u>*and they will be tormented day and night forever and ever.*</u>

Here are some additional verses for consideration:
- *Psalm 30:3*
- *Psalm 49:13–14*
- *Job 24:19*
- *Proverbs 15:24*
- *Matthew 5:22*
- *Matthew 10:28*

- *Mark 9:42–48*
- *Revelation 14:9–11*

In all of these verses, Jesus tells us about **a literal Hell**. In Matthew 25:41, God tells us whom Hell was prepared for: **not for man** but for the Devil and his angels. Unfortunately, when Adam and Eve sinned, after being enticed by Satan, the door to Hell was opened for man to enter. This was not God's intention, but man chose this option. This is why we so desperately need Jesus to save us.

To expand on an earlier point, the Lord presented the *"born again"* concept as a way to explain accepting personal spiritual rebirth. When individuals realize what sin really does within their souls, many seek out and desire a pardon—offered to mankind only through Jesus.

Romans 10:9-13 provides us with the steps an individual must complete to become *"born again."* These issues are personal between one individual and God, one on one.

Romans 10:9–13
⁹ that if you confess with your mouth Jesus as Lord, and believe in your heart that God raised Him from the dead, you will be saved; ¹⁰ for with the heart a person believes, resulting in righteousness, and with the mouth he confesses, resulting in salvation. ¹¹ For the Scripture says, whoever believes in Him will not be disappointed. ¹² For there is no distinction between Jew and Greek; for the same Lord is Lord of all, abounding in riches for all who call on Him; ¹³ for Whoever will call on the name of the Lord will be saved.

To become a true *"born again"* Christian, people must accept and understand some Godly characteristics of Jesus and some humbling truths about themselves:

1. Acknowledge they are a sinner.

2. Understand they need a pardon—possible only through accepting Jesus as their Savior.
3. Believe Jesus died on the cross for their sins.
4. Accept by faith Jesus' resurrection on the third day.
5. Accept by faith that God raised Him from the dead.
6. Accept by faith that Jesus sits at the right hand of God today.
7. Believe that Jesus is the King of kings and Lord of lords.

Then, one must do the following two easy steps listed in Romans 10:9. If you:

1. *"confess with your mouth Jesus as Lord"*
2. *"believe in your heart that God raised Him from the dead, you will be saved."*

After completing these two simple steps, I suggest offering up a verbal prayer to God similar to this:

Dear Jesus,
I am a sinner, and I am thankful for Your forgiveness. I accept You, Jesus, as my personal Savior. Thank you for taking my sins upon Yourself, on the cross, shedding Your blood for me, and for saving me through Your loving grace. I know You live today and are sitting at the right hand of the Father. Thank you, Jesus, for saving my life.
I love you, Lord.

Once a person completes these simple steps, they have entered into a new, perfect **spiritual relationship with Jesus**, thusly **born again**. At this point, new Christians obtain a full pardon, perfect eternal grace, and full forgiveness through Jesus, from God the Father. **They can never lose it!**

The Bible lists no other earthly actions or rituals that anyone must follow from this point forward to keep or maintain salvation. **Jesus completed everything on the cross.** If any church system requires anyone to do any kind of **works** or **actions** to maintain salvation, then grace has no true meaning. Proclaiming that God requires worldly **works** or **actions** to maintain salvation is **false doctrine**.

New **born-again** Christians can now freely work out their personal life issues directly with the Lord. This requires no third party; we need only to read the Bible and pray within a new, special loving relationship with Jesus. **Born-again** Christians receive a strong veil of protection from God:

Romans 8:38–39
[38] For I am convinced that neither death, nor life, nor angels, nor principalities, nor things present, nor things to come, nor powers, [39] nor height, nor depth, nor any other created thing, will be able to separate us from the love of God, which is in Christ Jesus our Lord.

Christianity is like a marriage proposal by Jesus to our souls . . . a very intimate thing. We can accept His proposal only prior to our physical death in this world. We have the ability to accept Jesus only until our last breath in this life. Because unexpected events might occur in our lives each day and with longevity unknown, this decision should not be taken lightly. At risk is eternal life with God, or eternal separation from Him (**Hell!**).

1 Thessalonians 5:3–6

3 *While they are saying, "Peace and safety!" Then destruction will come upon them suddenly like labor pains upon a woman with child, and they will not escape.* 4 *But you, brethren, are not in darkness, that the day would overtake you like a thief;* 5 *for you are all sons of light and sons of day. We are not of night nor of darkness;* 6 *so then let us not sleep as others do, but let us be alert and sober.*

APPENDIX C

IMMINENCE?

The Bible clearly tells us that the visual Rapture should not come as a surprise to Christians. We are to literally expect its arrival and be prepared to actually see Jesus coming in the clouds.

The **imminence doctrine** defines what we refer to as the Rapture as non-visual and in secret, something that will happen at any moment, without any warning—without any prophecies or **"signs"** preceding this event. Some Bible teachers justify this inaccurate doctrine by using Bible verses that include the phrases *"at hand"* or *"quickly"* in their texts. These teachers seem to imply the phrases *"at hand"* or *"quickly"* both mean "imminent," which is a weak interpretation of the original Greek Biblical text. In all of these verses, when we see the phrases *"at hand"* or *"quickly,"* they actually mean **it is certain to happen**—a large and very significant distinction.

The *"last days"* actually started at Pentecost (*the day the Holy Spirit came upon the disciples*) and, therefore, the Rapture could happen at any time with no *"signs"* needed beforehand (*therefore imminent*). A detailed study of Joel 2 completely dispels this concept.

I propose a couple of questions about imminence for those who still feel strongly in favor of this weak, secret Rapture concept. What Biblical text literally describes this theory? Might it possibly be the Scriptures telling us the Rapture happens in the *"twinkling of an eye"* or *"at a day and hour when we least expect it"*? What about *"nobody, not even Jesus, knows the day or time but only the Father"*? These proclamations from the Bible—when originally spoken by **Jesus, as a human man**, during His earthly life here—were, at that moment in history, true:

Philippians 2:5-9
5 Have this attitude in yourselves which was also in Christ Jesus, 6 who, although He existed in the form of God, did not regard equality with God a thing to be grasped, 7 but emptied Himself, taking the form of a bondservant, and being made in the likeness of men. 8 Being found in appearance as a man, He humbled Himself by becoming obedient to the point of death, even death on a

cross. *9 For this reason also, God highly exalted Him, and bestowed on Him the name which is above every name[.]*

When Jesus became a human man, He *"emptied Himself"* temporarily of some of the attributes of God and took on the *"likeness of man."* He needed to be a real man, with restricted knowledge to His authority, to be able to fulfill His mission on the cross.

John 17:1-5
1 Jesus spoke these things; and lifting up His eyes to heaven, He said, "Father, the hour has come; glorify Your Son, that the Son may glorify You, 2 even as You gave Him authority over all flesh, that to all whom You have given Him, He may give eternal life. 3 This is eternal life, that they may know You, the only true God, and Jesus Christ whom You have sent. 4 I glorified You on the earth, having accomplished the work which You have given Me to do. 5 Now, Father, glorify Me together with Yourself, with the glory which I had with You before the world was.["]

When Jesus completed His work on the cross, after His resurrection, in John 17:5, He asked God to **glorify Himself back together with the Father**, essentially asking the Father to give Him back all the authority He had in heaven *"before the world was."* Today, Jesus has full, unlimited knowledge. **He is a full equal part of our triune God** and knows all—including when the Rapture will happen.

What really happens in the *"twinkling of an eye"*? We addressed this earlier, it is not the Rapture, but all our bodies changing at the final trumpet. A group of people here on earth at the start of the visual Rapture event will get *"caught by surprise."* But not Christians; it is the secular nonbelievers, as also explained earlier.

God never planned for the Rapture to be a surprise event; it is Satan who wants us to think this. If we do not follow God's explicit teachings, we may experience some unwarranted fear and will not get our crown. Please do not be deceived.

Luke 12:35–37
³⁵ Be dressed in readiness, and <u>keep your lamps lit</u>. ³⁶ Be like men who are waiting for their master when he returns from the wedding feast, so that they may immediately <u>open the door to him</u> when he comes and knocks. ³⁷ Blessed are those slaves whom the master will find <u>on the alert</u> when he comes[.]

God wants us to "*keep our lamps lit*" and to know what the Bible tells us about the visual Rapture event, so we can stay alert in readiness to open the door for Him, so to speak, upon His return. But how can we know the process necessary to stay "*alert*" and ready to "*open the door for him*"? If God meant to hide the Rapture from us or for us not to expect it, He wouldn't have told us to prepare. Why would He have us stay alert, if the Rapture were a hidden surprise event? Those of us in the light must understand about the visual Rapture and its arrival. Putting our lamps on the lampstands means God is asking us to share this light with others. This includes telling our Christian friends to understand what will soon come upon the world.

Luke 21:34–36
³⁴ <u>Be on guard</u>, so that your hearts will not be weighted down with dissipation and drunkenness and the worries of life, and that day will not come on you suddenly like a trap; ³⁵ for it will come upon all those who dwell on the face of all the earth. ³⁶ But <u>keep on the alert</u> at all times, praying that you may have strength to escape all these things that are about to take place, and to stand before the Son of Man.

"*Be on guard.*" Do not let our earthly problems allow us to take our eyes off the ball. Stay alert and stand strong because God has given us all the information we need to know exactly when He will return. The Bible lights our way. God also wants us to pray for the strength to escape the horrors of the Tribulation. I did say *"escape"* because God Himself uses this word:

1 Thessalonians 5:1–5

¹ Now as to the times and the epochs, brethren, you have no need of anything to be written to you. ² For you yourselves know full well that the day of the Lord will come just like a <u>thief in the night</u>. ³ While they are saying, "Peace and safety!" Then destruction will come upon them suddenly like labor pains upon a woman with child, and they will not <u>escape</u>. ⁴ <u>But you, brethren, are not in darkness, that the day would overtake you like a thief</u>; ⁵ for you are all sons of light and sons of day. We are not of night nor of darkness;

1 Thessalonians 5:6–11

⁶ so then let us not sleep as others do, but let us be alert and sober. ⁷ For those who sleep do their sleeping at night, and those who get drunk get drunk at night. ⁸ But since we are of the day, let us be sober, having put on the breastplate of faith and love, and as a helmet, the hope of salvation. ⁹ For God has not destined us for wrath, but for obtaining salvation through our Lord Jesus Christ, ¹⁰ who died for us, so that whether we are awake or asleep, we will live together with Him. ¹¹ Therefore encourage one another and build up one another, just as you also are doing.

The *"thief in the night"* **does not refer to the Rapture**, but rather, specifically, to **the start of the Tribulation**. Again, God is going to *"steal away"* the secular world's supposed peace, not steal Christians away secretly in His visual rapture event.

God specifically asks all living believers not to sleep, which means staying aware, per Thessalonians 5:7–8. We are to stay alert and be ready.

God does not intend for the Rapture to be a secret event. It will be **fully visual** on a grand scale.

John 4:25–26

25 *The woman said to Him, "I know that Messiah is coming, He who is called Christ; when that One comes, He will declare all things to us."* 26 *Jesus said to her, "I who speak to you am He."*

APPENDIX D

IS JESUS THE MESSIAH?

Is Jesus truly the prophesied Jewish Messiah?

I am a Christian because of a young **Jewish rabbi**, who, along with 12 bold **Jewish young men** of His choosing, changed the world. This rabbi explained how He was the Son of God, the Promised One, not always recognized although all Biblical evidence points to Him as actually being who He said He was.

This paragraph is highly important! Again, I boldly proclaim, a true Bible-reading Christian is not the enemy of the Jew but a staunch advocate who loves the Hebrew people with great affection. As a Christians I am really an adopted Jew. I honor the God of **Abraham, Isaac, and Jacob: we're family!** The only difference between a Jew and a Christian is that the Christian has accepted **Jesus the Christ** as the Jewish God/man who was prophesied in the Tanakh—**the Jewish Messiah!** This young rabbi was a Jew, **is a living Jew today** sitting at the right hand of God the Father, and will always be a Jew, both inside a literal millennial age and then forever into the Eternal Order *(look at the new Jerusalem inside the Eternal Order in Revelations 21:10-14).* When I leave this earth to be with Jesus, I will become "**a perfect Jew**" in God's eyes, unblemished in every sense. **I look forward to this day with great joy and expectation!** Jesus is **my Messiah, my Lord and my God,** *Yahweh, Adonai, Elohim, Jehovah.*

All mankind, including the Jew, are saved by accepting Christ as our Savior, our Messiah. I tell you with great sadness that some Christian churches falsely teach that the Jews of today live under a different covenant. These churches say the Jews may have a separate path to God because Jesus never revealed His true identity to the Jewish leaders of His day. These churches maintain that, because Jesus **supposedly** never claimed to be the Messiah; Christians today do not need to try to share with the Jews regarding Him. **This view is Biblically incorrect!** Jesus did, in fact, tell the Jewish people and their leaders that He was the Christ.

I take the Scriptures literally and believe that throughout the Bible God makes it clear who the Messiah was, and still is, today. **He is Jesus Christ!** Some Scriptures from Mark and John:

Mark 14:60–63

60 The high priest stood up and came forward and questioned Jesus, saying, "Do You not answer? What is it that these men are testifying against You?" 61 But He kept silent and did not answer. Again the high priest was questioning Him, and saying to Him, "Are You the Christ, the Son of the Blessed One?" 62 And Jesus said, "I am; and you shall see the Son of Man sitting at the right hand of power, and coming with the clouds of heaven." 63 Tearing his clothes, the high priest said, "What further need do we have of witnesses?["]

John 4:25–26

25 The woman said to Him, "I know that the Messiah is coming He who is called Christ; when that One comes, He will declare all things to us." 26 Jesus said to her, "I who speak to you am He."

Jesus admitted to the Jewish high priest and the Sanhedrin that He was indeed the Messiah. They should have known Jesus spoke the truth, because they were Biblical experts and the scholars of their day. Clearly, Jesus fulfilled all the prophecies in the Tanakh confirming His identity. The Jewish rulers of the day did not accept Him as the Christ because Jesus did not fit within their limited earthly expectations. They thought (*intellectually*) God would make the Messiah a human king like David (*not an **eternal everlasting** God/man*). They considered it blasphemous that Jesus declared Himself the Messiah. These experts did not follow their own Scriptures and entirely dismissed Jesus at His first visit. The Jewish leaders did not recognize Him, due to a serious misunderstanding of what the Messiah should represent . . . the main reason Jesus will come back soon for His second coming. This time, Israel will not miss Him, to their ultimate eternal glory.

Romans 1:16–17

16 For I am not ashamed of <u>the gospel</u>, for it is the <u>power of God for salvation to everyone</u> who believes, <u>to the Jew</u>

first and also to the Greek. [17] For in it the righteousness of God is revealed from faith to faith; as it is written, "But the righteous man shall live by faith."

If God intended different paths for the Jews and the Greeks (*Gentiles*) for salvation, why did He tell us here in Romans 1:16 the *"gospel"* is the *"power of God for salvation"* (*Jesus*) *for "everyone"*? He even went so far as to say specifically *"to the Jew first."* Christians are required to witness Jesus to our Jewish family as God calls us to do. We all need Christ as our Savior. God has but one covenant given to us in the personhood and resurrection of Jesus, for all mankind, including our brothers, the Jews. In fact, in the book of Acts, God sent Paul to minister about Jesus the Messiah *"to the Jews first"* and then the Gentiles. **Paul, a Jew himself, always went to the Jews first to proclaim Jesus.** A couple of examples regarding Paul's Jewish ministry in sharing about the Messiah to the Jews of his day:

Acts 13:46

[46] Paul and Barnabas spoke out boldly and said, "It was necessary that the word of God be spoken to you first; since you repudiate it and judge yourselves unworthy of eternal life, behold, we are turning to the Gentiles.["]

Acts 14:1-7

[1] And it came about in Iconium they entered the synagogue of the Jews together, and spoke in such a manner that a large number of people believed, both of Jews and of Greeks. [2] But the Jews who disbelieved stirred up the minds of the Gentiles and embittered them against the brethren. [3] Therefore they spent a long time there speaking boldly with reliance upon the Lord, who was testifying to the word of His grace, granting that signs and wonders be done by their hands. [4] But the people of the city were divided; and some sided with the

Jews, and some with the apostles. ⁵ And when an attempt was made by both the Gentiles and the Jews with their rulers, to mistreat and to stone them, ⁶ they became aware of it and fled to the cities of Lycaonia, Lystra and Derbe, and the surrounding region; ⁷ and there they continued to preach the gospel.

As mentioned earlier and in Acts 14:1, Paul always went into the synagogue first. We also can see he did the same thing in **Acts 13:5, 13:13, 13:42, 14:1, 17:1, 17;17, 18:4–11, 19:8, 28:17, and 28:28.** This indicates how the concept of going to the Jews first is important to God. As an adopted member of the Jewish family, grafted in by God Himself, I accept and trust in my Jewish rabbi, my Messiah, **Jesus the Christ!**

If any of our current Jewish family chooses to dislike this news or even feels hate for Jesus or Christians by association for sharing about Him, please take the following information into serious consideration. Because of atrocities committed against the Jewish people in the **supposed name of Jesus** throughout history, please remember this: **misguided human beings** perpetrated all past atrocities on the Jewish people . . . **in severe contradiction to the Holy Scriptures**! As one gigantic example, **Hitler was not a Christian!** Although he claimed to be, his writings on the subject are evil, misguided non-Biblical garbage. Everything he did to the Jewish people during WWII was Satanic and had nothing to do with any valid interpretation of the true Biblical New Testament. He was a vile individual. Please do not let the actions of severely misguided, flawed, and obviously Satanically indwelled human beings cause any reason for any kind of justifiable separation from the one man who came to save us all: the Jewish man/God, Jesus the Christ.

For clarification, in reference to the Lord, Jesus Christ, these are not His first and last names. **Jesus** is **His name** and **Christ** is **His title. Christ translates as Messiah.** Actually, saying **Jesus the Christ** or **Jesus the Messiah** is more accurate.

Another interesting thought regarding the Messiah: the Jewish faith that currently does not recognize Jesus as the Messiah waits for some future leader, yet to come, through the bloodline of King David — the prophesied Messiah. This pertains to the Davidic Covenant, to my understanding, as referred to in 2 Samuel 7:

2 Samuel 7:8-13

[8] *"Now therefore, thus you shall say to My servant David, 'Thus says the Lord of hosts, "I took you from the pasture, from following the sheep, to be ruler over My people Israel. [9] I have been with you wherever you have gone and have cut off all your enemies from before you; and I will make you a great name, like the names of the great men who are on the earth. [10] I will also appoint a place for My people Israel and will plant them, that they may live in their own place and not be disturbed again, nor will the wicked afflict them any more as formerly, [11] even from the day that I commanded judges to be over My people Israel; and I will give you rest from all your enemies. The Lord also declares to you that the Lord will make a house for you. [12] When your days are complete and you lie down with your fathers, I will raise up your descendant after you, who will come forth from you, and I will establish his kingdom. [13] He shall build a house for My name, and I will establish the throne of his kingdom forever.["""]*

2 Samuel 7:16-17

[16] *["""]Your house and your kingdom shall endure before Me forever; your throne shall be established forever."""* [17] *In accordance with all these words and all this vision, so Nathan spoke to David.*

I have read about the importance of the Jewish Messiah coming through the bloodline of David. **Jesus, by the way, did fulfill this prophecy completely.** The entire Bible documents His precise lineage. As detailed earlier, in the Tanakh, God gives the significant genealogies of mankind and their ancestral relationships, in complete detail, from Adam to Abraham and Isaac in Genesis 5:1–32, 11:10–32, and 21:1–3. Interestingly, they all point to the lineage of Jesus. Is this all chance? **No.**

In the first book of the New Testament, Matthew 1:1–17, God completes the entire bloodline of Jesus by showing all accurate, verifiable genealogies from Abraham and Isaac to both Joseph and Mary. The lineage of Mary *(the correct bloodline)* Jesus' mother is pure. Joseph although the custodial earthly father of Jesus also traces back in the line of David with one flaw, **Jeconiah** (Matthew 1:12). He was not a worthy heir due to sin. By design this one flaw proved that Joseph could not be the real father of Jesus. God knew what he was doing. David appears within both genealogies — verification that Jesus was and is, to this very day, the Jewish Messiah prophesied in the Tanakh.

This now brings up some interesting questions. From the birth of Jesus by Mary, Joseph's wife, until today, have we any complete records of all the genealogies of all the 12 tribes of Israel? **No.** How would a possible future Messiah, someone other than Jesus, prove his heritage today as a direct descendent back through the bloodline of David without flaws? He couldn't. I can see no current way to prove the lineage of a future Messiah directly to David (*even through DNA*) unless our Jewish family will accept a possible bloodline relationship to David by faith alone. **Jesus is the Biblical prophesied Messiah.** He came once, and He will soon come again and prove His true identity, once and for all, to His beloved, Israel. God never abandons His family.

Did you know the world today has approximately **2.5 billion Christians** and **1.8 billion Islamic** believers? Do you know how many Jews live on the earth today? Only **14.5 million**, in a **7.7 billion total population** (2019) . . . **quite a minority**. Yet, God Himself says the **Jews are His chosen . . . His Glory**, and He wants them to acknowledge **the special Son** He sent **for their eternal blessing**.

Something unfortunate is happening today in Judaism, and it breaks my heart. Some rabbis today tell us that Mary, the mother of Jesus, was most likely a prostitute, and thusly, Jesus was a bastard child. **Do not accept this pure dreck (drek).**

The prophet Isaiah wrote one of the greatest books in the Bible. In Chapter 48, God talks about how He promises liberation for Israel. What God promises, He delivers. In Isaiah 48:16, God has foretold Israel about His Son. In fact, it is actually Jesus Himself talking to the Jewish people in this verse:

Isaiah 48:16
16 *"Come near to Me, listen to this: from the first I have not spoken in secret, from the time it took place, I was there. And now the Lord God has sent Me, and His Spirit."*

Notice in the verse above, *"And now the **Lord God** has sent **Me**, and **His Spirit**."* All through the Old Testament, *"the Lord God"* (*the Father*) refers to a sent second person, *"Me"* (*Jesus*), and a third entity, *"His Spirit,"* the Holy Spirit. The Tanakh clearly **acknowledges the Trinity**! God tells Israel today in the **Tanakh** who Jesus is and who He was from the beginning. God, as always, is **truthful** and **non-secretive** with His people, Israel. I hope today's Jews are indeed *"Coming near to God"* and *"listening"* regarding who God is, as required in Isaiah 48:16: the **God of Israel is the Trinity**!

One more highly profound verse from the prophet Isaiah offers the House of David a *"sign"* of who the Messiah will be:

Isaiah 7:13–14
13 *Then he said, "Listen now, O house of David! Is it too slight a thing for you to try the patience of men, that you will try the patience of my God as well? 14 Therefore the Lord Himself will give you a sign: Behold, a virgin will be with*

child and bear a son, and she will call His name
Immanuel.["]

The only person who has ever lived who fulfilled this prophetic sign scribed by the prophet Isaiah was **Jesus the Christ**. **God has told Israel all along who Jesus is.**

Because Israel did not recognize the Messiah, Jesus the Christ, at His first visit, Jesus tells us a Tribulation period, the 70th week of Daniel, must take place prior to His physical second coming. At the end of the Tribulation, Israel will finally accept that Jesus was and is indeed the living prophesied Messiah of the Old Testament.

In the following verses, God, through the Apostle Paul, explains how He granted Gentiles the greatest gift possible, due solely to the Jews rejecting Jesus as the Messiah at His first visit:

Romans 11:11–16
*11 I say then, they did not stumble so as to fall, did they? May it never be! **But by their transgression salvation has come to the Gentiles, to make them jealous.** 12 Now if their transgression is riches for the world and their failure is riches for the Gentiles, how much more will their fulfillment be! 13 But I am speaking to you who are Gentiles. Inasmuch then as I am an apostle of Gentiles, I magnify my ministry, 14 if somehow **I might move to jealousy my fellow countrymen and save some of them.** 15 For if their rejection is the reconciliation of the world, what will their acceptance be but life from the dead? 16 If the first piece of dough is holy, the lump is also; and if the root is holy, the branches are too.*

The Apostle Paul was a Jew, a Pharisee. He never relinquished his religion or heritage. He calls the Jewish people *"my fellow countrymen"* in Romans 11:14. The difference: he recognized Jesus to be the promised Messiah, per the Old Testament.

Just as with Paul, God requires Christians to share about Jesus with our Jewish family. Soon the world will witness the visual Rapture. So, it is imperative that we plant some seeds today, to help in the harvest of our Jewish family toward faith in Jesus, after we have departed.

At the conclusion of the visual Rapture, no Christians will remain in the world to help explain about Jesus. We must leave a strong legacy today through writings and teaching. Revelation 7:4–8 stipulates that, at the beginning of the Tribulation, 144,000 Jewish evangelists will come to know Jesus as their promised Messiah. Twelve thousand members from each of the 12 tribes of Israel make up this group. God's 144,000 will receive a seal of protection, and no harm will come to them. They will minister about the Messiah, Jesus, to the whole world for the entire Tribulation period. They will be transformed into 144,000 indestructible evangelists, vastly surpassing all contemporary counterparts — magnificent to behold.

Many Christians ask what role the United States might ultimately play in Biblical prophecy. I have seen no mention of direct involvement, but note: per the Biblical **Road Map** explained in this book, no country as defined today (*with the exception of Israel*) will retain its current identity when God allows the formation of the One World Government. The United States will have some new name in one of the new 10 kingdoms. The fact that the United States has no direct mention in the Bible lends more credence to the concept of the One World Government happening before the Tribulation begins.

In the book of Isaiah, chapter 24, God talks about the set of judgments that will come to the earth in the distant future. He talks about the judgments that will happen inside the coming Biblical Tribulation. In Isaiah 24:14–15, He explains something **interesting** and **joyful** within the midst of all the terrible troubles happening inside the Tribulation description:

Appendix D: Is Jesus the Messiah?

Isaiah 24:14–15
[14] They raise their voices, they shout for joy; <u>they cry out from the west concerning the majesty of the Lord.</u>
[15] Therefore <u>glorify the Lord in the east</u>, the name of the Lord, the God of Israel, in the coastlands of the sea.

Our Biblical assignment is to share end-time prophecy with the world so that, as events unfold, many will figure out the happenings and who Jesus really is . . . similar to helping plant some seeds for the beginning of the greatest harvest revival in all of human history. Did you know that during the Tribulation, **billions of people** living under the severe adversity of this very horrible time will come to a loving knowledge of Jesus?

Isaiah 26:9
[9] At night my soul longs for you, indeed, my spirit within me seeks You diligently; For when the earth experiences <u>Your judgments</u> the inhabitants of the world learn righteousness.

"Your judgments": the Tribulation.

I find true value in my life by offering the loving gift of an introduction of Jesus to others, especially my Jewish family. It is with humility that I ask any Jewish reader to please take a serious look at this wonderful individual, Jesus. He holds you in the highest regard and wants you to believe in Him through your free-will choice. He is at the door waiting for you to knock.

The Author

Pastor Rick Blomgren was born in Chicago, Illinois, in 1954. During his college years, an interest in end-time prophecies (*eschatology*) took shape. For more than 45 years, he has studied and researched multiple end-time prophetic theories in an effort to define what God has shared with us in His Word. **Rick's goal: to discover the most glorious version of end-times prophecy, using merely the complete Bible as his guide. To discover the version that is enlightening, joyful, and magnificent, representing the majesty, grandeur, and full glory of our Lord Jesus. Anything less is not acceptable.**

For 12 years, Rick studied with Dr. Fred Kenton (*Doc*) Beshore (*1926–2016*), until his passing on June 7, 2016. Doc was the president of the World Bible Society in Costa Mesa, California. Rick began his study work with Doc in 2004, attending his 300-person Bible study class on Sunday mornings. Study with this sagacious scholar expanded to a couple afternoons a week in his office or home, where together they explored God's prophecies in great depth on a more personal level.

Doc held five doctoral degrees in theology. He became an ordained minister in 1944 and published multiple books regarding end-times prophecy. Doc taught in multiple seminaries and pastored many churches across the nation. He honed and refined his skills under the tutelage of Dr. David L. Cooper (*1886–1965*). Dr. Cooper was a leading expert in Biblical prophecy related to Israel, during the first half of the 20th century. Doc was one of Dr. Cooper's Timothys from 1955 to 1965. Dr. Cooper developed the *Golden Rule for Biblical Interpretation*:

> *"When the plain sense of scripture makes common sense, seek no other sense; therefore, take every word at its primary, ordinary, usual, literal meaning unless the facts of the immediate context, studied in the light of related passages and axiomatic and fundamental truths indicate clearly otherwise."*

Through prayer and plain, literal *"common sense"* Bible interpretation, Rick developed a yearning to share with others what is happening in the world, explaining how today's current events purposefully validate God's Biblical prognostications for mankind's final days. For this reason, the book *Stunned* came to be.

Rick is the pastor for Revere Today Ministries in Newport Beach, California. He places a specific emphasis and passion on clear Biblical teaching of end-time prophecies. Rick is also an award-winning architect and a member of the American Institute of Architects. He has been in private practice for more than 33 years and is licensed in multiple states. Rick has been married to his wife, Jana, for 28 years.

Acknowledgments

I am deeply thankful for our Lord Jesus, who died on the cross, took away our sins, and provides grace, forgiveness, and salvation.

I am thankful for my beautiful, devoted, godly wife, Jana — the light of my life for 28 years. Without her love, support, and incredible patience, this book could not have happened.

I thank my parents, Richard and Mary Jane (*both with the Lord*), for the introduction to Jesus and planting solid roots early on.

Many thanks to my friend Burr, a bold, rugged, and graciously wise Arizonian. He provided wonderful generosity, moral support, suggestions, recommendations, and ebullient encouragement, which were vital factors in the creation of this book.

My friend Mark (*once a Catholic seminarian*) was instrumental also, as we attend Bible studies and talk about current events and how they connect with prophecies. I gained insight from his intellect, wisdom, and knowledge. He also studied with Doc Beshore along with me. Mark is a great friend, brother in Christ and a blessing from God in my life.

Also, Bob and Carol Z., kind friends for more than 30 years. I thank them for their generous financial support to this endeavor, through their Christian Charitable Organization. Bob just recently went home to be with the Lord.

Thank you, Sandy, for your tenacity, continually considering my initial writings to be a book. You finally got me to believe that a book is actually what they needed to be. I am eternally grateful.

My Beloved Teacher

In loving memory of Dr. Fred (*Doc*) Beshore (*1926–2016*)

I know God directed me to this wise, Godly sage whose knowledge of Jesus and His Word has changed my life in unimaginably profound ways.

My beloved teacher, mentor, and deeply loved friend Doc went home to be with the Lord on Tuesday, June 7, 2016.

His legacy is represented in a loving wife of 70-years Lois, a Godly family, multiple published books, and DVDs providing well-documented viewpoints regarding Biblical end-time prophecies. In this book, *STUNNED*, I have included my personalized student's perspective. In his books, he includes much more than the brief story I related.

Amazingly, when he passed, at 90 years of age, Doc still had almost total recall of the entire Bible. Sometimes it seemed as if his brain was online, maintaining a full Wi-Fi connection with the Lord . . . incredible to comprehend. I can handle a great deal of information at one time, as a detailed person, but it was almost impossible to keep up with him. He was amazing to watch. What an awesome blessing.

I am grateful that the Lord allowed me to fall within Doc's earthly orbit. Through his detailed knowledge of the Bible along with guidance from the Lord, I have been changed in fantastic ways for the service of Jesus my Christ. I am eternally grateful.

"Well done, good and faithful servant."

Love you, Doc.

For Our Skeptical Friends

If in the near future you see a major attack against Israel initiated by their neighboring enemy countries, including Russia, take note of a possible mysterious outcome. Initially, Israel will appear doomed; then miraculously, this aggression will be thwarted by **God Himself, RESCUING** Israel for His glory alone. When this happens,

THE WORLD WILL BE STUNNED!

**Mankind will have witnessed
God's two-minute warning confirming
we have arrived at the end of the age.**

After this amazing rescue occurs, if you desire to know more about what happened and the major events that must quickly follow, the Bible literally explains each of them.
This book chronicles this rescue of Israel and all the amazing prophecies we are told, in the Bible, must then soon arrive.

On this incredible day, please visit us at:
www.reveretodayministries.org

Humble Requests

If you enjoyed this book, please consider joining with me in a **grassroots effort** to get copies of *STUNNED*, the book, into the hands of all our family and friends. Many Christians are experiencing unnecessary fears about world events today. This is not God's intention for His family. God, in His Bible, is telling us what is happening today so we can *"comfort one another with these words,"* as directed in 1 Thessalonians 4:18.

WHAT IS A GRASSROOTS EFFORT?

"People at the grassroots are excited to do something amazing from the bottom up. They are especially excited to do something MEANINGFUL — in their own estimation. These are strong-minded people who, when they discover a truth or cause worthy of their time, energy, and means, are willing to let go of inhibitions, fears, and preconceptions and jump wholeheartedly into a given cause with great fervor and passion."

CONSIDER WRITING A REVIEW OF THIS BOOK ON AMAZON:

Please consider writing a **five-star** book review on Amazon. To do this, go to the book *STUNNED* on Amazon's website and share how the information in this book has positively affected your thinking regarding what God is doing in our world today.

BOLDLY SHARE THIS GOOD NEWS WITH OTHERS:

In Ephesians 6:19–20, we learn it is God's desire for us to *"boldly share His word with others."* This includes any and all good news we derive from the Lord through His entire Bible.

GOD TELLS US FEAR IS NOT AN OPTION:

In 1 John 4:16–18, God tells us *"perfect love casts out all fear."* This direction allows us to confidently offer comfort to our friends as the world severely changes in the near future.

Thank you for your consideration of these requests.
God Bless, **Rick A. Blomgren**

Revelation 22:16, 20–21

16 "I, Jesus, have sent My angel to testify to you these things for the churches. I am the root and the offspring of David, the bright morning star."

20 He who testifies to these things says, "Yes, I am coming quickly." Amen. Come, Lord Jesus.
21 The grace of the Lord Jesus be with all. Amen.

Glossary
Table of Contents

ABOMINATION OF DESOLATION – Daniel 12:11, Matthew 24:15, Daniel 11:31, Mark 13:14. This happens at the midpoint of the Tribulation, when the Antichrist appears to have been killed and comes back to life (*resuscitated*). He will enter the temple and declare himself the only true god. Everyone must take his mark (*666*), worship only him, or be put to death.

ABRAHAM (ABRAM) – Genesis 14:13. Abram is called the "Hebrew." The name Hebrew means *"the one who crosses over."* This is when God told Abram to move from Haran to Canaan, Genesis 12:1-7. God changes his name from Abram to Abraham in Genesis 17:5. He is told he will become the father of many nations.

ABRAHAMIC COVENANT – Genesis 15:18–21, Genesis 12:1-3, Genesis 17:9-14. This is God's promise to the Hebrews that He has a land prepared for them. The land extends from the Rivers of Egypt to the Euphrates River, in current-day Iraq. As part of this promise, God initiated circumcision as a requirement for all male children as an earthly sign that they were partakers of God's Abrahamic promise. (*See ISAAC; ISHMAEL*)

ABRAHAMIC PROMISE – Genesis 12:1-3. God told Abram (*Abraham*) to leave Haran with his entire family and head to the promised land of Canaan. God promised to make from Abram a great nation and to bless him and all his generations.

ADVANCE – GOD SHARED EVERYTHING IN ADVANCE – Mark 13:23, Amos 3:7, Luke 8:16–17. The BIBLE was fully completed in 95 AD when John scribed Revelation. There is no need for it to ever be updated or modified. God has clearly told us everything we need to know for our time, in advance.

A-MILLENNIALISM – The belief that Christ is presently reigning within the Church today, and that the "1,000 years" referenced in Revelation 20:1–6 is a metaphor referring to our present church age, which will culminate in Christ's return. This is not an accurate view from the Bible.

ALLAH – (*See QURAN*) Allah is the Arabic word for god. Prior to the completion of the Islamic holy book, the Quran (*632 AD*), the term Allah could have been used for any form of god. Upon completion of the Quran, this exact Arabic term took on a clear and defined meaning. Allah today describes the god of the Islamic faith and is clearly defined as a god who has no Son, a god who does not recognize the God of the Jews and Christians today.

ALL THE TREES – (*See UNITED NATIONS*)

ANALYSE OUR PRESENT TIME – Luke 12:54–56.

ANGELS – Heavenly beings created from the beginning for the service of the Lord. There are three levels of heavenly beings: the lowest are angels who have no wings; then higher are the seraphim, who have six wings; and the highest are the cherubim, who have two wings. They have many attributes. They were created for eternity (Luke 20:30), they do not marry (Matthew 22:30), they are wise (2 Samuel 14:17), they care for mankind (Luke 15:10), and they carry the good news of Jesus (Revelation 14:6). Satan was the most beautiful cherub. When he became prideful and thought he was equal to God, he fell from grace and was thrown down to earth with one-third of all the angels in heaven. (*See SATAN*)

ANGEL OF THE LORD – The Angel of the Lord is referenced all throughout the Bible. When God appears in angelic form, this is called a theophany. This angel appeared to Hagar in Genesis

16:10–13, Abraham in Genesis 22:12–15, Jacob in Genesis 31:11, Moses in Exodus 3:2–6, Stephen in Acts 7:30, and Joshua in Joshua 5:13–15. These are merely a few verses, but it is clear this represents God Himself.

ANY MOMENT – Refers to the Rapture being an IMMINENT event. This is the idea that there are no SIGNS that will precede the Lord's return in the RAPTURE based on a supposed "mystery" mentioned in 1 Corinthians 15:51–52. The problem with this is that this "mystery" was explained, by Paul, in 1 Thessalonians 4:13–18 at least 5 years earlier. (*See PROGRESSIVE REVELATION*)

APOSTASY – 2 Thessalonians 2:3, 1 Timothy 4:1, 2 Timothy 4:3–4, Hebrews 5:11–14. When the Christian Church "FALLS AWAY" from true faith in the inerrancy of the Bible and the belief that Jesus is the only way to salvation. This is when any Church places more faith in LOVE than in all Biblical TRUTH and accepts myths, false faiths, doctrines, and manmade traditions as contemporary reality in contradiction to the whole Bible.

APOSTLES – Also a term for teacher (*See DISCIPLES*). Twelve ordinary men selected by Jesus to take His gospel to the world. They are listed in Matthew 10:2 and are Simon (*Peter*), Andrew, James, John, Philip, Bartholomew, Thomas, Matthew, James, Thaddeus, Simon, and Judas. One was a devil, Judas, and would commit suicide after turning Christ over for crucifixion. These men were all appointed by Jesus Himself. After Judas' death, the apostles drew lots to elect a new replacement. They selected Matthias, per Acts 1:26. The problem was they did not have the authority to do this; only Jesus did. We find later in Acts 9:15–16 and Romans 1:1, 1:15, and 11:13 that Jesus Himself selected Paul as the new final 12th apostle, so Paul is the correct replacement.

Glossary

ANTICHRIST – Daniel 7:23–24. This is the evil leader who will come on the scene after the One World Government forms and breaks into 10 divisions. He signs the "covenant" with Israel that starts the Tribulation. At the midpoint of the Tribulation, he is apparently killed, comes back to life, and is indwelled by Satan for the last half of the Tribulation. Some distinctions: the prefix **anti-** has two meanings. In the English language, it means **against** someone or something. However, in the **original Greek** text, the prefix *"anti-"* when attached to the title given to Jesus, *"Christ,"* or *"**Messiah**,"* means *"instead of"* or *"in place of."* Therefore, using the original Greek interpretation, the **Antichrist** does not mean **against Christ**; it means **in place of Christ**. The end goal of the Antichrist is not to merely be against Christ, but to **completely replace Jesus**, making Himself God. He will proclaim himself as the only one and true god.

ANTI-SEMITISM – Psalm 83:1–4. Hostility toward or discrimination against the Hebrew people or Jews as a religious, ethnic, or racial group; basically, hatred of the Jewish people.

APOCRYPHAL BOOKS – (253) These seven books were added into the Catholic Bible, at the Council of Trent in 1546 AD. These books all intertwine within the Old Testament. They include the books of *Tobit, Judith, Wisdom, Sirach, Baruch, 1 Maccabees,* and *2 Maccabees. (See LAWS OF MOSES, THE PROPHETS, AND THE PSALMS)*

ARMAGEDDON – Ezekiel 39:17–29, Revelation 19:17–21. The battle between Jesus and all the nations of the world remaining at the end of the 7-year Tribulation after His GLORIOUS APPEARING. Jesus fights this battle on His own without any help and achieves a rapid and decisive final victory over evil. We all come back with Jesus but are only bystanders.

ARMOR OF GOD – Ephesians 6:10–13. The *"Armor of God"* is His Word, the full and complete CANON, the BIBLE.

BABYLON – An ancient city that is about 50 miles southeast of Baghdad in current-day Iraq. This was the first major civilization after the flood of Noah and was ruled by Nimrod (*a bad guy*). He was killed by a wild animal, and his wife, Semiramis, became Ishtar, the Queen of Heaven. She had a son, by a quasi-virgin birth, named Tammuz, a sun god. This was the first BABYLON MYSTERY RELIGION. The church of the last days will be similar. It will have a prominent god-like mother with a godly son. It will transform into a false unbelieving church through Biblical compromises, false doctrines, and false traditions. It will go into the 7-year Tribulation for its watering down of truth and faith in Jesus alone.

BABYLON MYSTERY RELIGION – (*See BABYLON*)

BELIEVE – See John 14:29.

BIBLE – 2 Timothy 3:16–17, John 1:1–5, 2 Peter 1:20–21, Hebrews 4:12–13. The perfect inspired Word of the God of Abraham, Isaac, and Jacob. It (*the Word*) was in the beginning; God wrote it before all creation as He knows everything from the beginning to the end of time. The Bible is not writings of men but through men inspired by the Holy Spirit.

BIRTH – (*See ISRAEL*) Matthew 24:32–24, Isaiah 66:8. In prophecy, this has turned out to be the prophesied rebirth of the State of Israel that occurred on May 14, 1948. In Isaiah, we are told about a land being born in one day. Who has heard of such a thing? We have seen this happen in our time.

BIRTH PAINS – Matthew 24:4–8. God tells us there will be birth pains (*plural*) and a birth (*See BIRTH*). This is the first of God's 24 end-time prophecies, discussed in Chapter 2.

BLESSED ARE YOUR EYES BECAUSE THEY SEE . . . – Matthew 13:16–17. God is telling us in the last days we will see His end-time prophecies happening. We are blessed and we are very lucky and special to be living at this specific moment in history. Many prophets wished they could have been alive to see all of the things happening today, fulfillments of prophecy.

BLOOD OF THE LAMB – Revelation 12:7–11. This is how we, as believers, overcome our accuser, Satan. It is through the *"Blood of the Lamb"* (*Jesus*) and *"the word of our testimony."* Also see 1 Peter 1:19, Revelation 7:14.

BOASTING – Jeremiah 23:28-32

BOLDLY TEACH (*OUR DIRECTIVE AS CHRISTIANS*) – Ephesians 6:19–20, Acts 9:27–28, Acts 14:3, Acts 18:26. All these verses indicate that teaching about Jesus with boldness is something that the Lord expects of us.

BONES OF PETER – (*See PETER'S BONES*)

BORN AGAIN – John 3:3, John 3:7, 1 Peter 1:3, 1 Peter 1:23. Jesus tells us specifically a person cannot be a saved Christian unless they are born again. To become born again, a person must confess and believe in Jesus, as directed in Romans 10:9–13.

BORN IN ONE DAY – (*See ISRAEL*). Isaiah 66:7–9. In prophecy, this has turned out to be the rebirth of the State of Israel that occurred on May 14, 1948. In Isaiah, we are told about a land being born in one day. Who has heard of such a thing? We have seen this happen in our time.

BRIDE OF JESUS – **"Christians"** Revelation 21:9, 2 Cor. 11:2.

BRIDE OF GOD – **"Israel"** Jer. 31:31-33, Jeremiah 3, Hosea 2.

CANON – Commonly referred to as the Divine collection of books that make up our current-day Bible, 66 books total in the Protestant version and 73 books in the Catholic version. (*See BIBLE*)

CALVINISM – (*See T.U.L.I.P.*). This is a false belief system established by the French theologian John Calvin (*1509–1564*). It is the belief that God "predestined" a part of the human race, without merit or any free will choice on their part, to eternal salvation. It is also Calvinists' belief that if you are not in the "elect," you are "predestined" for eternal damnation. The flaw with this belief system is John 3:16. (*See APOSTASY*)

CATCHING UP – For the purposes of this book, this is known as the prophesied pre-Tribulation Rapture of Christians. (*See RAPTURE*)

CATHOLIC CHURCH (*END-TIME CHURCH*) – The word *Catholic* translates to "universal." This current-day church follows many of the traditions of the first Babylonian church formed by Nimrod after the Flood of Noah. Its model of operation leads to a belief that it will become the Universal Church, incorporating all religions within it, and will be the church entity that will go into the Tribulation, the Church of Laodicea, as described in

Revelation 3:14–22. This church will rule out of the true Babylon located in current-day Iraq.

CATHOLIC CHURCH *(MOVE TO BABYLON?)* – Currently, this church is located in Rome on a site directly over the believed burial site of the Apostle Peter's bones. After Ezekiel 38, they may discover Peter's bones are actually buried in the true city of Babylon. If this proves to be true, the Catholic Church will be required to move to Babylon in Iraq. If this happens, this will prove that the Catholic Church is the end-times church of Laodicea.

CHRISTOPHANY – The terminology used for the physical pre-incarnate appearance of Jesus in the Old Testament. He appears to Abraham in Genesis 22:1–19, then to Jacob in Genesis 31:11–13 and 32:24–37, and to Moses in Exodus 3:1–4:17. There are also many other occurrences.

CHURCH OF PHILADELPHIA #6 – Revelation 3:7–13. This is the sixth of the seven church periods that make up the Christian Age. It is the "loving Church" *"kept from the hour of testing,"* the Tribulation. It will end at the Rapture.

CHURCH OF LAODICEA #7 – Revelation 3:14–22. This is the seventh and final church period inside the Christian Age. It is the *"lukewarm"* Church, neither hot nor cold. God will spit this church out of His mouth. This church goes through the Tribulation and purposefully overlaps with Philadelphia. (*See SHINAR*)

COME OUT OF HER *(FLEE FROM FALSE CHURCHES)* – Revelation 18:4–5. When we see Christian churches start to join together for world unity, be very careful as God is telling us this is a very bad sign of the times. Weigh every church's viewpoints on God and the Bible, and make sure there are no compromises. If you see compromises, God tells us that church has left Him and we need to flee so we do not suffer the consequences of their folly. Again, please be very careful and watch diligently. (*See ONE WORLD CHURCH*)

COMFORT ALL THAT MOURN – Page 30, Isaiah 61:2(c) This is the 1,000-year MILLENNIUM PERIOD after the TRIBULATION period has been completed. It is the third of three time periods listed in Isaiah 61:2.

COMFORT ONE ANOTHER – (*See ENCOURAGE ONE ANOTHER*). 1 Thessalonians 4:13–18, specifically verse 18. Encouragement is yet another directive similar to comfort, and this is listed in 1 Thessalonians 5:1–11. These 1 Thessalonians verses explain about the Rapture, indicating that God wants us to fully anticipate the "visual" Rapture's arrival and to comfort one another with this glorious information.

COPYRIGHT *(GOD'S WARNING)* – Revelation 22:18–19. God placed a strict Copyright on His Bible. He tells us **not to add** anything or to **take anything away** from His perfect completed Word. It has been perfect from the beginning of time. If anyone adds anything to His book, all the plagues listed in the Bible will be added to that person. One of the major plagues is the Tribulation. If anyone subtracts anything, God will take away that person's part from the tree of life. Be very careful, as this is a severe warning. There are no mysteries listed in the Bible that have not already been fully explained within its full text. (*See EVERYTHING; BIBLE; MYSTERIES*)

COUNCIL OF TRENT – From 1545 to 1563, during the Protestant Reformation, the Catholic Church responded to this Reformation with their Council of Trent. They considered the Biblical interpretations and beliefs of the new Protestant movement to be blasphemous and wanted to clarify their positions on the Bible. Many current-day false doctrines within the Catholic Church came into existence as a result of this council.

CREATED OR MADE – *(See CREATION)*

CREATION – In Genesis 1, God talks about two actions He performed. These actions were to create (*Hebrew-bara*) and make (*Hebrew-asah*). These words mean two different things. In Genesis 1:1, "God created the earth in the beginning." In Genesis 1:2, the already-created earth *was formless, void, and dark, and water covered the earth.* This was not the flood of Noah. This occurred at the fall of Satan per Isaiah 14:12, when God threw him down to earth and destroyed His creation out of disdain. God now took the already-created, messed-up earth and "made," restored it, from existing created matter and light, using elements He had already created long ago. How do we know? 2 Peter 3:3-7 tells us this specifically. Also see Colossians 1:16, Hebrews 11:3, Psalm 33:6-9, Genesis 2:7, Genesis 2:19–23, and John 1:3.

CROWNS – (216–218) God offers five individual crown rewards for service over and above the call of duty. For Bible prophecy students, there is the **CROWN OF RIGHTEOUSNESS**, 2 Timothy 4:7-8. The other four are **LIFE**, James 1:12; **GLORY**, 1 Peter 5:1-5; **EXULTATION**, 1 Thessalonians 2:19; and the **INCORRUPTIBLE CROWN**, 1 Corinthians 9:25-27.

CYRUS – Ezra 1:1-5, Isaiah 44:28-45:4. Cyrus' decree to rebuild Jerusalem and the Second Temple started the 70 weeks of Daniel; to bring an end to all sin and seal up prophecy. The first year of the reign of Cyrus was 434 BC. Some believe it was 536 BC based on Ptolemy's calculations, in the mid 100's AD. His calculations, based on astrology, are incorrect. *(See 70 WEEKS OF DANIEL)*

DAY (*A DAY IS A LITERAL DAY*) – (148–150) Genesis 7:11, Genesis 8:13. This has been highly debated, but God has answered this question for us clearly in the two Genesis verses above. God tells us Noah's age during and after the flood in years, months, and days. The Hebrew word for days is "yom," and this is used more than 350 times in Genesis. There is no Biblical confusion as to a day being a literal 24-hour day in the Bible. God used years, months, and days, again a second time, in Genesis 8:13–14, when Noah exits the ark. Clearly, a day is a day. There can be no possible confusion; a day is meant to be a 24-hour day.

DAY (*CREATION DAYS*) – (158–160) Genesis 1:3–31. Actually six literal 24-hour days. (*See DAY [A DAY IS A LITERAL DAY]*)

DAY (*NOAH, LOT, and the RAPTURE*) – (204–206) Luke 17:26–17, Matthew 24:37–41 (Noah), Luke 17:28–29 (Lot), Luke 17:30–36 (the Rapture and Tribulation begin). The flood and destruction of Sodom happened on single days. The verses above define how the Rapture will happen the same day the Tribulation begins, by God's design.

DAY OF THE LORD – (*See TRIBULATION*). Zephaniah 1:15.

DAY OF JEHOVAH – (*See TRIBULATION*)

DAY OF WRATH – (*See TRIBULATION*). Zephaniah 1:14, Revelation 6:17.

DAY OF VENGEANCE OF OUR GOD – Page 30 Isaiah 61:2(b). This is the 7-year TRIBULATION period that starts the day the PRE-TRIBULATION RAPTURE occurs, mere hours later. Jesus will announce the arrival of this period when He returns in the clouds to Rapture Christians on one magnificent day.

DANIEL'S 70TH WEEK – (*See 70 WEEKS OF DANIEL*).

DAY DAWNS – (195, 201) 2 Peter 1:19. This occurs the day the Rapture will take place. It is the assurance, in a Christian's heart, that the Rapture is about to take place. This assurance is for Christians who are aware of the signs God provides on this specific day. For prophecy students, we will see God's signs in the sun, the moon, and the stars as described in Joel 2:30–31 and Luke 21:25–28. (*See DAY STAR*)

DAY OF JACOB'S DISTRESS – (*See THE TIME OF JACOB'S DISTRESS*)

DAY STAR – (192–196) 2 Peter 1:19. When we see God's signs the day the Rapture will arrive, God will give us the Day Star in our hearts so we will know when to "literally" look up, as directed in Luke 21:28. Note the arrival of the Rapture should not come as a surprise to Christians. We are to expect it, as we are told in 1 Thessalonians 5:1–11.

DEATH GATE – (212–214) The Rapture is not intended to be a surprise to Christians. Those who know to look up will be Raptured, alive, at the last trumpet. Those who do not understand prophecy and hide in their houses will be put to death first and immediately Raptured with the first group, those already dead after the first trumpet. They will not know this happened until they get to heaven and understand they missed one of God's greatest blessings, the Crown of Righteousness.

DECEPTIONS – (167) Romans 1:18–21 and Romans 1:28–32. Additionally, (131–171). Any and all false beliefs and doctrines that the Deceiver will use in the last days to make people believe that

Jesus is not real and that both God and His Bible are antiquated fables and myths.

DISCIPLES – Also the term for a student. (*See APOSTLES*). The terms *disciples* and *apostles* are often thought to be interchangeable. This is not actually correct, as they have two different meanings. A disciple is a follower, pupil, and student. An apostle is a student who has been selected to become a vigorous advocate and teacher of the Word of God. The original 12 disciples were trained, and then Jesus assigned all but Judas to become special apostles to teach the world about Himself. By definition, those today who study the Word are disciples, albeit at a much different level. Those who are called to teach become apostles, again at a much different level. Not all disciples are apostles, but all apostles are disciples. All students today are disciples, Acts 6:7.

DEISTS – We are being falsely told today (*See APOSTASY*) that our country was not founded on a Judeo-Christian model. Therefore, Jesus is not relevant as a true representation of the founding fathers' "rock" for the formation of the United States. Deists believe in the existence of a supreme being, specifically of a creator who does not intervene in the universe. The term is used chiefly of an intellectual movement of the 17th and 18th centuries that accepted the existence of a creator on the basis of reason but rejected belief in a supernatural deity who interacts with humankind.

DINOSAURS – (164-166) Job 40:15–18, Job 41 (the entire chapter).

DWELLING SECURELY – (*See ISRAEL DWELLING SECURELY*)

EARS TICKLED – 2 Timothy 4:3–4. In the last days, *"they will not endure sound doctrine"* and will *"turn away from truth."*

EARTH *(OLD EARTH CONCEPT)* – Genesis 1:1–2, 2 Peter 3:3–7. God tells us the Earth is very old; however, man is not. In Genesis 1:1–2, we see the world is formless and void; no life could possibly exist on it. This is the result of the fall of Satan long ago. God fixed the Earth 6,000 years ago and created man. Evolution is not possible based on this scenario. Also see Genesis 5:5–8 *(plants and man)* for some additional support.

EARTH *(YOUNG EARTH CONCEPT)* – This concept is the belief system that all of creation happened only 6,000 years ago, and it contradicts what is listed above in the (OLD EARTH CONCEPT). The problem with this concept is that it does not address the story of the fall of Satan and his being cast down to Earth. Remember, Satan and his fallen angels were/are spirit beings, not flesh and blood, so this also indicates how evolution is not a viable alternative.

ECUMENICAL MOVEMENT – The modern ecumenical movement (ecumenism) throws open a "wide" gate, beckoning everyone to come in with a great emphasis on uniting all professing Christians of all denominations and beliefs into one church entity. A One World Church! The message is that we're not so different after all, so we can work together for unity and brotherhood. Setting aside theological differences, we can help each other in the things we all agree upon. This is exactly how the One World Church will form through the Catholic Church in the last days. God warns us about this concept as a danger in Matthew 24, verses 4, 11, and 24. (*See CATHOLIC CHURCH*)

ELECTION – John 6:70–71. We need to be very careful with this word or the word "elect." *Elect* does not mean saved. Jesus tells us something very important regarding the 12 apostles: He chose all of them, yet one was a devil. This appears to tell us that even though Judas was "elected," he was not saved.

ELIJAH *(Different from Elisha)* – Matthew 17:10–13. Elijah will come in the last days "*to restore all things.*" The Lord tells us that a form of Elijah has already come; he was John the Baptist. We know that Jesus cannot be talking about John coming at the time the Lord was speaking about this, because John the Baptist had already been dead about a year. We are also told about the return of Elijah just prior to "*the great and terrible day of the Lord,*" the Tribulation in Malachi 4:5–6 and Luke 1:17. (*See 144,000*)

ENCOURAGE ONE ANOTHER – 1 Thessalonians 5:1–11. This passage explains about the visual Rapture, showing God wants us to be in the know and comforted by what is coming. It is not coming in secret. (*See COMFORT ONE ANOTHER*)

END TIMES – Actually relates to the 70 weeks of Daniel that started with the decree by Cyrus to rebuild both Jerusalem and the second temple after the Hebrews Babylonian captivity. The end time officially started in 454 BC. 69 of the 70 weeks were completed *(483 years)* at Jesus triumphal entry and crucifixion. The 70th week was put on a long time out *"the favorable year of the Lord,"* Isaiah 61:2(a) and Luke 4:12. We are about to witness the arrival of Daniel's final 70th week. 24 prophecies were designed to show us the 70th week is on the way; the Lord is about to return to finish Daniel's 490 year prophecy for Israel alone. Christians were not any part of the first 69 weeks and will not be a part of the final 70th week either, designed for Israel's benefit as God tells us. Christians will be Raptured allowing God to deal specifically with His glory Israel. For Christians we should look forward to the Lord's return with great excitement and anticipation. This is why understanding prophecies, designed to indicate the restarting of the 70th week timeclock, is so vital for believers today. (See 24 END TIME PROPHECIES)

ESCAPE – Joel 2:28–32. These verses are talking about the Rapture just prior to the start of the Tribulation. In verse 32, God says "*those that call upon His name*," before the Tribulation starts and signs in the heavens become evident, shall be delivered. God says that "*there will be those that escape*" – escape: His words, not mine. God desires for believers in Jesus to escape the Tribulation. Also see Luke 21:36, 1 Thessalonians 5:3.

ESCAPISM – (*See ESCAPE; RAPTURE; PRE-TRIBULATION RAPTURE; MATTHEW 24*). A term used by some Christian groups that believe living Christians at the time of the Rapture must go into the Tribulation for cleansing. Their thinking is that Christians who believe in the Rapture are in denial or "wishful thinking" and that judgment by God is coming only to those Christians unfortunate enough to be alive when the Rapture happens. These people use Matthew 24 as the basis for this thinking; however, this is not what Matthew 24 truly says.

ESCHATOLOGY – A branch of theology concerned with the study of final events in the history of the world and mankind.

ETERNAL ORDER – After the completion of the Millennium, God's job with sinful mankind is completed. This is where all those who have accepted Jesus will live for all eternity.

EVANGELICALS AND CATHOLICS TOGETHER – In 1994, prominent Protestant Church leaders signed a document called *Evangelicals and Catholics Together* basically stating that our differences are insignificant. This is part of the apostasy that will soon become more and more rampant in the last days.

EVIL GOOD AND GOOD EVIL – Isaiah 5:20–21. In the last days, everything good and true in the Bible will be seen as bad and wrong. Everything bad and wrong will be seen as good. This is a cruel deception that will severely expand in the last days.

EVOLUTION – (*See CREATION*). Genesis 1:1–2. Evolution where mankind evolved from early primal ancestors over millions of years. This flies in the face of what God tells us, and this concept is totally incorrect Biblically.

EZEKIEL 38:1–39:16 – A battle God causes to happen where the enemies of Israel come against the country to destroy it. God saves Israel and defeats the enemies on His own without the help of mankind, rescuing Israel from all harm. (*See Chapter 4*)

EZEKIEL 38 ATTACK *(IT SHALL BE DONE)* – Ezekiel 39:8.

EZEKIEL 38 ATTACK *(GOD MAKES HIS NAME KNOWN)* – Ezekiel 39:7.

EZEKIEL 38 ATTACK *(PRE-TRIBULATION)* – Ezekiel 30:1–5 and five pre-Tribulation justifications, Ezekiel 38:8.

FALL AWAY FROM FAITH – 1 Timothy 4:1. This happens in the last days just prior to the Rapture and the beginning of the Tribulation. (*See APOSTASY*)

FALSE DOCTRINE – (*See DECEPTIONS*)

FALSE PROPHET/S – Deuteronomy 18:20–22, Jeremiah 23:28-32. God warns about false prophets who will tell us things, in the last days, that are not in the Bible. Some will proclaim they were imparted with new "divinely inspired" unknown truths God kept secret until our time. God gives us a way to know about them because what they tell us will not come true. Unfortunately, many believers today follow these people as if they have some mystical authority and totally discount God's own Bible. (*See COPYRIGHT*)

FALSEHOODS – Jeremiah 23:28-32

FAVORABLE YEAR OF OUR LORD - Page 30 Isaiah 61:2(a), Luke 4:12. This is the 2,000-year period from the time of the ascension of Jesus and His Return at the Rapture.

FIG TREE – (*See ALL THE TREES; BIRTH*). Matthew 24:32, Luke 21:29.

FINAL GENERATION – (*See GENERATION*). Psalm 90:10. This Psalm tells us a generation is 70 to 80 years. Genesis 15:12-16 tells us a generation could be 100 years. It is believed the final Biblical generation started with the rebirth of the State of Israel in 1948. Everything in end-time prophecy must be completed before Israel turns 100 in 2048, including the Rapture and the entire 7-year Tribulation. This is up to God so stay tuned.

FLOOD OF NOAH – (*See NOAH*)

FOREVER – When used in Scripture, this word does not always represent endless duration. It can represent continuity, perpetuity, or duration. One example is in Isaiah 32:14–15. Note that the word "forever" is used and then it is qualified with the phrase *"until the Spirit is poured out."* This cannot be an endless period.

FRUITS OF THE SPIRIT – Galatians 5:22-25

GAP *(Between Rapture and Tribulation, not the old and young earth gap theory)* – Luke 17:26–36, specifically Luke 17:30–31. Commonly referred to as an undetermined timeframe between the Rapture and the start of the Tribulation. **There is no gap!** The Rapture will happen hours before the signing of the agreement between the Antichrist and Israel within one 24-hour period. This signing event will start the 7-year Tribulation period.

GENERATION – Psalm 90:10 tells us "a lifespan" is 70 to 80 years. Genesis 15:12-16 tells us a "generation" could be 100 years. In Matthew 24:34, we are told *"this generation shall not pass away until all these things be accomplished."* This means everything explained in Matthew 24. The Greek word for "generation" is "Ganeah," which translates as born one. Isaiah 66:7–8 explains about a *"man-child," "a land born in one day,"* and a *"nation brought forth at once."* This is a prophecy explaining Israel's future rebirth as a nation, which occurred on May 14, 1948.

GENTILES *(TIME OF THE GENTILES FULFILLED)* – Luke 21:24. This verse tells us that the people "Israel" will be scattered until Jerusalem is regained. This occurred in June of 1967 as a result of the Six-Day War. This is another sign that the end days are now in motion.

GENERATION WILL NOT PASS AWAY . . . – Matthew 24:34.

GOD OF ABRAHAM, ISAAC, AND JACOB – *(See TRINITY)*

GOD IS LOVE, FEAR NOT – 1 John 4:16–18.

GOG AND MAGOG *(Ezekiel 38:1–39:16)* – Typically known as Russia *(Magog)* and the ruler of Russia *(Gog)*, they will play a vital role in the Ezekiel 38 attack. *(See EZEKIEL 38)*

GOG AND MAGOG *(Revelation 20:7–8)* – A metaphor, not the real attack known as the battle of Gog and Magog in Ezekiel 38. This event described in Revelation happens at the end of the millennium. *(See RUSSIA)*

GOSPELS – The first four books of the New Testament: Matthew, Mark, Luke, and John.

GOVERNMENTS ESTABLISHED BY GOD – Romans 13:1–3.

GOVERNMENTS – PRAY FOR THEM – *LEAD A QUIET AND TRANQUIL LIFE* – 1 Timothy 2:1–3.

GOVERNMENTS – SUBMIT YOURSELVES – 1 Peter 2:13–17.

GLORIOUS APPEARING – 2 Thessalonians 2:9. Jesus, the Son of God, returning to the earth physically at the end of the 7-year Tribulation.

GLORY – *(See ISRAEL GOD'S GLORY)*. God holds Israel in high esteem. In Isaiah 46:12, He declares *"Israel is His Glory."* In Isaiah 48:11, God tells us *"and My glory (God's) will I not give to another."* Israel is the apple of God's eye to this very day. These statements make it Biblically clear that the Christian church today **has not** replaced Israel. Also, Romans 11.

GREAT AND AWESOME DAY OF THE LORD – *(See TRIBU-LATION)*. Joel 2:31.

HARLOT – (*See BABYLON MYSTERY RELIGION*). The corrupt evil church of the last day that will be in control for the first half of the Tribulation. (*See THE CHURCH OF LAODICEA #7*)

HELL – (271–278) Matthew 24:41, Psalm 30:3, Psalm 49:13–14, Job 24:19, Proverbs 15:24, Matthew 5:22, Matthew 10:28, Mark 9:42–48, Revelation 14:9–11. These are but a few of the multiple descriptions by God of a literal Hell. This is a real place. Please do not let anybody fool you into thinking it is only a fable.

HERMENEUTICS – The art and science of Biblical interpretation. There are two main principles of hermeneutics that are important in Bible interpretation. They are double reference and recurrence.

HOLY SPIRIT – The third member of the Holy Trinity. (*See TRINITY*)

HOOKS – (*Plural, not hook*) Ezekiel 38:4. Hooks are defined as the drawing or enticement by God Himself that will bring the enemy armies around Israel to war against Israel. God will win this war for Israel on His own without the help of mankind. (*See EZEKIEL 38:1–39:16*)

HOUR OF TESTING – (*See TRIBULATION*). Revelation 3:10–11.

IMPOSSIBLE FOR GOD TO LIE – Hebrews 6:17–20.

IMPRECATORY PRAYERS – (*See PSALM 83*). Prayers by David: Psalms 35, 55, 58, 59, 69, 109. Prayers by Asaph: Psalms 79, 83, 137. These prayers ask for God Himself to bring punishments, in some form, upon certain sets or classes of individuals at some time in the future. All for God's glory alone.

IMMINENCE DOCTRINE – Refers to the Rapture being THE TAKING OF Christians by the Lord at any moment, a surprise event. This belief system claims there can be no prophetic "signs" that will precede the Lord's Pre-Tribulation return based on a supposed "mystery" mentioned in 1 Corinthians 15:51–52. The problem with this is that this "mystery" was explained, in full, by Paul in 1 Thessalonians 4:13–18 at least 5 years earlier. The Bible tells us the Rapture should not come as a surprise to "informed" Christians. It will only come as a surprise "like a thief" to unbelievers per 1 Thessalonians 5:1–11. Imminence will be rendered inaccurate once we witness the rescuing of Israel from Islam in Ezekiel 38. This will be a monumental clarification of Bible prophecy for those in doubt. (*See PROGRESSIVE REVELATION*)

INERRANCY – Jeremiah 36:22–32 tells of the writings of Jeremiah. Jeremiah was told to hide and surrogates showed the king Jeremiah's writings; the king burned them. But then God allowed and helped Jeremiah per verse 32 to rewrite the entire book that had been burned up and to then finish the book. It was identical because it was only a copy. The original Bible was written before time existed. God has the full original copy in heaven and has protected it for all eternity. It is inerrant, perfect.

IN THE BEGINNING – (*See CREATION*). Genesis 1:1–2.

ISAAC – The second son of Abraham (*See ISHMAEL*). He is the son of promise listed in Genesis 21:12, leading to the birth line of Jesus. God asked Abraham to offer Isaac for sacrifice. Note in Genesis 22:5 that he and Isaac went to worship and Abraham told his young men that had accompanied him that they (*both*) would come back again. Abraham had full faith and trust that if he were to kill Isaac as God requested, God would raise him to life again, which is similar to what He (*God the Father*) would later do with his own son. This is a beautiful picture of obedience and unfettered faith. (*See ABRAHAMIC COVENANT*)

ISHMAEL – Genesis 16:1–15. The first son of Abram, conceived with Sarah's maidservant Hagar. He <u>is not</u> the son of promise per Genesis 21:12–13, but he is promised a great nation (*large nation in numbers, not a righteous one*), which is Islam today. Genesis 16:1–15, 25:12–17. (*See EZEKIEL 38:1–39:16*)

ISHMAELITES – (120–125) (*See ISHMAEL*). The descendants of Ishmael. This group today represents Islam. Mohamed, who we are told spoke the words of the Quran into existence in 632 AD, claimed to be an Ishmaelite.

ISHTAR – (55–57) The wife of Nimrod, mother of Tammuz, and self-proclaimed Queen of Heaven. She was the figurehead of the first Babylonian Mystery Religion.

ISLAM – (120–125) (*See EZEKIEL 38:1–39:16*). The religion that is practiced today by the descendants of Ishmael, the son of Abraham and Hagar.

ISRAEL – (*Isaiah 66:7–9*) The name of the current country in which Israelites, Jews, the Hebrew people live today. Reborn on May 14, 1948, Israel is the fulfillment of a major end-time prophetic super sign. This term is also commonly used to define the majority of the people who live in this country: the Jews inside Israel. (*See THE FIG TREE; BORN IN ONE DAY*)

ISRAEL *(GOD'S GLORY)* – In Isaiah 43:14–21, verse 20, God tells us Israel is His chosen land and people. In Isaiah 46:13, God calls *"Israel His Glory."* And finally, in Isaiah 48:11, God tells us *"His glory He will not give to another."* To this day, Israel is God's chosen and always will be.

ISRAEL *(DWELLING SECURELY)* – Ezekiel 38:8, Ezekiel 38:11, Ezekiel 38:14. Biblical prophecy explaining that Israel is dwelling safely within unwalled villages: not in peace, a "shalom" arrangement, but securely, a "batach" situation, which is what is happening in Israel today. This is in place today and happens just prior to the Ezekiel 38 attack.

ISRAEL *(THE FIG TREE)* – Luke 21:29–32, Matthew 24:32–34. Referred to as "the fig tree." (*See* UNITED NATIONS)

ISAAC – Genesis 21 and 22:17–18. The second son of Abraham with his wife, Sarah. Isaac is also the half-brother of Ishmael. Isaac is the legitimate heir and the son of promise in the Bible.

JEALOUSY – Romans 11:11–16. After the Jews rejected Jesus, the Gentiles were grafted (*adopted*) into God's family. Paul tells us the reason is so that we might make the Jews jealous, leading some of them to salvation. Our assignment is to help our Jewish family discover Jesus is the promised Messiah.

JERUSALEM, COMFORT MY PEOPLE . . . – Isaiah 40:1–2.

JERUSALEM, PRAY FOR THE PEACE . . . – Psalm 122:6–7.

JESUS the CHRIST – The Son of God. A third part of the Holy Trinity (*one God in three parts*), which is the Father, Son (*Jesus*), and

Holy Spirit. Jesus is His name and Christ His title. Christ translates as Messiah. He was born of a virgin and lived the only perfect life in human form in our world. He willingly went to the cross, taking all of the sins of the world on Himself, and died to save mankind. On the third day, he rose from the dead and conquered death and to this day lives and sits at the right hand of God the Father in heaven. He will soon return in clouds at the Rapture and 7 years later to the earth in his GLORIOUS APPEARING at the end of the Tribulation.

JESUS CHRIST IS THE SAME FOREVER – Hebrews 13:8.

JESUS CHRIST *(ONLY SINLESS HUMAN)* – Hebrews 4:14–16. It is impossible for the Virgin Mary to be sinless. (*See VIRGIN MARY*)

JESUS EMPTIED HIMSELF – Philippians 2:5–11. As a man on earth, although God, Jesus emptied Himself of some of His Godly attributes and knowledge to be a man susceptible to sin. This way, he experienced all we do and was able to withstand all temptations. This is also the state of being He was in when we are told that He does not know the day or the hour of the Rapture. (*See JESUS REGAINS ALL AUTHORITY*)

JESUS REGAINS ALL AUTHORITY – John 17:1–5. When Jesus completed His mission on earth, He asked God the Father to restore to Him the full glory that He had had with Him before the world was. He regained a full equal share within the Trinity. Jesus knows everything today, including exactly when the Rapture will arrive. (*See JESUS EMPTIED HIMSELF*)

JEWISH BOY – (*See GENERATION; BORN IN A DAY*). The Jewish boy is a reference to the final generation that started with the rebirth of the State of Israel on May 14, 1948.

JEWS – God's chosen people, the Hebrews. *(See ISRAEL GOD'S GLORY)* Today there is 1 Jew on earth for every 521 people. Meeting a Jew is a great blessing from God.

KINGDOMS – (77–79) Daniel 7:24. In prophecy, in the last days, we will see a One World Government that breaks into 10 kingdoms.

LAND BORN IN A DAY – *(See BORN IN A DAY)*

LAST DAYS – *(See END TIMES)*

LATTER YEARS – *(See END TIMES)*

LAWS OF MOSES, THE PROPHETS, AND THE PSALMS – Luke 24:44. Jesus during His ministry on earth taught "only" from these three sections of the Old Testament. The Apocryphal books are not a part of the Bible that Jesus used for His ministry.

LEAVEN *(GROWTH OF SIN WITHIN THE CHURCH)* – 1 Corinthians 5:6–9; Mark 8:15; Luke 12:1, 13:8, 13:21. Leaven suggests the implanting of wrong interpretation and thinking that markedly alters the true nature and intent of God's truth. Leaven in the church is altering truth to a point where the desires of God are no longer followed or recognized as significant. This also relates to apostasy.

LEADERS *(WORLD'S POLITICAL LEADERS)* – (28–29) Romans 13:1-3, 1 Peter 2:13-17. All world leaders are selected by God

Himself, not by mankind. His plans for humanity are fully set, so we have nothing to fear. God is in full control.

LEFT & RIGHT – (276–277) Ecclesiastes 10:2; Matthew 25:33–34, 25:41, 25:46. Today in the political realm in the United States, the two major political parties are referred to as either the "left" or the "right." In looking at the verses above, it is interesting how God uses these two specific words. Does this mean something? You decide.

LIVING SECURELY *(Israel)* – Ezekiel 38:8, 11, 14. Israel is living securely today within "unwalled villages." We are told this will be the situation in the last days just prior to the Rapture and Tribulation. Please note that this could be possible only when the State of Israel is in existence. This was not the case, and was not possible, prior to May 14, 1948.

LOOK UP – 2 Peter 1:19, Luke 21:27–28, Matthew 21:28. The specific and literal request God has for living Christians on the day the Rapture arrives. (*See Chapter 6*)

LOT *(THE DAY SODOM WAS DESTROYED)* – Luke 17:26–30, specifically Luke 17:28–29. Just prior to the Rapture and Tribulation, the world will appear peaceful as in the days of Lot, until **"the day"** destruction and travail came upon Sodom. So will it be in **"the day"** of the Son of Man. (*See NOAH*)

MADE OR CREATED – (*See CREATION*)

MAN OF LAWLESSNESS – (*See ANTICHRIST*)

Glossary

MAMERTINE PRISON – The name of the prison where the Romans kept Paul until they beheaded him due to his faith, sometime around 68 AD. Some say Peter was there also, but Peter was never in Rome, as he was the apostle to the Jews inside the true city of Babylon. (*See PAUL; PETER*)

MARK OF THE BEAST – Revelation 13:15–18. For the last half of the Tribulation (*not at any time before this period*), a person will need to take this mark of allegiance to the Antichrist in order to buy or sell. It is a terrible thing and guarantees that a person will not go to heaven. Once this mark is taken, a person cannot change their mind and is doomed for eternity. Seven is God's perfect number. The mark of the beast is 666, which is like saying 6.66, the number of man, just short of 7, falls short enough to lose salvation.

MARY (*VIRGIN MOTHER OF JESUS*) – (66–69) Luke 11:27–28, 1 Timothy 2:3–6, Hebrews 4:14–16. Some say Mary remained a virgin all her life; the Bible contradicts this in Matthew 1:24–25. Married to Joseph, she had multiple children with him after the virgin birth of Jesus. This is highly disputed within the Catholic Church but solidly supported within the actual Bible.

MATTHIAS (*REPLACEMENT APOSTLE FOR JUDAS. Appointed by the remaining 11 apostles*) – (*See PAUL; APOSTLES*)

MATTHEW 24 – This chapter does not tell us that Christians must live through the Tribulation. A basic understanding of two hermeneutical principles, "double reference" and "recurrence," is required to interpret this chapter accurately. In short, verses 1–7 are a question asked by the disciples. Verse 8 is a time-out period, per the words **"these things."** Verses 9–31 jump into the future where Jesus explains how terrible the future Tribulation will be. In verse 32, by "recurrence," He comes back to their present time using the words "**these things**" again, then again, one more time, for clarity in verse 34. In verses 34–51, Jesus answers the original question asked in verses 1–7 and fills in the time-out period left back in verse 8, explaining the signs to look for before a pre-Tribulation Rapture.

MILLENNIUM – The 1,000-year period, after the completion of the Tribulation, when Christ will rule on the earth.

MORNING STAR – In Isaiah 14:12, Satan was referred to as the "star of the morning, son of the dawn." After his fall, he no longer qualified for this title. Christ is also the "bright Morning Star," as referenced in Revelation 22:16. One is God (Jesus); the other is a creation, a fallen angel (Satan).

MYTHS – 2 Timothy 4:3–4. In the last days, "**they will not endure sound doctrine**" and will "*turn away from truth.*"

MYSTERIES – Matthew 13:11. There are no mysteries in the Bible that God has not shared with us. Unbelievers are not able to understand the Bible. (*See PROGRESSIVE REVELATION; COPYRIGHT*)

NARROW GATE, WIDE GATE – Matthew 6:13–14 tells us the path to God is narrow and the path to destruction is broad. God is telling us only a few are going to spend the time to figure things out. This is very sad.

NOAH (*THE DAY THE FLOOD CAME*) – Genesis 7:17–24 tells us that God blotted out every living thing on the face of the land at that time in a "**single day**" except Noah's family and the animals on the ark. He did not say in the ocean. (*See LOT*)

NOAHIC COVENANT – Genesis 9:16–17. The Noahic covenant laid out in Genesis is a covenant made with all of humanity, and it marks a new beginning for the world after the flood. A sacrifice ratifies this covenant, Genesis 8:20–21, and God promises never again to use a flood to destroy all life with water. The Lord promises that the seasonal cycle will continue while the earth remains per Genesis 8:22.

NON-CANONICAL PROPHETS – 1 Chronicles 29:29. Some people tell us that we can only use canonical prophetic writings in the Bible to determine what the Bible explains. There are good prophets of old who provided solid information for the prophets whose writings are in the Bible. God acknowledges some of them. In 1 Chronicles 29:29, God mentions two, Nathan and Gad.

NOT EVERY SUPPOSED CHRISTIAN WILL BE SAVED – Matthew 7:21–23. If someone professes to be a Christian but does not know or follow His true Word, there is a chance that without being "born again" a person will not see God. He will tell you, "*I never knew you: depart from me.*" (*See BORN AGAIN*)

ONE GOD AND ONE MEDIATOR – 1 Timothy 2:5. One God and one mediator, Christ Jesus.

ONE WORLD CHURCH – Revelation 17:1–5. Soon after Ezekiel 38 is completed, a one world church forms. With the Islamic faith potentially neutralized, the last major church to mop up the carnage will be the Catholic Church. It will become the leading church in the world, and it will and must, per the Bible, fall from true faith in Jesus. Their consolidation will appear as a good thing but will be the exact opposite. As Christians, we will know this because Jesus will begin to be severely scorned and marginalized. When you see this scorning and marginalization occur, be very careful of what you do and whom you believe. This is Biblically prophesied. (*See UNIVERSAL CHURCH*)

ONE WORLD GOVERNMENT – Daniel 7:24. Shortly after the completion of Ezekiel 38, a One World Government will quickly form and break into 10 divisions. Then, an 11th leader will come on the scene; this will be the Antichrist. As Christians, we will get to see him and know who he is shortly before we depart in the Rapture. The secular world will have no idea who he is until he reveals himself at the midpoint of the Tribulation.

OMMISSION – Jeremiah 26:2 – God tell us to *"not omit a Word"* when studying the Bible. (*See COPYRIGHT*)

PAUL *(THE FINAL 12TH APOSTLE)* – (70–73) Ephesians 3. Formerly Saul, a man who hated and killed Christians. He had a conversion to faith on a Damascus road. His name was changed to Paul, and he became the man who wrote by God's inspiration more than half of the New Testament. After Christ's ascension, Paul was assigned as the apostle to the Gentiles in Rome until he was put to death for his faith around 68 AD. Paul is the true replacement 12th apostle after the death of Judas, not Matthias. (*See APOSTLES; MATTHIAS; MAMERTINE PRISON*)

PEACE AND SAFETY – 1 Thessalonians 5:1–3. The world will appear to be at peace (*a decadent peace*) until **the very day** the Rapture occurs and the Tribulation begins. Both of these things happen within the same 24-hour day. The unbelieving world will be caught off guard when God, as a thief, steals this false peace away from mankind.

PENTATEUCH – Referred to as the "five vessels," the Torah meaning "the Law" or "instruction." The first five books of the Tanakh (*Old Testament*): Genesis, Exodus, Leviticus, Numbers, and Deuteronomy.

PENTECOST – Acts 2:1–4. Shortly after the ascension of Jesus into heaven, after His resurrection, the Lord sent the Holy Spirit to descend upon the apostles. This is known as the day of Pentecost. As a result, the Holy Spirit or "comforter" is with all Christians today.

PERSECUTED FOR LIVING GODLY IN CHRIST –
2 Timothy 3:12–13.

PETER *(THE APOSTLE)* – (70–75) Matthew 16:17–19, 1 Peter 5:13. Simon Peter is the "**small rock**" upon whom Jesus would build His church. The Catholics got this wrong. Jesus "**the rock**" did not make him their first pope. Peter was assigned as the apostle to the Jews. Prior to the destruction of the second temple in 70 AD, the majority of the Jews who were not in Jerusalem were located in the actual city of Babylon (*currently in Iraq*). Peter lived there with his son Mark as we discover in 1 Peter 5:13. Peter did not live or minister in Rome. (*See PAUL; MAMERTINE PRISON*)
PETER'S BONES – 1 Peter 5:13. Peter sends a greeting along with Mark his son from the true Babylon (*not Rome*). Because Peter was an apostle to the Jews, they predominantly lived in Babylon (*SHINAR*) after the destruction of the Jerusalem temple in 70 AD. Peter lived in Babylon (*Iraq today*), where he ministered. This would surely mean his bones are buried there. If true, this will be a monumental discovery very soon and a strong reason for the Catholic Church to move their headquarters to Babylon, where their first pope's bones will have been discovered.

PLANTS ON THE EARTH – (*See EARTH – OLD EARTH CONCEPT*). Genesis 2:5–8.

PNEUMATIKON CHARISMA – 1 Corinthians 12:8–10. Upon the ascension of Jesus into heaven, the Bible (*that which is perfect*) had not yet been completed. Jesus gave the apostles the Pneumatikon Charisma, which was the full knowledge of the Bible, so they could teach about Him accurately. The apostles could impart this to others, but these others, who received this power, could not pass it on. Upon the death of all the apostles and all those who had been given these gifts, the Pneumatikon ended and the perfect Bible took its place. We have the perfect Word of God today, the Bible, as our tool to teach the Word of God.

POST-MILLENNIALISM – The belief that the millennium is an era, not necessarily a defined literal 1,000-year period. This belief system says Christ is currently reigning, not literally on earth but through the gradual increase of the Gospel and its power to change lives. After this gradual Christianization of the world, Christ will return and immediately usher the church into their eternal state after judging the wicked. Postmillennialists believe Christ will return after some undefined version of the millennium, not before. This is not an accurate view of the Bible. It is assigned to the Jew to minister to the world.

PREACHING – 2 Timothy 4:1-2 – Be ready in all seasons to preach the word accurately.

PROGRESSIVE REVELATION – The belief that God has provided the full history and the complete story of the future of mankind in sequential order; He has "revealed" it for us (*See ADVANCE*). Through the study of the entire Bible, as a complete unit, the chronology of mankind from Adam through to the second coming of Jesus can be fully explained and understood.

Additionally, many Christians say the Rapture is imminent because God mentions a mystery in 1 Corinthians 15:51–52. This mystery is not actually a mystery because it is explained in 1 Thessalonians 4:13–18, which was written 5 years prior to the Corinthians verses.

PROPHECY – Prognostications by God in the Bible to tell us what is coming in the future. One-third of the Bible is prophecy, so it should not be taken lightly, John 14:29.

PROPHETS – FALSE – (See FALSE PROPHTES)

PROPHETS – NON-CANONICAL - 1 Chronicles 29:29-30 – There are prophecies God shares with us through Prophets, who do not have formal writings included in the Biblical Canon. As an example, in the verses listed above, we see Nathan and Gad. These men were God inspired Prophets, who in God's design, did not need to have their written works become a part of the completed Bible.

PRE-MILLENNIALISM – The belief that the second coming of Jesus will occur before a literal 1,000-year reign of Christ from Jerusalem upon the earth. If you believe in a pre-Tribulation Rapture, as I do, you would be considered a dispensational pre-millennialist. The Catholic Church and many current-day contemporary churches believe in historical pre-millennialism, which states that the Rapture occurs at the end of the 7-year Tribulation. I believe this to be incorrect.

PROPHETS *(CANONICAL)* – These are the special men God has used in both the Old and New Testaments to scribe His 66 canonical books that make up our Bible today. (*See NON-CANONICAL PROPHETS*)

PROPHETS *(CURRENT DAY)* – Revelation 22:18–19. The Bible is complete in its original form, finished around 95 AD. There are no new mysteries or prophecies that God plans to share with us today that are not already in the Bible. There are no new current-day prophets in our time.

PSALM 83 – (120–124) This chapter is an imprecatory prayer by Asaph asking God Himself to come against the Ishmaelites, the enemies of Israel, to wipe them out and remove them from the world for God's glory alone. This chapter **is not** a prophecy telling us Israel, on their own, will instigate the Islamic removal.

PURGATORY – A holding place after death, according to a Roman Catholic belief (*tradition or doctrine*) in which the souls of people are placed in an intermediate location so they can be made pure through suffering before going to heaven. **This is false doctrine that is not supported by anything within the canonical Bible.** At death, we go straight to heaven or somewhere else that is not a wonderful location: hell.

QURAN – This is the holy book of the Islamic faith. It was written by scribes who translated verbal messages from Mohamed into a final written form. Completed around 632 AD, it was written more than 500 years after the Bible was completed. It contains revised and altered versions of many dates, timeframes, and concepts used in the Bible. A severe difference is their God Allah claims to have no son. This means that their version of god, Allah, cannot possibly be the same as the God of the Bible, who in the New Testament claims to have a Son, Jesus.

RAPTURE – (*Entire Chapter 6, Pre-Tribulation*). 1 Thessalonians 5:1–11 (*See PROGRESSIVE REVELATION*). The Bible tells us the Rapture should not come as a surprise event to "informed" Christians. It will come as a surprise "like a thief" only to unbelievers. As Christians, we are told by our Lord to exhort one another and build up each other with this information. I believe in a PRE-TRIBULATION RAPTURE of the true Christian church (*all born-again believers today*) mere hours before the Tribulation begins on the same day (*See 75 DAYS*). I also firmly believe God intends for the Rapture event to be seen by all of mankind; it will not be a secret event. There are many theological reasons for this to be true. Here are brief descriptions of the three prominent theories of when the Rapture will occur:

> **PRE-TRIBULATION RAPTURE:** The belief that the Rapture of Christians will occur before the Tribulation begins. This is my belief system. I also believe this will occur the same day the Tribulation begins. (*See 70 WEEKS OF DANIEL*)

> **MID-TRIBULATION RAPTURE:** The belief that the Rapture occurs at the midpoint of the 7-year Tribulation.

> **POST-TRIBULATION RAPTURE:** The belief that the Rapture occurs at the end of the 7-year Tribulation.

(*See UNSAVED SOULS AT THE RAPTURE*). Zephaniah 2:1–3.

REFORMATION – The 16th-century religious movement that led to the establishment of the Protestant Church. This was very unpopular within the Catholic Church because it eliminated the need for intermediary communications with God through priests. It allowed mankind to go directly to God personally, as the Bible directs of us.

REPLACEMENT THEOLOGY – The thinking that after Christ the Jews are no longer relevant, that the Christian Church has replaced Israel in God's eyes. This is incorrect doctrine. The Book of Revelation and the Tribulation is all about bringing Israel back to God. (*See GLORY*)

RESTRAINER – (186–187) 2 Thessalonians 2:3–7, Mark 12:9–11. We are told there is a restrainer that holds back the Antichrist in the last days. Many think this is the Christian Church. Some believe it is the Holy Spirit. Both thoughts are incorrect. 2 Thessalonians 2:3–7 tells us the Antichrist is restrained until the time when he will be revealed. This happens at the midpoint of the Tribulation. The restrainer is the three kings who are defeated at the midpoint of the Tribulation. They will hold him at bay for only the entire first half of the Tribulation.

RIGHT & LEFT – (*See LEFT & RIGHT*)

RIGHT IS WRONG AND WRONG IS RIGHT – Isaiah 5:20–21.

RUSSIA (*MAGOG?*) – The battle of Gog and Magog is generally referred to as the event described in Ezekiel 38:1–39:16. In Revelation 20:7–10, this battle is referenced as a "metaphor." Note verse 7 starts out "*when the thousand years are completed.*" This refers to an event involving Satan that will happen very quickly, at the end of the Millennium, in a similar fashion as the Ezekiel 38 battle that will have happened 1,000 years earlier. How might we know that Russia is the army from the north (*Magog*) referenced in Ezekiel 38? Look at Joel 2:20. The army from the north is driven into an eastern sea and a western sea. There is only one country north of Israel that touches both a western sea (*the Atlantic*) and an eastern sea (*the Pacific*). This one country is Russia.

RIGHTEOUSNESS – Isaiah 26:9, when "*God's judgments are upon the earth*" (*See TRIBULATION*) "*the inhabitants of the world learn righteousness.*"

--- S ---

SAINTS – (211–212) Ephesians 4:11–12, Matthew 27:52, Philippians 1:1, and Hebrews 6:10. The saints are all believers in Jesus Christ. They are not only those selected by the Catholic Church or elected to be called saints.

SATAN – (231–233) He was the most beautiful of God's created angelic beings. He was consumed by arrogance and pride and considered himself to be equal with God. God threw him out of heaven with one-third of all the angels as a punishment for this arrogance. Satan is the ruler of earth today. God will soon put an end to his evil at the conclusion of the Tribulation and finally at the end of the Millennium. Satan is a real being; please do not be fooled into thinking he is mythical.

SCOURGE (*OVERWHELMING SCOURGE*) – God's army mentioned in Joel 2. It is not literally called "the scourge" in Joel; this descriptive word "scourge" is a description, explaining the results of what the Joel 2 army will do in the last days. See Isaiah 28:14–15 and Isaiah 28:18–19.

SCRIPTURE (ALL) INSPIRED BY GOD . . . – 2 Timothy 3:16–17.

SEASON OF EVENTS – Luke 12:54–56. God tells us to be watching what is happening in the world and to "analyze" our season of events through Biblical prophecy. He is literally telling us what is going on if we are willing to both look and notice.

SECOND ADVENT – The second coming of Jesus Christ.

SECOND COMING – This is the literal return of Jesus Christ, which will be discernible through end-time prophecies. The second coming is a 7-year period bookended by two events. The first event is the Rapture, where Christ comes in the clouds to take Christians home with him and starts the 7-year Tribulation in motion on that same day. The second is His glorious appearing at the end for the Tribulation, where He will defeat evil and start the 1,000-year Millennium.

SECOND EXODUS – Ezekiel 38:8, Jeremiah 16:14–15. The First Exodus was when *"God brought the Children of Israel out of Egypt."* The second Exodus is happening today; God is bringing "Israel together from the land of the north and all the countries where he had scattered them" in 70 AD, bringing them home into their own land. The reassembled State of Israel was established on May 14, 1948. Also see Ezekiel 37:11–14, Zephaniah 2:1–2, Jeremiah 31:8.

SECOND VATICAN COUNCIL (VATICAN II) – From 1962 to 1965, the Catholic Church held the Second Vatican Council (*Vatican II*)—a pastoral convention, convened to update and review the disciplines, policies, doctrines, and attitudes of the Catholic Church relating to the modern world.

SECURELY – (*See PEACE AND SAFETY*) Ezekiel 38:8, 11, and 14. Israel is *"living securely"* in *"unwalled villages"* just prior to EZEKIEL 38:1–39:16. This in Hebrew is a *"betach"* arrangement: they are in a place of refuge and safety. This is not a *"shalom"* arrangement, which would be at peace.

SEVEN MOUNTAINS *(HILLS)* – (72–75) Revelation 17:9–11. We are told the *"seven mountains"* (*hills*) actually represent seven kings, not geography. Five had fallen already when John wrote Revelation, and one existed in his time. And a seventh, by its description in the book of Revelation, depicts the coming One World Government of the end times.

SHINAR – Zechariah 5:5–11 tells us that at some time in the near future an apostate version of possibly the Catholic Church will be carried in an *"ephah container"* by *"two storks,"* Apostate Protestantism and Judaism, to *"the plains of Shinar,"* which is Babylon in current-day Iraq. This will be the church of the end times. (*See CHURCH OF LAODICEA*)

SHREWD AS SERPENTS, INNOCENT AS DOVES –
Matthew 10:16.

SIGNS *(YES – ONLY FOR BELIEVERS)* – (*See Chapter 2*). God offers believers 24 end-time signs for us to witness so we can know that Jesus is about to arrive. How might it be possible to see signs? Chapter 2 explains all of this in detail; it is amazing.

SIGNS *(NO – PRE-RAPTURE SIGNS FOR UNBELIEVERS)* – In Luke 17:20–21, God is talking with the Pharisees, who were the bad guys in His day. He knew they would not be looking for "signs," so none will be given to them. No signs for unbelievers, only for true Christians. Unbelievers do not desire to know, and God is not going force them to understand what is happening. So this "one single" verse says **"no signs"** but there are 75 other verses that say "yes" there **"are signs"** for BELIEVERS.

SODOM – (*See LOT*)

STONE – When used in the Bible, typically refers to Jesus.

STUDENT – *(See DISCIPLES)*

SUPER SIGNS – In Chapter 2, I show 24 end-time prophecies, signs of the last days. Three of them, #4, #13, and #24, are classified as "super signs" of the end times.

TAMMUZ – A child of a false god in the original counterfeit Babylonian religion. He was the son of Ishtar. *(See ISHTAR)*

TANAKH – This is the Hebrew name used by our Jewish family for what Christians call the Old Testament. Jews today do not use the terminology "Old Testament" in reference to their Holy book. *(See PENTATEUCH)*

TEACHER – *(See APOSTLES)*

TEMPLE *(JERUSALEM)* – Revelation 11:1-2, 2 Thessalonians 2:3-4. The third Jewish temple in Jerusalem will be rebuilt after Ezekiel 38 (*this clears the Temple Mount*). Biblically, this must occur before the Rapture and Tribulation. This will not be a good temple in God's eyes. This temple will be the place where the Antichrist will perform the Abomination of Desolation and declare himself to be the only God at the midpoint of the Tribulation.

THE FIG TREE – *(See ISRAEL THE FIG TREE)*

THE GREAT TRIBULATION – *(See TRIBULATION)*. Revelation 7:14. Tribulation, by definition, is always a period of severe trials. The word "great" is used to express the tremendous added difficulty experienced in the last half of the Tribulation. It is not a second event.

THE TIME OF JACOB'S DISTRESS – (*See TRIBULATION*). Jeremiah 30:7.

THIEF IN THE NIGHT – (*See Chapter 6*). 1 Thessalonians 5:1–11. Often thought to refer to God taking Christians secretly at the Rapture. When looking at 1 Thessalonians 5:1–4, it is clear that the thief is when God takes a false peace and safety from the secular world. The Rapture is not to come as a thief or even a surprise to knowledgeable Christians.

TIME OF JACOB'S DISTRESS – (*See THE TIME OF JACOB'S DISTRESS*)

THREE DAYS IN THE GRAVE *(JESUS)* – In the Jewish culture, a day starts at 6:00 PM and goes through to 6:00 PM the following day. Any portion of a day, even a few minutes, is considered a full day. We are told Jesus was in the grave for three days. Using the explanation above, it is possible this was only about 26 hours. Here is how. Jesus could have been buried at 5:00 PM on Friday, then entombed all day Saturday and risen at 7:00 PM Saturday night. This would be considered three full days.

TONGUES – Referenced in Isaiah 28:11–13 and then specifically in Acts 2, verses 3–4, 6, and 8–11. "Tongues" literally means known "languages" in almost all situations. Note in Acts 2:3 *"tongues distributing themselves."* Then as we continue in verse 8 these "tongues" were heard by everybody in *"their own language."* Verses 9–11 list 16 different specific dialects that were heard, all known languages. The apostles did not know these languages, but God allowed them to speak in these different dialects without being taught; this is a miracle. It is possible for someone to speak in an unknown tongue, but God desires for this to be done in private, with Him alone, not in public.

TORAH – (*See PENTATEUCH*). The first five books of the Tanakh, or Old Testament.

TRADITIONS – Beliefs or theories created by man and established as Biblical truth by various denomination of the Christian Church. These are manmade theories and often do not follow sound Biblical doctrine. Traditions believed or accepted as Biblical truth can carry severe consequences. (*See COPYRIGHT*)

TRAVEL AND KNOWLEDGE INCREASE – Daniel 12:4. This is another sign that the last days are upon us.

TRIBULATION – Revelation 3:10, a 7-year period where God will judge the wicked people remaining after the Rapture in righteousness, Isaiah 26:9. God tells us the Tribulation occurs in two periods of 1,260 days. The first half is described in Revelation 11:2 and the second half in Revelation 13:5. The GLORIOUS APPEARING happens on day 2,520, after these two periods are completed. Jesus' actual return to ground will not be a surprise to anybody. There is a period of 75 days after the GLORIOUS APPEARING described in Daniel 12:11–12. The second half of the Tribulation is listed in Daniel as 1,335 days: another 1,260 days + 75. These 75 days are two additional periods of time, one 30 days long and the second 45 days. This 75-day period is where the Lord will set everything up for the coming 1,000-year MILLENNIUM PERIOD. Tribulation: Jeremiah 30:4–7, Daniel 9:27, Daniel 12:1, Matthew 24:15–22. (*See 70 WEEKS OF DANIEL*) In context, due to translation issues, sometimes the word "tribulation" only means daily trials and problems.

Glossary

TRIBULATION (PEACEFUL FIRST HALF – NO!) – (104–105) Some Christians believe the Tribulation will be peaceful for the first 3½ years. This is a severe error. Twenty-one judgments come upon the world in these 7 years of horror. Fourteen occur in the first 3½ years. Half of the souls living after the Rapture will die in the first half of the Tribulation. No peace, pure distress.

TRINITY – One God in three parts: the Father, Son (Jesus), and Holy Spirit. In Genesis 18–19:28, Jehovah is spoken to as a singular entity while appearing as three distinct men. This was God in His three forms. In Isaiah 48:16, "*and now the Lord God (Father) has sent Me (Jesus) and His Spirit (the Holy Spirit).*" This represents the triune God that has existed before time began, the Holy Trinity. This God is also the God of Abraham, Isaac, and Jacob.

TRUTH – (*See LOVE*). It is "impossible for God to lie," Hebrews 6:18. Love of the truth is greater than love alone, 2 Thessalonians 2:10. John 8:31–32. Jeremiah 23:28-32.
T.U.L.I.P. – (*See CALVINISM*). Calvinists believe in what is referred to as the "five points" of Calvinism. These five points form the acronym T.U.L.I.P.: **"T"** = Total Depravity, **"U"** = Unconditional Election, **"L"** = Limited Atonement, **"I"** = Irresistible Grace, **"P"** = Perseverance of the Saints. Note: Calvinism is not a Biblically correct form of Christian doctrine.

TWINKLING OF AN EYE – **This is not the Rapture itself.** In 1 Corinthians 15:51–52, God tells us about something that happens at the last trumpet, which means there must be a first. The only thing that occurs in a twinkling is our changing into heavenly bodies, not the Rapture event itself. (*See RAPTURE*)

UNITED NATIONS *(ALL THE TREES)* – Luke 21:29–32. These verses refer to *"the fig tree"* and *"all the trees."* The fig tree represents Israel and all the trees the United Nations. Note in these verses we are told when we see both of these things happen we are to know the summer is near. In other words, the last days have arrived. All the trees came to be in 1945, the fig tree in 1948. *(See ISRAEL [THE FIG TREE])*

UNITED STATES *(IN PROPHECY)* – Why isn't the United States mentioned in the Bible? It is because in the last days there will be a new One World Government that will break into 10 new kingdoms. This is explained in prophecies #16 and #19 in God's 24-prophecy sequence *(Chapter 2)*. With the exception of Israel, all countries in the last days will lose their national sovereignties and will fall under some new names. The United States will no longer exist as we know it today just prior to the Lord's return. This is not a bad thing, however, if you understand what is happening and why.

UNPARDONABLE SIN – Matthew 12:32. The only unpardonable sin today after Christ died for us on the cross is not to accept Jesus as your personal Savior during your lifetime on earth. *(See BORN AGAIN)*

UNSAVED SOULS AT THE RAPTURE – Micah 7:1–6 talks about the pain when, in verse 2, *"the godly person has perished from the land, and there is no upright person among men."* After the Rapture, for a brief moment, every person on the earth will be an unbeliever. This will be a dark moment.

UNIVERSAL CHURCH – *(See ONE WORLD CHURCH; CATHOLIC CHURCH)*. The word "Catholic" means universal.

Glossary

VATICAN II – (*See SECOND VATICAN COUNCIL*)

VIRGIN MARY – Luke 11:27-28, 1 Timothy 2:3-6. The mother of Jesus. In the Catholic Church, she holds a very high level of authority. Many times, prayers for mediation on our behalf are made directly to God in her name instead of the name of Jesus. Please be careful here and read the two verses listed above, in God's own words. It is then up to you to determine from God's Word if this authority placed today on Mary is justified or possibly incorrect human doctrine. You decide. (*See JESUS SINLESS*). See Matthew 1:24-25, Acts 1:14, Galatians 1:19, Matthew 13:53-56, Mark 3:31-32, Luke 8:19-21.

WARNING SIGNS – (*See SIGNS*)

WEST, WESTERN POWERS – Isaiah 24:14-15. It is interesting that in these verses we are told the west will cry out concerning the majesty of the Lord to glorify those in the east. Might this mean that even though the United States may no longer exist, the Christians in this new kingdom formerly known as the United States may still play a strong role in helping Israel in the last days? Only time will tell. (*See UNITED STATES*)

WORD IS PASSING AWAY . . . – 1 John 2:15-17.

WORD OF GOD IS LIVING . . . – Hebrews 4:12-13.

WRONG IS RIGHT AND RIGHT IS WRONG – Isaiah 5:2-21.

YEAR OF JEHOVAH'S FAVOR – Isaiah 61:2(a), Luke 4:19. This is a long period of time that spans from PENTECOST and will end at the PRE-TRIBULATION RAPTURE. Jesus announced the arrival of this period in the synagogue, per Luke 4:19, and sat down.

YOM – (148–149) The Hebrew word for day used predominantly in Genesis. (*See the multiple references to DAY*)

ZIONIST MOVEMENT – Around 1897, the Jewish people developed a strong desire to come back and have a homeland in Israel. Started by Theodor Herzl, the movement felt that due to the anti-Semitism that was growing during the 1880s it was time to have a safe place to live, Israel. All of this was the precursor for the formation of the new State of Israel on May 14, 1948.

--- NUMBERED ITEMS ---

3rd – TEMPLE IN JERUSALEM – Revelation 11:1–2. This is prophecy #18 in God's 24-event Road Map. These verses indicate another temple will be built. Ezekiel 38 will clear the Temple Mount so this third temple can be erected. With prefabrication, it could go up very quickly. This is not a good temple, as it will allow the Jews to reestablish the animal sacrificial system, which is a slap in the face to Jesus, who died once for all sins.

7 – CHURCH AGES EXPLAINED IN REVELATION – Revelation 2 and 3. These are both seven literal churches in Christ's day and a representation of seven time periods from the ascension of Christ to His second coming at the Rapture. The sixth church, Philadelphia, is the current loving church that will be Raptured. The seventh church is Laodicea, which exists today, also overlapping with Philadelphia. This is the lukewarm church that will enter the Tribulation. (*See CATHOLIC CHURCH*)

7 – HILLS – Revelation 17:9–11. This is not Rome because these verses tell us they are kings. Five were prior to the time of Jesus, one was during the time of Jesus, and one is to come just prior to His second coming. The last one will be the final Roman form of government (*not in physical Rome*) of the Antichrist. It will be inside Babylon in the land of Shinar. (*See SHINAR*)

7 – MOUNTAINS – (*See 7 – HILLS*)

10 – WORLD DIVISIONS AND KINGS – Daniel 7:24. This is the 19th prophecy in God's list of 24. After the One World Government forms, it will break into 10 kingdoms with 10 kings. When we see this happen, the end is near.

12 – TRIBES OF ISRAEL – (84–85) (*See 144,000; ELIJAH*). The following map shows an approximation of the land mass areas given to the original 12 sons of Jacob that make up the 12 tribes of Israel. The land mass shown on the map is a little larger than the land area currently occupied by Israel today. This may soon change after Ezekiel 38. Note on the map the lands of "Ephraim" and "Dan." These tribes are not listed in Revelation 7. In Revelation 7, the two tribes not shown are "Levi" and "Joseph." I am not sure which areas they will occupy. This map is provided to show a general geographic land map of where all 12 tribes should be generally located.

144,000 – During the entire Tribulation, there will be 144,000 Jewish evangelists who will accept Jesus and preach for the full 7-year Tribulation period. They will be made up of 12,000 members from each of the 12 tribes of Israel. This means the 12 tribes must be in existence before the Tribulation starts. These 144,000 individuals will accept Jesus almost immediately after the Rapture occurs. (*See ELIJAH*)

24 – PRE-TRIBULATION END-TIME PROPHECIES – Chapter 2: God offers 24 end-time prophecies that started in 1914 and will lead us to the Rapture and Tribulation. Twelve have been fulfilled; 12 additional items will soon arrive.

21 – TRIBULATION JUDGMENTS – Isaiah 26:9 and Chapter 7: When God's 21 judgments are in the world, His people learn righteousness. The purpose for the Tribulation is to bring Israel to the knowledge that Jesus is their Messiah. They will acknowledge this during the last three days of the Tribulation, accept Him, and invite Him back, and He will return.

70 AD *(DESTRUCTION OF THE SECOND TEMPLE)* – The second temple was destroyed in 70 AD. There has been no temple since that time. This will soon change after Ezekiel 38, which will be a fulfillment of prophecy #18 along God's 24-event Road Map.

70th WEEK OF DANIEL – Daniel 9:24–27. God tells us 69 of Daniel's prophesied 70 weeks, or 483 of the 490 years, were completed at the time of Christ's crucifixion. Then God placed a long time-out on mankind before a distant future day when Jesus will come back and initiate the 70th week of 7 years, the Tribulation. This is a key prophecy that supports a Pre-Tribulation Rapture but why? Because Daniel's 70 weeks **are only intended for Israel**! The Christian "Church" was not around for any of the first 69 weeks **purposefully**! By simple logic, **the Christian Church is not going to**

be here for the 70th week either, as again this period **is for Israel alone**! Christians will be removed to safety, by design, in a Pre-Tribulation Rapture event. (*See TRIBULATION*)

75 DAYS *(AFTER THE END OF THE TRIBULATION)* – Daniel 12:11–13. At 2,520 days after the start of the Tribulation, Jesus comes back in the Glorious Appearing and wins an earthly battle with Satan. There are two added periods of time listed in Daniel 12, a 30-day period and a second one lasting 45 days, for a total of 75 added days before the Millennium starts. This is a time for Jesus to clean things up and make everything ready for the Millennium.

10-243
2 Peter 1:2

Made in the USA
Middletown, DE
06 August 2020